VOLUME 528

JULY 1993

THE ANNALS

of The American Academy *of* Political
and Social Science

RICHARD D. LAMBERT, *Editor*
ALAN W. HESTON, *Associate Editor*

CITIZENS, PROTEST, AND DEMOCRACY

Special Editor of this Volume

RUSSELL J. DALTON

University of California
Irvine

 SAGE Periodicals Press *NEWBURY PARK LONDON NEW DELHI*

THE ANNALS

© 1993 *by* The American Academy *of* Political *and* Social Science

Editorial Office: 3937 Chestnut Street, Philadelphia, PA 19104.

For information about membership* (individuals only) and subscriptions (institutions), address:

SAGE PUBLICATIONS, INC.
2455 Teller Road
Newbury Park, CA 91320

From India and South Asia, write to:	*From the UK, Europe, the Middle East and Africa, write to:*
SAGE PUBLICATIONS INDIA Pvt. Ltd.	SAGE PUBLICATIONS LTD
P.O. Box 4215	6 Bonhill Street
New Delhi 110 048	London EC2A 4PU
INDIA	UNITED KINGDOM

SAGE Production Staff: LINDA GRAY, LIANN LECH, and JANELLE LeMASTER
*Please note that members of The Academy receive THE ANNALS with their membership.
Library of Congress Catalog Card Number 92-62092
International Standard Serial Number ISSN 0002-7162
International Standard Book Number ISBN 0-8039-5110-8 (Vol. 528, 1993 paper)
International Standard Book Number ISBN 0-8039-5107-8 (Vol. 528, 1993 cloth)
Manufactured in the United States of America. First printing, July 1993.

The articles appearing in THE ANNALS are indexed in *Book Review Index, Public Affairs Information Service Bulletin, Social Sciences Index, Current Contents, General Periodicals Index, Academic Index, Pro-Views,* and *Combined Retrospective Index Sets.* They are also abstracted and indexed in *ABC Pol Sci, Historical Abstracts, Human Resources Abstracts, Social Sciences Citation Index, United States Political Science Documents, Social Work Research & Abstracts, Sage Urban Studies Abstracts, International Political Science Abstracts, America: History and Life, Sociological Abstracts, Managing Abstracts, Social Planning/Policy & Development Abstracts, Automatic Subject Citation Alert, Book Review Digest, Work Related Abstracts, Periodica Islamica,* and/or *Family Resources Database,* and are available on microfilm from University Microfilms, Ann Arbor, Michigan.

Information about membership rates, institutional subscriptions, and back issue prices may be found on the facing page.

Advertising. Current rates and specifications may be obtained by writing to THE ANNALS Advertising and Promotion Manager at the Newbury Park office (address above).

Claims. Claims for undelivered copies must be made no later than three months following month of publication. The publisher will supply missing copies when losses have been sustained in transit and when the reserve stock will permit.

Change of Address. Six weeks' advance notice must be given when notifying of change of address to ensure proper identification. Please specify name of journal. Send address changes to: THE ANNALS, c/o Sage Publications, Inc., 2455 Teller Road, Newbury Park, CA 91320.

Origin and Purpose. The Academy was organized December 14, 1889, to promote the progress of political and social science, especially through publications and meetings. The Academy does not take sides in controverted questions, but seeks to gather and present reliable information to assist the public in forming an intelligent and accurate judgment.

Meetings. The Academy occasionally holds a meeting in the spring extending over two days.

Publications. THE ANNALS is the bimonthly publication of The Academy. Each issue contains articles on some prominent social or political problem, written at the invitation of the editors. Also, monographs are published from time to time, numbers of which are distributed to pertinent professional organizations. These volumes constitute important reference works on the topics with which they deal, and they are extensively cited by authorities throughout the United States and abroad. The papers presented at the meetings of The Academy are included in THE ANNALS.

Membership. Each member of The Academy receives THE ANNALS and may attend the meetings of The Academy. Membership is open only to individuals. Annual dues: $42.00 for the regular paperbound edition (clothbound, $60.00). Add $9.00 per year for membership outside the U.S.A. Members may also purchase single issues of THE ANNALS for $13.00 each (clothbound, $18.00). Add $2.00 for shipping and handling on all prepaid orders.

Subscriptions. THE ANNALS (ISSN 0002-7162) is published six times annually—in January, March, May, July, September, and November. Institutions may subscribe to THE ANNALS at the annual rate: $132.00 (clothbound, $156.00). California institutions: $141.57 paperbound, $167.31 clothbound. Add $9.00 per year for subscriptions outside the U.S.A. Institutional rates for single issues: $24.00 each (clothbound, $29.00). California institutions: $25.74 paperbound, $31.10 clothbound.

Second class postage paid at Thousand Oaks, California, and additional offices.

Single issues of THE ANNALS may be obtained by individuals who are not members of The Academy for $17.00 each (clothbound, $26.00). California residents: $18.23 paperbound, $27.89 clothbound. Add $2.00 for shipping and handling on all prepaid orders. Single issues of THE ANNALS have proven to be excellent supplementary texts for classroom use. Direct inquiries regarding adoptions to THE ANNALS c/o Sage Publications (address below).

All correspondence concerning membership in The Academy, dues renewals, inquiries about membership status, and/or purchase of single issues of THE ANNALS should be sent to THE ANNALS c/o Sage Publications, Inc., 2455 Teller Road, Newbury Park, CA 91320. Telephone: (805) 499-0721; FAX/Order line: (805) 499-0871. *Please note that orders under $30 must be prepaid.* Sage affiliates in London and India will assist institutional subscribers abroad with regard to orders, claims, and inquiries for both subscriptions and single issues.

Printed on recycled, acid-free paper

THE ANNALS

of The American Academy of Political
and Social Science

RICHARD D. LAMBERT, *Editor*
ALAN W. HESTON, *Associate Editor*

--------------- FORTHCOMING ---------------

See page 3 for information on Academy membership and
purchase of single volumes of **The Annals.**

CONTENTS

BOOK DEPARTMENT CONTENTS

UNITED STATES

SOCIOLOGY

ECONOMICS

PREFACE

In the past decade, most Western democracies have experienced a flowering of citizen action groups and social movements concerned with environmentalism, women's rights, peace, consumerism, life-style choices, and other issues of advanced industrial societies. These groups have attempted to mobilize the public's changing values and issue interests into a new political force that can challenge governments and the dominant social paradigm. Through their advocacy of new issue demands and their reliance on new forms of protest and direct citizen action, these groups have disrupted the political status quo in an effort to expand the normal boundaries of democratic politics.

This issue of *The Annals* focuses on how such citizen groups are transforming the nature of contemporary democratic politics. When citizen protest groups first emerged in large numbers during the turbulent 1960s in the United States, they were initially seen as a sign of these stormy times. Often, they were treated as political novelties; sometimes, they, or at least subgroups within these movements, faced outright opposition and hostility from the political establishment. It was just 30 years ago from this year that the free-speech movement was seen as a revolutionary cause in Berkeley and the civil rights movement was suffering bitter repression in parts of the American South. In both their nonviolent and violent forms, these new examples of citizen action generally were seen as lying outside the bounds of normal politics, representing an unconventional style of political action.

Similar types of citizen interest groups began to appear in Europe in the 1970s, where they are known as "new social movements." Many of the issues are the same: the environment, feminism, human rights, and alternative life-style choices. Furthermore, the political methods of these groups, ranging from nonviolent protest to politically based acts of violence, tested the limits of the democratic process. These groups appeared to be even more unconventional in the highly structured political systems of most European states. Green activists, for example, were often castigated as undemocratic extremists; politicians and bureaucrats frequently responded to these new interests as if they were threats to the established political order. Several well-known political scientists cited these groups as illustrations of the "excess of democracy" that threatened the very vitality of the democratic process. Indeed, for many political systems based on neocorporatist or consociational models of interest representation, the populist and direct-action methods of these new movements did seem to represent a fundamental challenge to the existing political order, even if one of the claimed goals of citizen action groups was to make the system more democratic.

As the contributors to this issue and other scholars now agree, these citizen interest groups and new social movements have become part of the political process in most Western democracies—and the democratic process has endured. Yet these new groups and new social movements are transforming the process. These groups spring from the new political controversies of advanced industrial societies and the new levels of political resources existing in these same societies. In merging these new political demands and new orientations toward democratic politics, these groups seek to expand the accepted methods of political participation to include new forms of direct action and new forms of interest representation—they signify a new repertoire or new technology of political action.

This issue of *The Annals* assembles a learned interdisciplinary group of social scientists to provide an assessment of how 30 years of this new form of citizen action has affected advanced industrial democracies. We emphasize the groups and activities identified as new social movements in the European context or more loosely labeled as New Left-oriented "public interest groups" in the United States. Of course, we realize that the methods of protest and direct action are now used by a broad array of societal interests, ranging from the Gray Panthers to schoolchildren. In addition, these new social movements may take many forms, and there are countergroups that oppose these interests and represent a different political dynamic. Still, we focus upon the groups that are identified with the new political forces of advanced industrial societies, such as environmentalists and the women's movement.

The contributions to this issue address two general questions: what are the implications of new social movements for the theory and practice of democracy, and how are these groups actually affecting the style of democratic policymaking?

Herbert Kitschelt introduces the first question, on the implications of citizen action groups for democratic theory, by outlining three models of democratic politics: liberal democracy, organized democracy, and direct democracy. Kitschelt specifies how, as representatives of a new form of direct democracy, citizen action groups deviate from existing political models—and their implications for polities based upon these models. In a provocative article, Jeffrey Berry builds upon this theme. Berry maintains that citizen action groups represent a challenge to the past style of democratic policymaking, but that this derives from their attempt to expand the democratic process and not to subvert it. Carol Hager's analysis of citizen movements in Germany reinforces this point. Hager describes how these groups have presented a dual challenge to the German political system: first, to change the content of the policy process and, second, to change the nature of the process itself. The similarity between the evolution and orientations of citizen action groups in the American and German examples is striking, and the roots of these similarities are described by Doug McAdam and Dieter Rucht. These two authors trace the common intellectual heritage of these movements, providing a unique comparative study of the diffusion of social action as an international phenomenon.

Despite the strong negative criticisms that are often directed at citizen action groups and their activities, these articles are surprisingly uniform in their positive assessment of the implications of these groups for Western democracies. In part, these authors reach this conclusion because they see most citizen action groups as advocating an expansion of the democratic process as one of their ultimate goals. Certainly there are exceptions, especially in the countermovements that have arisen in reaction to new social movements. But on the whole, these are not antidemocratic movements. In addition, these authors observe that as most citizen groups become involved in the political process, they have gradually shed their prior advocacy for revolutionary ideology and violent methods in favor of a more pragmatic political orientation. One year, for instance, Josef Leinen is the head of an anti-system environmental group in Germany; the next, he is environmental minister in the Saar. Ironically, by shedding their revolutionary goals of fundamentally transforming society and the political system, these citizen groups have strengthened the vitality of democracy. The incorporation of these new social movements into a more pluralist pattern of policymaking revitalizes the democratic process by expanding political access and increasing democratic legitimacy. Kitschelt, Berry, and Hager all see this transition from revolution to reform as an ongoing feature of contemporary citizen groups.

The second question we ask is how citizen groups have transformed the policy process with their new issue interests and new styles of political action. Here the authors' conclusions are more varied. Thomas Rochon and Daniel Mazmanian review the experiences of the nuclear freeze movement and environmental groups in the United States. In the latter case, they find that rather than remaining outside the established political process, as their unconventional rhetoric would suggest, environmental groups in California have become quite successful by playing in the game of conventional politics.

The article by William Gamson and Gadi Wolfsfeld on the relationship between protest groups and the media reinforces the image of the conventionality of citizen action groups. In order to obtain the type of positive media coverage that reinforces the goals and image of the movement, citizen groups must maintain public—and media—sympathy for the movement and must emphasize specific issues that can easily be represented in a newspaper article or short television news report. The need for media coverage is thus one factor that encourages citizen action groups to develop a more conventional political profile. Dennis Chong reinforces the point that social movements are forced toward pragmatism if they wish to endure—and succeed. Chong argues that social movements must assure potential participants that their efforts have a reasonable likelihood of generating desired results. To maximize such assurances, groups may attempt to build links to established political figures, draw upon the resources of other political groups, and avoid global ideological goals in favor of simple objectives. As Gamson argued in his earlier study of social movements in America, *The Strategy of Social Protest*, the key to success is "to think small."

Together, these articles suggest that citizen action groups generally have joined the conventional process of policymaking as new actors. The groups are therefore changing policy outcomes, but they have not fundamentally altered the process itself.

A contradictory view of the conventionality of citizen protest groups is offered in the chapter by Ronald Shaiko. Greenpeace seems to epitomize the new issue interests and new confrontational style of citizen action groups: it is one of the largest, and arguably one of the most visible, environmental groups in the United States and several other Western democracies. Shaiko finds that Greenpeace U.S.A. remains largely outside the bounds of conventional politics—a sharp contrast to the pragmatic environmentalists described by Rochon and Mazmanian. Despite a national membership of nearly 2 million, Shaiko reports that Greenpeace is a virtual nonentity to policymakers in Washington.

Diarmuid Maguire's comparative study of the dynamics of protest politics in Italy and Northern Ireland also portrays a less sanguine image of the consequences of citizen protest. Maguire's first caveat is to remind us that the use of protest can evoke a cycle of political violence, as seen in graphic terms in the Italian and Northern Ireland experiences. Maguire's second reminder is that the outcome of protest cycles does not always reinforce and restore the democratic process. Italy was able to integrate the political interests of the new social movements; Northern Ireland has not been able to achieve this democratic transition, and this has had disastrous consequences for the population. As Maguire notes, the technology of protest can be used to redress grievances and gain political access, but under some circumstances, these same techniques can result in the denial of these rights for the original protestors or their opponents. Indeed, the continuing conflicts over abortion rights in the United States, or minority rights in Europe, attest to the potential destructiveness of political action that takes to the streets.

Because political parties are so central to the democratic process, this volume includes two articles that consider how the rise of citizen action groups has affected prior patterns of party government. Initially, citizen action groups were seen as a threat to political parties, usurping their interest-articulation function and transforming elections into single-issue contests. Both Marjorie Hershey and Robert Rohrschneider are more sanguine about these developments. Focusing on the case of women's groups, Hershey finds that the American political parties have largely integrated both sides of these interests into their party platforms and electoral constituencies. The 1992 U.S. presidential election campaign provides clear evidence to support this position. Rohrschneider's analysis of European party systems provides striking parallels to the American evidence. He notes that new social movements initially presented challenges to the programs, electoral position, and political structure of European party systems. By focusing on their programmatic objectives and downplaying their broader structural demands, new social movements generally have been effective in bringing their issues onto the agenda of the established parties. Again, the moderation of goals was rewarded with results.

What, in summary, are the lessons that can be drawn from the research presented in this volume? First, it is clear that the claims of revolutionary change made by some citizen protest groups, and the dire forecasts of their opponents, were exaggerated. The vitality of democracy is that it is an open system that can accommodate new political interests, though we must add that Maguire's article suggests that the stability and strength of preexisting democratic institutions may influence a system's ability to integrate these new political forces. Most of the articles in this volume focus on stable democracies, and they stress how citizen action groups have become a force of political reform, broadening and revitalizing the democratic process. This, indeed, is a significant accomplishment of the past 30 years.

It is also true, however, that some groups remain outside the democratic process. Unconventional environmental action is tolerable within the bounds of democratic politics; ecotage is not. The general transformation of citizen action groups into semiconventional participants in the political process does not apply in all cases. Having observed these variations, we should ask what explains the tactical choices that groups make and the response of counterprotestors and the authorities. This is a question that is only partially answered by the work presented here, and further research remains to be done.

Furthermore, having witnessed this accomplishment—the opening of the political process to broader citizen interests and even the partial reform of political processes to institutionalize this input—we should not be blinded to the new questions raised by these developments. Several of the chapters in this issue describe a new style of policymaking that is developing to accommodate representation by citizen groups, what Berry terms "issue networks." If the integration of citizen action groups leads to the creation of relatively closed policymaking networks in specific issue domains, this can have negative consequences. Closed issue networks limit political access to interests not defined as members of the network. The disaggregation of policymaking to issue networks also may create the type of ossified political system described in Mancur Olson's *Decline of Nations*. We already know, for instance, how issue networks respond to a collective national problem like the budget deficit: they want to cut the other guy's benefits.

It is not enough for citizen action groups to become actors in the political process and then have the process continue as in the past. As Jeffrey Berry notes in the conclusion to his article, the incorporation of citizen interest groups creates new problems of complex governance for democracies. Now we need to look at the implications of this expansion of the boundaries of democratic politics.

RUSSELL J. DALTON

ANNALS, *AAPSS*, **528**, July 1993

Social Movements, Political Parties, and Democratic Theory

By HERBERT KITSCHELT

ABSTRACT: New left-libertarian social movements invoke an ancient communitarian democratic theory against the contemporary practice of competitive elite democracy. Two explanations for this phenomenon are explored. First, in a cyclical model, challenges to representative democracy are viewed as recurring expressions of dissatisfaction with representative institutions. Second, in a structural differentiation model, the practices of left-libertarian movements trigger a pluralization of political decision modes in advanced capitalist democracies, even if such participatory innovations fall short of the direct democratic ideal expressed by movement activists. Although the cyclical model has some merit, on the whole, the structural differentiation model provides an analytically more powerful explanation of recent social movement activity.

Herbert Kitschelt is professor of political science at Duke University and Humboldt University in Berlin, Germany. He has published books and articles on technology policy, political parties and party systems, and social movements in Western Europe. His most recent books are The Logics of Party Formation *(1989),* Beyond the European Left *(1990), and* The Transformation of European Social Democracy *(1993). He has recently begun to study the development of Eastern European party systems.*

13

IT is probably one of the very few valid generalizations in the literature on social protest and collective mobilization that social movements arise only when aggrieved groups cannot work through established channels to communicate new claims into the political process of authoritative decision making. The closure of existing avenues of participation, such as those provided by political parties or interest groups, is a necessary, though not a sufficient, condition for the emergence of unconventional, disruptive, and sometimes violent collective mobilization.[1]

In this vein, the so-called "new" social movements in advanced capitalist democracies in the 1970s and 1980s responded to a situation in which novel demands inspiring important constituencies at least initially did not strike a responsive chord in the existing vehicles of interest intermediation. Whereas political parties and established interest groups have been primarily organized around economic-distributive issues, that is, the allocation of scarce monetary resources to political constituencies, new social movements are predominantly concerned with the procurement of pure public goods characterized by both joint production and nonexcludability from consumption. Such goods are typically intangible in the sense that individuals cannot claim particular shares of the good in the same way that distrib-

utive collective goods can be pocketed by the recipients of pensions, higher wages, medical benefits, farm subsidies, and most of the other collective goods produced in the run-of-the-mill distributive political struggle.

New social movements appear in at least two forms. On the one hand, they engage in a politics of space. In the politics of space, citizens mobilize against the physical and natural consequences of how space is organized by a political economy that is primarily concerned with distributive issues. Environmental protection, land-use planning, urban zoning, transportation, industrial siting, minimizing waste disposal, and the like are typical issues involved in the politics of space. On the other hand, new movements practice a politics of social identity, in which participants work toward a redefinition and reconstitution of individual and collective identities as well as social relations that would go beyond the stereotypes generated by contemporary market relations, political institutions, and cultural conceptions. This politics of social identity is expressed particularly in the women's movements—abortion, anti-pornography, sexual harassment, marital abuse, and so on—and the movements of cultural and physical minorities, such as gays, ethnic minorities, and the handicapped.

Both currents of new movements oppose the commodification of society in a capitalist market economy, be it through the undervaluation of nature and space or the transformation of individual and collective identities by economic exchange relations. They are on the left in their opposi-

---

1. Of course, the intensity of deprivation, the resources of the mobilizing actors, the leaders' strategic skills, and the opponents' counterstrategies contribute to the extent of mobilization and the success or failure of such efforts.

tion to markets as the dominant social governance structure. Moreover, both strands of these movements oppose the bureaucratization of society in economics and politics that allegedly suffocates the ability of individual citizens to participate in the definition of collective goods and identities. Instead, they call for a culturally libertarian transformation of social institutions that gives more leeway to individual choice and collective self-organization outside the economic commodity cycle or bureaucratic political organization. This political thrust is reinforced by the experience that it is precisely the highly bureaucratized political party machines and interest groups—business, labor, professions, churches, and so on—that have been unresponsive to the demands of the left and libertarian social movement sector.[2]

The stakes and the struggle of the left and libertarian social movements thus invoke an ancient element of democratic theory that calls for an organization of collective decision making referred to in varying ways as classical, populist, communitarian, strong, grass-roots, or direct democracy against a democratic practice in contemporary democracies labeled as realist, liberal, elite, re-

publican, or representative democracy. I have no intention of presenting yet another abstract confrontation of the two alternative conceptions of democracy, together with some kind of synthetic blend that can overcome these polarities.[3] Nor do I intend to measure the distance between the direct democratic ideals and the practices of contemporary left-libertarian social movements. Instead, I wish to explain the reasons why contemporary social movements still invoke the image of direct democracy and the possible consequences this may have for democratic institutions. Two hypotheses about the relationship between established democratic procedures and the images and practices of contemporary social movements may be advanced. First, in a cyclical model, challenges to representative democracy are viewed as recurring expressions of dissatisfaction with representative institutions. Second, in a structural differentiation model, the practices of left and libertarian social movements are hypothesized to alter the democratic process in advanced capitalism and trigger a pluralization of political decision modes, even if the participa-

---

2. Frank L. Wilson points out that the strength of new social movements is not directly related to the incidence of corporatist interest intermediation. I would add that regimes with pronounced partocracy—Belgium, Germany, Italy, the Netherlands—also display strong movement mobilization. See Frank L. Wilson, "Neo-Corporatism and the Rise of New Social Movements, " in *Challenging the Political Order*, ed. Russell J. Dalton and Manfred Kuechler (New York: Oxford University Press, 1990), pp. 67-84.

3. For good reviews of these issues, see Benjamin Barber, *Strong Democracy* (Berkeley: University of California Press, 1984); Robert Dahl, *A Preface to Democratic Theory* (Chicago: University of Chicago Press, 1956), chaps. 1-3; Robert A. Dahl, *Democracy and Its Critics* (New Haven, CT: Yale University Press, 1989), chaps. 1-2; David Held, *Models of Democracy* (Stanford: Stanford University Press, 1987); William H. Riker, *Liberalism against Populism* (Prospect Heights, IL: Waveland Press, 1982); Claus Offe and Ulrich K. Preuss, "Democratic Institutions and Moral Resources," in *Political Theory Today*, ed. David Held (Oxford: Polity Press, 1991), pp. 143-71.

tory innovations fall short of the direct democratic ideal expressed by movement activists.

SOCIAL PROTEST AND CYCLES OF DEMOCRATIC DECISION MAKING

The idea that cycles play a role in democratic decision making was first introduced into contemporary debates by Kenneth Arrow.[4] If individuals have different preference rankings over a given set of alternatives and always vote on pairs of alternatives with simple majority as their collective decision rule, no unique collective preference may exist that best reflects the preference rankings of the participating individuals and wins in all runoffs between alternatives—the "Condorcet winner." Arrow then went on to prove that this paradox cannot be remedied unless at least one of several intuitively rational principles of democratic decision making—such as nondictatorship, Pareto optimality, unrestricted domain, and independence of preference rankings from irrelevant alternatives—are violated.

The response of political theorists and empirical political scientists to this formal result has varied. Some have claimed that the practical relevance of cycling majorities is quite limited and does not apply to the key political alternatives contested in contemporary democracies. Among those who accept the relevance of cycling, one group argues that cycling

is actually good for stable democracy because it assures that losers in one round of the political game can be winners in a later round. Pluralist systems with cycling majorities thus can detach the popular legitimacy of specific decisions and rulers from the legitimacy of the political constitution.[5] Other theorists, however, argue that cycles endanger democracy because they undermine citizens' faith in the rationality of democratic decision rules and undercut the stability of constitutional governance. As a remedy, they recommend institutions, that is, enforced rules of the game that constrain the range of alternatives submitted and the probability of alternatives to be accepted in democratic decision making. Such institutions include all the mechanisms of political representation and agenda building advocated by realist democratic theories to overcome the shortcomings of direct democracy among which cycling majorities and indecisiveness rank high: a predominance of elected representatives over citizen participation, discriminating electoral systems to limit the fragmentation of preferences represented, and rules of decision making in parties and legislatures that centralize control over political agendas.[6]

4. Kenneth J. Arrow, *Social Choice and Individual Values* (New York: John Wiley, 1951). The central underlying idea of Arrow's paradox was, of course, provided by the Marquis de Condorcet over 150 years earlier.

5. Nicholas R. Miller, "Pluralism and Social Choice," *American Political Science Review*, 77(3):734-47 (1983).

6. See Riker, *Liberalism against Populism*; Joseph A. Schlesinger, *Political Parties and the Winning of Office* (Ann Arbor: University of Michigan Press, 1991); Kenneth J. Shepsle, "Studying Institutions: Some Lessons from the Rational Choice Approach," *Journal of Theoretical Politics*, 1(2):131-47 (1989).

Advocates of institutions that are designed to overcome the instability of participatory democracy, however, are vulnerable to the counterargument that if citizens cannot agree on stable collective preference functions, they may also be unable to choose stable institutional rules. If the choice of institutional rules biases policy choices in favor of or against some alternative, rational actors will prefer the institutions that maximize their chances to win at the policy level. Thus institutions inherit disagreements about policies and cannot provide stability.[7] A cycle of decision alternatives may be superseded by a cycle of institutions and decision rules, unless stricter decision rules are imposed that make it impossible to change the institutions themselves. In this vein, provisions that constitutions can be altered only with qualified majorities—such as three-fifths or two-thirds—avert cycling but violate Arrow's nondictatorship postulate because they give a minority veto rights over rule changes.

The rigidity of institutions provides the bridge between cycles of democratic choice and social movements. If the established democratic institutions systematically underprivilege certain policy preferences and if the rules themselves are impossible to change even if a majority of citizens so desires, dissenters can only step outside the established framework of political governance and engage in protest. The role of institutions in democracy thus explains a mechanism by which social movements come about. Institutions may be necessary to overcome democratic instability, yet at the same time they constrain democratic principles.[8] This mechanism inducing citizens to switch from normal rule-guided participation to exceptional protest politics does not by itself yield a cycle of political practices that returns to its origin. We need a second mechanism that explains how citizens move back from exceptional to normal democratic politics. This mechanism has to do precisely with the disappointments of direct democratic practice. It has been explained in the works of Albert Hirschman and Sidney Tarrow.

Albert Hirschman's analysis of "shifting involvements"[9] postulates endogenous mechanisms that push citizens back and forth between a preference for private individual—market—choices, accompanied by a constrained sphere for collective decision making within representative democracy and a desire for public collective choices through deliberation and direct democratic participation. Each of the alternative decision modes brings about its own disappointments. These disappointments

7. This point has been made against Riker's liberal conception of democracy by Dahl, *Democracy and Its Critics*, p. 154, based on the work of Jules Coleman and John Ferejohn, "Democracy and Social Choice," *Ethics*, 97(1):11-22 (1986).

8. For a lucid discussion of this central contradiction of democracy that democratic rules may not have been arrived at by and may not be based on democratic support but only enable democracy to function, see Stephen Holmes, "Precommitment and the Paradox of Democracy," in *Constitutionalism and Democracy*, ed. John Elster and Rune Slagstad (New York: Cambridge University Press, 1988), pp. 195-240.

9. Albert O. Hirschman, *Shifting Involvements* (Princeton, NJ: Princeton University Press, 1981).

may be rooted in human nature, but Hirschman wishes to emphasize the causal priority of economic structure and development as the engine behind the cycle.[10] Thus the advent of material abundance for a considerable share of the population has made the search for more abundance less meaningful and has generated serious consumer disappointments. These experiences are likely to lower the perception of the costs of participation in collective decision making and to increase the value of the democratic process as an end in itself. Public life, however, produces its own frustrations, such as the extreme efforts required to bring about even modest collective decisions, let alone leaving a personal imprint on the process and the outcome. Hirschman concludes, "In short, the trouble with political life is that it is either too absorbing or too tame."[11]

Hirschman's argument is empirically illustrated by Sidney Tarrow's incisive study of collective action in Italy that identifies a cyclical dynamic of mobilization in which the first sparks of collective protest feed on themselves, set a precedent that enables others to enter the social movement sector, expand the scope of contestation, and thus improve the opportunity structure for protest.[12] Analogous to a business cycle, however, this self-reinforcing dynamic eventually reaches a peak when slack resources have been spent, some demands and movement representatives are co-opted by the politi-

cal elites, disappointments with the effectiveness of protest set in, and movements experience internal divisions, leading to a demobilization of most participants.[13] Tarrow empirically shows how Italian movements began to mobilize for reform from the early 1960s on and how more and more new causes crystallized around new repertoires of protest action that peaked in the late 1960s and then declined to the mid-1970s.

While Tarrow's penetrating and empirically meticulous study convincingly describes and analyzes the rise and decline of the Italian movement sector and its most important components over a span of more than a decade, it is questionable whether this wave of mobilization conforms to the image of a cycle that returns to its origin. For one thing, had Tarrow carried the analysis forward through the 1970s and 1980s, the empirical evidence would have revealed continued protest activities and oscillating levels of mobilization that may not abide by a cyclical pattern. Social movements appear to be caught up in the structural change of the Italian polity and have left a lasting impact on the nature of politics that plays a role even in periods when manifest movement protest is relatively dormant. I will pursue the theoretical underpinnings of this argument in

10. Ibid., p. 14.
11. Ibid., p. 119.
12. Sidney Tarrow, *Democracy and Disorder: Protest and Politics in Italy, 1965-1975* (New York: Oxford University Press, 1989).

13. Of course, cyclical models of political mobilization already underlie a cohort of natural-history studies on revolution, the major representatives of which are Crane Brinton, *The Anatomy of Revolution* (1938; reissued, New York: Harper & Row, 1965); Lyford Edwards, *The Natural History of Revolution* (1927; reissued, Chicago: University of Chicago Press, 1972); George S. Pettee, *The Process of Revolution* (New York: Harper & Row, 1938).

the next section. For now, I wish to focus on a different argument. Both Hirschman and Tarrow appear to suggest that the cycle has two phases that involve the hegemony of representative democracy (phase 1) and contestation by advocates of direct democracy (phase 2). Instead, I wish to argue that the two-phase model characterizes democratic decision-making cycles incompletely. There is a third mode of democratic decision making within such cycles that is rarely distinguished in the literature on democratic theory and social movements but that has considerable importance for the self-transformation of new social movements.

The evolution of Western democracies reveals considerable institutional variation over time and across space that is amenable to reconstruction in terms of democratic theory. The general idea that contemporary democracies reflect realist conceptions of democracy is too simplistic. Under the realist umbrella, at least two different modes of democratic decision making exist that can be roughly associated with Arend Lijphart's distinction between majoritarian and consensus democracies.[14] I will refer to them as the "liberal" and the "organizational" conceptions of democracy, both of which are distinct from the direct conception of democracy. In at least four respects, each of these three views of democracy conceives of political actors and institutions in different ways.[15] Moreover,

each conception singles out different achievements of democracy. I will argue that citizens really want the achievements of all three modes of democratic choice and that what triggers their dissatisfaction with any existing institutional form is that each delivers only one achievement. This sets the stage for institutional cycles among three forms of democracy and three phases of disappointment and political transformation.

The three forms of the democratic process systematically vary in terms of who the competitors are, conception of citizenship, institutional design, and conception of interests.

1. The democratic competitors: For liberal democrats, the main competitors are candidates for and incumbents of elected office who are independent of special interests and relatively unconstrained by party activists. In contrast, the organized view of democracy sees mass parties with internally recruited leaders as the main competing entities. Mass parties treat leaders as spokespersons for the entire collective and maintain close ties to external mass organizations.[16] Finally, direct de-

Joseph A. Schumpeter, *Capitalism, Socialism, and Democracy* (New York: Harper, 1950). Organized democracy is primarily supported in the socialist or the Catholic tradition and in recent writings is represented by Adam Przeworski, *Capitalism and Social Democracy* (New York: Cambridge University Press, 1985). The direct democratic tradition is rooted in anarchosyndicalism and has been recently updated by Barber, *Strong Democracy*, and in a particularly inventive manner by John Burnheim, *Is Democracy Possible?* (Oxford: Polity Press, 1985).

14. Arend Lijphart, *Democracies* (New Haven, CT: Yale University Press, 1984).

15. Representatives for the liberal view of democracy are Dahl, *A Preface to Democratic Theory*; Riker, *Liberalism against Populism*;

16. In spite of allegations going as far back as Robert Michels, *Political Parties* (New York:

mocracy refuses to draw a clear line between citizens, rank-and-file activists, and leaders in the democratic process. Relations to organized constituencies are only ad hoc, based on personal rather than formal ties and intermittent coalitions around particular issue positions supported by both parties and external groups.

2. Conception of citizenship: Liberal democrats see citizens as self-regarding individuals who experience political involvement as a burden to be delegated to a specialized group of professionals. Organizational democracy sees citizens as other-regarding and therefore contributing to mass parties; yet it also assumes that for most individuals, politics is a burden that is left to an accountable group of political specialists at the helm of the party. Finally, advocates of direct democracy consider citizens to be other-regarding and involved in politics as an opportunity for self-realization and self-transformation, not as a burden on one's time and energy.

3. Institutional design: The liberal democratic model presumes competitive majoritarian politics with plurality electoral systems, separation of powers, presidentialism, competition between party elites, and no formal role for special interest groups in the legislative process. The role of the electorate is to eliminate unpopular incumbents in periodic elections. For organizational democrats, the ideal type of democracy combines propor-

tional representation of parties in the legislature, a functional division of government power, parliamentarism, bargaining and cooperation between party elites, and top-level ties to important interest groups.[17] For direct democrats, council democracy, popular referenda (initiatives, plebiscites), maybe representatives chosen by lottery from the entire citizenship, and the absence of special interest groups approximate the ideal set of institutions.

4. Conception of interests: Each set of democratic institutions is shaped by and promotes a different process of interest formation. For liberal democrats, citizens' preferences are formed in the prepolitical sphere, and the task of politicians is to aggregate such interests. For organizational democrats, parties shape the constituencies' preferences and interests through educational processes tied to the party organization as a potter shapes clay with his or her hands.[18] For advocates of direct democracy, preferences and interests are generated as a continuous process in the enactment of democratic choice. Actors discover their common objectives in a communicative process of political deliberation.

Free Press, 1962), a systematic divergence between party leaders and party activists, particularly in formally organized mass parties, cannot be systematically proved. See Herbert Kitschelt, "The Internal Politics of Parties: The Law of Curvilinearity Revisited," *Political Studies*, 37(3):400-421 (1989).

17. For the empirical characterization of liberal-majoritarian and organizational-consensual democracies, see Lijphart, *Democracies*, esp. pp. 214-16; Arend Lijphart and Marcus M. L. Crepaz, "Corporatism and Consensus Democracy in Eighteen Countries: Conceptual and Empirical Linkages," *British Journal of Political Science*, 21(2):235-46 (1991).

18. See, e.g., Przeworski, *Capitalism and Social Democracy*, chaps. 1-2, for his quasi-Leninist analysis of class formation as a political process that is consciously molded by political parties.

In a well-known article on American political bureaucracy, Herbert Kaufman argued that citizens want an institutional design that delivers representativeness, competence, and executive leadership all at once. Yet closer inspection reveals that each administrative arrangement involves trade-offs between the three desirable objectives: decentralization of governance promotes representativeness but hurts competence and executive leadership; rule by a corps of expert professionals enhances competence but undercuts representativeness and executive leadership; centralization of administrative control, finally, boosts leadership, but reduces representativeness and competence.[19]

A similar set of trade-offs applies to the democratic institutions favored by liberal, organizational, and direct participatory democrats. Citizens expect democracy to provide (1) rationality in the sense of Pareto-optimal stable collective choices, (2) responsiveness to the demands of mobilized citizens, and (3) politicians' accountability to voters, even though the latter may not be directly mobilized. Liberal democracy delivers stable collective choice, although it also claims to be accountable. But citizens' ability to remove political leaders from office does not by itself establish a linkage of accountability. Accountability is the strength of organizational democracy, because mass parties provide a continuous mechanism to tie political leaders to a broad rank-and-file organization

that mutually adjusts leaders' and followers' demands and expectations. Given that organizational democracy usually involves complex and shifting coalitional arrangements and policy compromises among government parties, democratic rationality, in the Arrovian sense of a unique collective welfare function, is not always served by the institutional arrangements.[20] Both liberal and organizational democrats attribute little weight to a democracy's capacity for responsiveness to mobilized citizens' demands. This is the emphasis of direct democracy. Yet direct democracy, lacking filters that constrain the range of choices, cannot guarantee collective rationality, nor is it particularly accountable to vast unmobilized constituencies.

Although this sketch overstates trade-offs by contrasting ideal types, it provides an instructive formulation of the trilemma of choosing democratic institutions. Existing democratic institutions trigger dissatisfaction that *may drive citizens in one of two different directions, depending on the concrete circumstances*. If liberal democracy prevails, there may be calls for organizational or direct par-

19. See Herbert Kaufman, "Emerging Conflict in the Doctrines of Public Administration," *American Political Science Review*, 50(4):1057-73 (1956).

20. This point was made in Anthony Downs, *An Economic Theory of Democracy* (New York: Harper & Row, 1957), chap. 9. He shows that two-party democracies permit party leaders to be rational and locate themselves near the median voter, whereas voters have no rational choice between different political positions—and hence cannot make leaders accountable to their preferences. In multiparty systems, voters can rationally choose parties close to their ideal position, but this rationality is undercut by the compromise policies that leaders must negotiate with other parties in order to join government coalitions.

ticipatory democracy.[21] Conversely, organized democracies may be challenged by liberal conceptions or direct participatory visions.[22] Finally, direct democracy is besieged by calls for liberal reform or organizational structure.

These alternatives also influence the self-transformation of social movements, once disappointments set in with direct democracy. Activists and critical observers usually assume that contemporary social movements proceed from direct democracy to an organizational democracy with strong bureaucratic control. Michels's striking analysis of the self-transformation in socialist trade unions and parties at the beginning of the twentieth century has left its imprint on the mind of today's activists and scholars. Instead, I wish to argue that direct democracy in left-libertarian movements and parties will not be replaced by organizational democracy, but by liberal democratic institutions with personal representation inside small-framework par-

ties that attract few members.[23] I am basing this hypothesis less on the conventional argument that the importance of the mass media and campaign technology in the electoral competition has rendered mass party organizations and organized democracy irrelevant.[24] More important are the entrenched individualism and voluntarism among movement and party activists that are detrimental to any effort to build centralized mass organizations, enforce formal rules, establish internal division of labor, and cultivate solidarity sentiments. As a consequence, left-libertarian political practices are more likely to become small framework associations in the hands of tiny coteries of individualist movement entrepreneurs and politicians with more or less political charisma.

The discourse on intraparty referendums in left-libertarian ecology parties, such as the German Greens and other European green parties, may demonstrate this logic of self-transformation.[25] Left-libertarians advocate popular referendums to overcome the constraints of partocracy. At the same time, however, they

21. Much of the debate about constitutional reform in Britain in the early 1990s is inspired by the apparent success of the European continent's more organizational democracies, while direct participatory demands are only an undercurrent. Conversely, in the United States it appears to me that the critique of the dominant liberal democratic conception usually calls for more grass-roots responsiveness and participatory decentralization rather than more organized democracy, a preference apparently confined to corporate technocrats and a considerable number of political scientists.

22. Especially partocracies such as Austria, Belgium, Italy, and most of the Scandinavian countries have witnessed left-libertarian challenges with a direct democratic inspiration, but also liberal democratic challenges from a New Right.

23. I have empirically substantiated this claim only for green parties, but not for social movements. See Herbert Kitschelt, *The Logics of Party Formation* (Ithaca, NY: Cornell University Press, 1989); idem, "New Social Movements and the Decline of Party Organization," in *Challenging the Political Order*, ed. Dalton and Kuechler, pp. 179-208.

24. The earliest representative of this position is Leon D. Epstein, *Political Parties in Western Democracies* (New York: Praeger, 1967). Such arguments overlook the multiple roles that mass party organizations play beyond the electoral process.

25. I am drawing on interview materials collected in the mid-1980s.

refuse to employ intraorganizational plebiscites among all members to settle major policy or strategic disputes and to nominate leaders or candidates for elected office (primaries). Intraorganizational plebiscites and primaries would give a voice to those who do not regularly participate in political deliberation and thus do not benefit from the main advantage of direct democracy. Yet advocates of this view become intellectually insecure when confronted with the counterargument that democratic citizenship based on deliberation relapses into an elitist exclusionary form of political rule because it violates basic principles of democratic equality by disenfranchising all those who lack the resources—time, education, money —for effective participation.

Formal ballots and strict rules of intraorganizational representation of unmobilized rank-and-file members, however, would introduce mechanisms of organized democracy into left-libertarian parties vigorously rejected by the activists. As a consequence, left-libertarian movements and parties have made few efforts to overcome the perverse effects of direct democracy to be responsive to mobilized activists, but they deny accountability to broader citizens' constituencies. Where direct democracy has been displaced by other procedures, not organized democracy but liberal mechanisms of individualist representation and entrepreneurship have filled the void.

The argument that social movements are caught up in a cycle of democratic practices thus may yield quite different cycles depending on the ideological outlook and historical circumstances of social movements. Whereas working-class politics, inspired by a strong commitment to solidarity and compliance with the collective, moved from experiments with direct democracy to organized democracy, left-libertarian protest politics, driven by the quest for a decommodification and debureaucratization of society, are more likely to adopt patterns of liberal democratic politics. As a consequence, contemporary social movements in continental European democracies are not caught up in a cycle that leads back to the full affirmation of organized democracy. Rather, they infuse elements of a liberal-individualist and competitive tradition of democracy into democracies that have been dominated by mechanisms of inter-elite bargaining and consensus building through large encompassing organizations of interest intermediation.

THE STRUCTURAL DIFFERENTIATION OF DEMOCRATIC PRACTICES AND SOCIAL MOVEMENTS

My critique of cyclical models of democratic institutionalization and social movements has challenged the proposition that, at the end of each cycle, the status quo ante will be reaffirmed. Beyond this defensive, negative argument, I would now like to take the offensive and suggest that some residues of direct democratic practices persist in the self-transformation of contemporary social movements, even though in a muted and constrained way. My hypothesis is based on the theory that issues of collective decision making are characterized by qualitative differences.

Different democratic choice procedures are better or worse equipped to handle certain classes of collective choice problems.

The dominant actors in three democratic decision modes have already been introduced: individual legislators (liberal democracy); mass parties (organized democracy); individual citizens and social movements (direct democracy). I will now add a fourth mode of decision making—corporatist interest intermediation—whose dominant actors are large encompassing interest groups that hammer out policy compromises in top-level bargaining with the assistance of state authority.[26] The key question, then, is, Why are there parties, individual legislators, interest groups, and social movements all at once and not one single type of political actor? Further, why are there different modes of interest articulation, aggregation, and decision making in democracies?

The cyclical view of social movements essentially claims that the differentiation of political actors and decision modes is transitory and that, in equilibrium, only one mode will persist. An alternative theory that insists on the structural differentiation of the modern polity affirms the coexistence of different decision modes and types of political actors, including social movements. It is

26. There is no democratic theory that corresponds to corporatist decision making because this type of decision making does not share the basic premise of democracy that all citizens should have equal weight in the decision process. On the political theory of corporatism, see Peter J. Williamson, *Varieties of Corporatism: A Conceptual Discussion* (New York: Cambridge University Press, 1986).

based on the idea that each decision mode has particular comparative advantages for handling a class of decision problems.

Collective decision problems may be distinguished with respect to their substantive and their temporal complexity. In substantive respects, political issues may present discrete or interdependent problems of choice. Discrete problems can be resolved without taking into account the issue's ramifications for other policy choices, whereas interdependent issues spill over onto a wide range of other issues. In temporal respects, political issues may require permanent attention by democratic decision makers and a continuous demand for collective decisions, or they may require intermittent attention and decisions. Where setting policy objectives and implementation are closely intertwined, issues require permanent democratic monitoring. Intermittent problems, in contrast, involve point decisions that define the policy, which then is either self-enforcing or easily monitored in the implementation process. Overall, then, there are four ideal typical decision problems: intermittent and interdependent; intermittent and discrete; permanent and interdependent; and permanent and discrete.

Liberal democratic institutions giving individual legislators a prominent role are likely to deal best with intermittent-interdependent issues and are likely to define or redefine problems of collective decision making as intermittent-interdependent. Individual legislators have a short time horizon and are thus more capable of dealing with intermittent decision matters, yet they are predisposed to examining issue interdependence. Because voter choices are affected by a multitude of issue positions signaled by a legislator, the latter must monitor issue interdependence in order to maintain his or her chances for reelection. Issues that lend themselves to logrolling on a case-by-case basis, such as pork barrel politics over budgets and projects, are most easily handled in settings with dominant legislators. Liberal representation can cope with substantive complexity (interdependence) but not with temporal complexity (permanence of decision making).

Substantively and temporally complex problems are handled better by integrated political parties in parliamentary democracies that instill a long time horizon in their legislative representatives and leadership; these circumstances allow parties to make more robust commitments to long-term policies while being less deterred by short-term opportunistic considerations of this or that politician's popularity.[27] In fact, the rationality of strong parties is to develop a reputation for a general political outlook that allows rational voters to commit themselves to the party in the anticipation that it will continue to propagate the implementation of its main tenets. This same rationality makes it difficult for large mass parties to respond quickly to temporally intermittent or substantively highly discrete policy issues.

In contrast to mass parties, interest groups focus on a narrower range of policy issues and dedicate a greater amount of their organizational resources to limited causes. This greater asset specificity of interest groups permits them to mobilize contributors and members in a more targeted way than parties can. This advantage, however, also prevents them from entering electoral politics, in which they would be compelled to take into account the interdependence of their most cherished causes with other policy issues. The corporatist participation of interest groups in public policymaking thus works only in functionally specific policy areas and presupposes relatively encompassing interest groups. Mass parties do well to cultivate their ties to interest groups, yet also to keep their distance from them in order to maintain their reputation for addressing the complex interdependence of policy issues.

Interest groups, like parties, are capable of engaging in issues that require a steady stream of policy decisions and monitoring of implementation. Both have few incentives to invest scarce political resources into intermittent and functionally specific issues that mobilize constituencies only briefly. It is with this type of decision problem that social movements have a clear competitive advantage over interest groups and parties. The asset specificity of social

27. It is no accident, therefore, that organized democracies have typically invested more in collective goods such as infrastructure and comprehensive social welfare institutions than liberal-competitive democracies, which have tended to provide more rents for special interests. My argument resembles Olson's claim that "encompassing" groups have a greater capacity to pursue collective goals than narrow interest groups do. See Mancur Olson, *The Rise and Decline of Nations* (New Haven, CT: Yale University Press, 1982), pp. 47-53.

movements concerns both the temporal and the substantive dimension. The character of the decision problem also explains why movements often prefer popular referenda to parliamentary decisions or bargaining among parties and interest groups as the appropriate democratic mechanism of authoritative decision making. The popular referendum is uniquely geared to intermittent and functionally independent point decisions.[28]

Social movements thrive on intermittent and discrete decision problems for a number of reasons. It is comparatively costless to mobilize large numbers of individuals around clearly defined, discrete, and visible issues, particularly if these decisions (1) involve a step good in which the choice is between providing all or none of the good, and (2) organize against a collective ill, giving the movement a protective mission, rather than demand a new collective good that engages the group in a proselytizing mission.[29] Fights against particular instances of discrimination, abuse, pollution, or repression illustrate this dynamic particularly sharply. Their concern for discrete and intermittent issues also means that it is not worthwhile for social movements to invest in lasting organizational as-

sets, such as charters, office space, and permanent staff. This reduces pressures on movement entrepreneurs to develop a complicated machinery of decision making despised by many grass-roots activists. Avoiding organization investments maintains the homogeneity of participants' preferences and lowers the burdens of raising finances, a need that usually forces an organization to attract not just purposively motivated activists but also contributors who primarily respond to marginal selective incentives—material, social—and thus burden the movement with dead weight. Overall, then, discrete intermittent decision problems tend to facilitate a more communicative, fluid, deliberative internal decision process in movements in which the main rewards of membership are intrinsic to the process of mobilization itself.

In light of these considerations, the organizational logic and internal differentiation of contemporary social movements such as those focused on ecology or feminism become intelligible. Within each issue domain, the nature of the decision problem interacts with the movement's organizational form. In environmental movements, there is a clear division between movements fighting about particular projects and facilities—nuclear installations, industrial plants, toxic waste disposal, and so on—and efforts to develop and legislate long-term environmental policies that take into account the temporal and substantive complexity of the subject matter. While project-oriented environmentalists stay close to the direct democratic movement

28. Benevolent evaluations of the usefulness of popular referenda therefore defend this decision mode against a general critique by advocates of representative procedures, but they admit that the appropriateness of this approach varies across decision arenas. See Thomas E. Cronin, *Direct Democracy: The Politics of Initiative, Referendum, and Recall* (Cambridge, MA: Harvard University Press, 1989), esp. chap. 8.

29. See Russell Hardin, *Collective Action* (Baltimore, MD: Johns Hopkins University Press, 1982), pp. 55-66.

structures, long-term ecological policymaking is usually developed by often highly professionalized ecological interest groups, research institutions, and even parties.[30]

In the feminist sector, a similar structural differentiation can be recognized. On the one hand, there are movements supporting or opposing particular point decisions—abortion rights, restriction of pornography, equal rights amendments, and so on—that clearly favor fluid direct democratic practices. The same applies to women's groups whose intrinsic goals are oriented more toward cultural change than toward pure policy decisions. Such groups tend to develop a communal infrastructure of bookshops, coffeehouses, media projects, child care initiatives, or shelters for battered women that only intermittently engages in political activity. On the other hand, feminist groups concerned with women's employment opportunities and other issues that require constant involvement in policy formulation and monitoring of implementation have developed formal interest group structures or have established themselves inside parties and interest groups. A similar division of labor among different organizational forms can probably be found in other movements, such as those of ethnic and cultural minorities.

A comparison of the different expressions of environmental and feminist concerns is likely to show that environmental groups have developed a greater propensity to accept formal interest groups than have women's movements. The ecological issue belongs to a politics of space in which questions of self-organization, deliberation, consensus, and preference change through consciousness-raising are held important but not essential to the attainment of the movements' objectives. In contrast, for movements engaging in the politics of social identity, such as most women's groups, means and ends, processes of mobilization and objective, cannot be clearly differentiated. To a large extent, the objective of the movements' practices is embodied in the process itself. In such groups, not only the orientation toward point decisions but the interdependence between process and goals inhibit instrumental organization in ways instituted by parties and interest groups. Maybe for this reason, there are many ecology parties, yet hardly a single successful women's party.[31]

The importance of cultural practices and the orientation of contemporary social movements toward intermittent and discrete policy issues suggests that, in empirical investigations, it is insufficient to examine movements' overt protest activities. Instead, it is vital to explore the persistence of "latent movements" embodied in interpersonal networks and nodes of communications that former activists maintain throughout periods with relatively few manifest protest engagements.[32] When new issues

30. An interesting hybrid that may therefore be unstable is Greenpeace. This group has made the effort to build a lasting organization around primarily discrete and intermittent activities and causes.

31. The Icelandic women's party is the exception.

32. See Alberto Melucci, *Nomads of the Present: Social Movements and Individual*

arise, participants can call upon such networks to mobilize for protest action. Latent social movement networks maintain a cultural and political capacity to monitor societal developments. In this vein, they constitute a threat potential that parties and interest groups have begun to reckon with. For example, this threat potential also surfaced in opinion polls in the late 1980s, revealing that the popular predisposition to participate in social movements had increased even at times when actual manifest protests had subsided.[33]

In advanced capitalist democracies, citizens' personal resources to engage in direct democratic practices have increased. At the same time, the scope and depth of policy issues that give rise to discrete point decisions vulnerable to challenge by social movements appear to have increased. Furthermore, if the latent readiness of fluid social networks to mobilize protest activities is taken into account, in addition to citizens' manifest protest behavior, it is difficult to get around the conclusion that in the 1980s and 1990s advanced industrial democracies exhibit qualitatively new patterns of democratic politics and an increasing differentiation of the avenues of political involvement.

This new configuration, however, indicates less a polarization of differ-ent modes of participation and democratic decision making than the opportunity for a new complementarity. As Olsen argued in his study of Norwegian democracy in the early 1980s, advanced democracies face the problem not of replacing complex political and economic institutions with social movements but of finding ways to accommodate spontaneity, individuality, entrepreneurship, and responsiveness in a bureaucratic and commodified society.[34] Both scholars of comparative politics and of political theory therefore are well advised to go beyond conventional dichotomies and study the complex interaction of and the contingent role played by specific modes of democratic participation and decision making in different policy arenas.[35]

CONCLUSION

As Lijphart has shown, Western democracies embody different conceptions of democracy. Some come closer to a liberal-democratic competitive and majoritarian model of democracy, others to that of an organ-

---

Needs in Contemporary Society (Philadelphia: Temple University Press, 1989), esp. pp. 70-75.

33. See the analysis of West German survey data in Dieter Fuchs, "The Normalization of the Unconventional: New Forms of Political Action and New Social Movements," in Political Participation and Democracy in Poland and West Germany, ed. Gerd Meyer and Franciszek Ryszka (Warsaw: Wydawca, 1991), pp. 148-69.

34. Johan P. Olsen, Organized Democracy: Political Institutions in a Welfare State: The Case of Norway (Bergen: Universitetsforlaget, 1983), esp. pp. 30-31.

35. Mark Warren has taken a first step in this direction in democratic theory by arguing that the chances of direct democratic and deliberative modes of decision making are affected by the nature of the goods discussed in politics. His typology of collective goods, however, is much more complex than my own modest proposal. See Mark Warren, "Democratic Theory and Self-Transformation," American Political Science Review, 86(1):8-23 (1992). Another effort to grasp the structural differentiation of modern democracy has been made by Held, Models of Democracy, chap. 9.

ized and more consensual democracy. Interestingly, the only variable in Lijphart's study that reflects a trace of direct participatory democracy, the frequency of referendums in a country, is unrelated to liberal or organized features of democratic institutions.[36] This suggests that there are indeed three different and independent modes of democratic governance that comparative political scientists and political theorists should distinguish as well.

In this article, I have argued that contemporary social movements represent an effort to redress the balance between the three modes of democracy in favor of direct participatory methods. Yet the thrust of my argument has also been directed against overly enthusiastic expectations that direct democracy could supplant liberal and organized modes of democratic decision making.[37] An infusion of direct democratic elements results from a differentiation of political issues and decision modes, not from a wholesale displacement of existing institutions. Furthermore, Hirschman's and Tarrow's insight into the wavelike distribution of social movements should be taken seriously. Even within a system of democratic differentiation, the relative impact of social movements and participatory politics will vary over time. Nevertheless, all this should not distract from the qualitative changes in the practice and opportunities for democratic participation evidenced by advanced capitalist democracies since the advent of collective protest mobilization in the 1960s.

36. See Lijphart, *Democracies*, p. 214.

37. Barber's *Strong Democracy* represents one of the most recent efforts to revive an all-but-unrestrained call for direct democracy.

Citizen Groups and the Changing Nature of Interest Group Politics in America

By JEFFREY M. BERRY

ABSTRACT: The rise of liberal citizen groups that began in the 1960s has had a strong impact on the evolution of interest group advocacy. The success of these liberal organizations was critical in catalyzing the broader explosion in the numbers of interest groups and in causing the collapse of many subgovernments. New means of resolving policy conflicts had to be established to allow for the participation of broader, more diverse policy communities. Citizen groups have been particularly important in pushing policymakers to create new means of structuring negotiations between large numbers of interest group actors. The greater participation of citizen groups, the increased numbers of all kinds of interest groups, and change in the way policy is made may be making the policymaking process more democratic.

Jeffrey M. Berry is professor of political science at Tufts University. He is the author of Lobbying for the People; The Interest Group Society; *and* Feeding Hungry People: Rulemaking in the Food Stamp Program *and coauthor of* The Challenge of Democracy *and* The Rebirth of Urban Democracy.

MANY protest movements have arisen in the course of American history, each affecting the political system in its own way. The social movements that took hold in the 1960s had their own unique set of roots but seemed to follow a conventional life span. The civil rights and antiwar groups that arose to protest the injustices they saw were classic social movements. Their views were eventually absorbed by one of the political parties, and, after achieving their immediate goals, their vitality was sapped. The antiwar movement disappeared, and black civil rights organizations declined in power. The most enduring and vital citizen groups born in this era of protest were never protest oriented. Consumer groups, environmental groups, and many other kinds of citizen lobbies have enjoyed unprecedented prosperity in the last 25 years. Never before have citizen groups been so prevalent in American politics, and never before have they been so firmly institutionalized into the policymaking process.

The rise of citizen groups has not only empowered many important constituencies, but it has altered the policymaking process as well. This article focuses on how citizen groups have affected interest group politics in general and how these organizations have contributed to the changing nature of public policymaking. A first step is to examine the initial success of liberal advocacy organizations as well as the conservative response to this challenge. Next, I will look at the impact of this growth of citizen group politics on the policymaking process. Then I will turn to how Congress and the executive branch have tried to cope with a dense population of citizen groups and the complex policymaking environment that now envelops government.

Finally, I will speculate as to how all of this has affected policymaking in terms of how democratic it is. The popular perception is that the rise of interest groups along with the decline of political parties has had a very negative impact on American politics. Analysis of the decline of parties will be left to others, but a central point here is that the growth in the numbers of citizen groups and of other lobbying organizations has not endangered the political system. There are some unfortunate developments, such as the increasing role of political action committees in campaign financing, but the rise of citizen groups in particular has had a beneficial impact on the way policy is formulated. The overall argument may be stated succinctly: the rise of liberal citizen groups was largely responsible for catalyzing an explosion in the growth of all types of interest groups. Efforts to limit the impact of liberal citizen groups failed, and the policymaking process became more open and more participatory. Expanded access and the growth in the numbers of competing interest groups created the potential for gridlock, if not chaos. The government responded, in turn, with institutional changes that have helped to rationalize policymaking in environments with a large number of independent actors.

THE RISE OF CITIZEN GROUPS

The lobbying organizations that emerged out of the era of protest in the 1960s are tied to the civil rights and antiwar movements in two basic ways. First, activism was stimulated by the same broad ideological dissatisfaction with government and the two-party system. There was the same feeling that government was unresponsive, that it was unconcerned about important issues, and that business was far too dominant a force in policymaking. Second, the rise of liberal citizen groups was facilitated by success of the civil rights and antiwar movements. More specifically, future organizers learned from these social movements. They learned that aggressive behavior could get results, and they saw that government could be influenced by liberal advocacy organizations. Some activists who later led Washington-based citizen lobbies cut their teeth as volunteers in these earlier movements.

For liberal consumer and environmental groups, an important lesson of this era was that they should not follow the protest-oriented behavior of the civil rights and antiwar movements. There was a collective realization that lasting influence would come from more conventional lobbying inside the political system. For consumer and environmental organizers, "power to the people" was rejected in favor of staff-run organizations that placed little emphasis on participatory democracy.[1] This is not to say that these new organizations were simply copies of business lobbies; leaders of these groups like Ralph Nader and John Gardner placed themselves above politics-as-usual with their moralistic rhetoric and their attacks against the established political order.

While there was significant support for these groups from middle-class liberals, a major impetus behind their success was financial backing from large philanthropic foundations. The foundations wanted to support social change during a time of political upheaval, but at the same time they wanted responsible activism. This early support, most notably from the Ford Foundation's program in public interest law, was largely directed at supporting groups relying on litigation and administrative lobbying. The seed money for these organizations enabled them to flourish and provided them with time to establish a track record so that they could appeal to individual donors when the foundation money ran out. Other groups emerged without the help of foundations, drawing on a combination of large donors, dues-paying memberships, and government grants. Citizen lobbies proved remarkably effective at raising money and at shifting funding strategies as the times warranted.[2]

Citizen groups emerged in a variety of areas. In addition to consumer and environmental groups, there were organizations interested in hunger and poverty, governmental reform, corporate responsibility, and many other issues. A number of new women's organizations soon followed

1. Jeffrey M. Berry, *Lobbying for the People* (Princeton, NJ: Princeton University Press, 1977); Michael W. McCann, *Taking Reform Seriously* (Ithaca, NY: Cornell University Press, 1986).

2. Jack L. Walker, Jr., *Mobilizing Interest Groups in America* (Ann Arbor: University of Michigan Press, 1991).

in the wake of the success of the first wave of citizen groups, and new civil rights groups arose to defend other groups such as Hispanics and gays. As has been well documented, the rise of citizen groups was the beginning of an era of explosive growth in interest groups in national politics. No precise baseline exists, so exact measurement of this growth is impossible. Yet the mobilization of interests is unmistakable. One analysis of organizations represented in Washington in 1980 found that 40 percent of the groups had been started since 1960, and 25 percent had begun after 1970.[3]

The liberal citizen groups that were established in the 1960s and 1970s were not simply the first ripples of a new wave of interest groups; rather, they played a primary role in catalyzing the formation of many of the groups that followed.[4] New business groups, which were by far the most numerous of all the groups started since 1960, were directly stimulated to organize by the success of consumer and environmental groups. There were other reasons why business mobilized, but much of their hostility toward the expanded regulatory state was directed at agencies strongly supported by liberal citizen groups. These organizations had seemingly seized control of the political agenda, and the new social regulation demanded increased business mobilization.[5] New conservative citizen lobbies, many focusing on family issues such as abortion and the Equal Rights Amendment, were also begun to counter the perceived success of the liberal groups.

The swing of the ideological pendulum that led to a conservative takeover of the White House in 1980 led subsequently to efforts to limit the impact of liberal citizen groups. The Reagan administration believed that the election of 1980 was a mandate to eliminate impediments to economic growth. Environmental and consumer groups were seen as organizations that cared little about the faltering American economy; President Reagan referred to liberal public interest lawyers as "a bunch of ideological ambulance chasers."[6] Wherever possible, liberal citizen groups were to be removed from the governmental process.

This attitude was manifested in many ways. Offices in administrative agencies that facilitated citizen participation through hearings and other public involvement procedures had their budgets cut severely, and most became completely ineffectual. Liberal groups were often excluded from boards and informal advisory groups consulted by agencies. The small number of agency programs that subsidized citizen groups for participation in rate-making and rule-making procedures were terminated. Efforts

3. Kay Lehman Schlozman and John T. Tierney, *Organized Interests and American Democracy* (New York: Harper & Row, 1986), pp. 75-76.

4. Jeffrey M. Berry, *The Interest Group Society*, 2d ed. (Glenview, IL: Scott, Foresman/ Little, Brown, 1989), pp. 16-43.

5. David Plotke, "The Political Mobilization of Business," in *The Politics of Interests*, ed. Mark P. Petracca (Boulder, CO: Westview Press, 1992), pp. 175-98.

6. Michael S. Greve, "Why Defunding the Left Failed," *Public Interest*, 89:91 (Fall 1987).

were also made to defund the Left by cutting programs that offered grants to organizations to do training or community organizing. Conservative critics argued that it made no sense for the taxpayers to support advocacy organizations that took federal grants and then turned around and worked against the government, sometimes even suing it.[7] At the time that the liberal advocacy groups were under attack, conservative citizen groups were being given extensive access to the White House and agencies.

The Reagan administration certainly succeeded in reducing the liberal groups' access to the executive branch. On a broader level, however, the conservative counterattack against the liberal groups was a failure. The reasons go far beyond the more accommodating stance of the Bush administration or the attitude of any conservative administrations that may follow. These organizations have proved to be remarkably resilient, and they are a strong and stable force in American politics. Most fundamentally, though, the Reagan attempt failed because the transformation of interest group politics led to large-scale structural changes in the public policymaking process.

CONSEQUENCES

The rise of citizen groups and the rapid expansion of interest group advocacy in general have had many important long-term consequences for the way policy is formulated by the national government. Most impor-

tant, policymaking moved away from closed subgovernments, each involving a relatively stable and restricted group of lobbyists and key government officials, to much broader policymaking communities. Policymaking in earlier years is typically described as the product of consensual negotiations between a small number of back-scratching participants.

Policymaking is now best described as taking place within issue networks rather than in subgovernments. An issue network is a set of organizations that share expertise in a policy area and interact with each other over time as relevant issues are debated. As sociologist Barry Wellman states, "The world is composed of networks, not groups."[8] This is certainly descriptive of Washington policymaking. Policy formulation cannot be portrayed in terms of what a particular group wanted and how officials responded to those demands. The coalitions within networks, often involving scores of groups, define the divisions over issues and drive the policymaking process forward. Alliances are composed of both old friends and strange bedfellows; relationships are built on immediate need as well as on familiarity and trust. Organizations that do not normally work in a particular issue network can easily move into a policymaking community to work on a single issue. The only thing constant in issue networks is the changing nature of the coalitions.

7. James T. Bennett and Thomas J. DiLorenzo, *Destroying Democracy* (Washington, DC: Cato Institute, 1985).

8. Barry Wellman, "Structural Analysis: From Metaphor to Substance," in *Social Structures*, ed. Barry Wellman and S. D. Berkowitz (New York: Cambridge University Press, 1988), p. 37.

The result of issue network politics is that policymaking has become more open, more conflictual, and more broadly participatory.[9] What is crucial about the role of citizen groups is that they were instrumental in breaking down the barriers to participation in subgovernments. Building upon their own constituency support and working with allies in Congress, citizen groups made themselves players. They have not been outsiders, left to protest policies and a system that excluded them. Rather, they built opposition right into the policymaking communities that had previously operated with some commonality of interest. Even conservative administrators who would prefer to exclude these liberal advocacy groups have recognized that they have to deal with their opponents in one arena or another. The Nuclear Regulatory Commission, the epitome of an agency hostile to liberal advocacy groups, cannot get away with ignoring groups like the Union of Concerned Scientists. The consensus over nuclear power has long been broken. Critics and advocacy groups like the Union of Concerned Scientists have the technical expertise to involve themselves in agency proceedings, and they have the political know-how to get themselves heard on Capitol Hill and in the news media.[10]

Issue networks are not simply divided between citizen groups on one side and business groups on another. Organizations representing business usually encompass a variety of interests, many of which are opposed to each other. As various business markets have undergone rapid change and become increasingly competitive, issue networks have found themselves divided by efforts of one sector of groups to use the policymaking process to try to gain market share from another sector of the network. Citizen groups, rather than simply being the enemy of business, are potential coalition partners for different business sectors. A characteristic of the culture of interest group politics in Washington is that there are no permanent allies and no permanent enemies.

Citizen groups are especially attractive as coalition partners because they have such a high level of credibility with the public and the news media. All groups claim to represent the public interest because they sincerely believe that the course of action they are advocating would be the most beneficial to the country. Since they do not represent any vocational or business interest, citizen groups may be perceived by some to be less biased—though certainly not unbiased—in their approach to public policy problems. This credibility is also built around the high-quality research that many citizen groups produce and distribute to journalists and policymakers in Washington. Reports from advocacy organizations such as Citizens for Tax Justice or the Center for Budget and Policy Priorities are quickly picked up by the media and disseminated across the country. Most business groups would

9. This argument is outlined in Jeffrey M. Berry, "Subgovernments, Issue Networks, and Political Conflict," in *Remaking American Politics*, ed. Richard A. Harris and Sidney M. Milkis (Boulder, CO: Westview Press, 1989), pp. 239-60.

10. Margaret E. Kriz, "Nuclear Wind-Down," *National Journal*, 31 Aug. 1991, pp. 2081-85.

love to have the respect that these citizen groups command in the press. For all the financial strength at the disposal of oil lobbyists, no representative of the oil industry has as much credibility with the public as a lobbyist for the Natural Resources Defense Council.

Despite the growth and stability of citizen groups in national politics, their reach does not extend into every significant policymaking domain. In the broad area of financial services, for example, citizen groups have played a minor role at best. There are some consumer groups that have been marginally active when specific issues involving banks, insurance companies, and securities firms arise, but they have demonstrated little influence or staying power. There is, however, a vital consumer interest at stake as public policymakers grapple with the crumbling walls that have traditionally divided different segments of the financial services market. Defense policy is another area where citizen groups have been relatively minor actors. But if citizen groups are conspicuous by their absence in some important areas, their overall reach is surprisingly broad. They have become major actors in policy areas where they previously had no presence at all. In negotiations over a free trade agreement with Mexico, for example, environmental groups became central players in the bargaining. These groups were concerned that increased U.S. investment in Mexico would result in increased pollution there from unregulated manufacturing, depleted groundwater supplies, and other forms of environmental degradation.

To its dismay, the Bush White House found that the only practical course was to negotiate with the groups.[11]

The increasing prominence of citizen groups and the expanding size of issue networks change our conception of the policymaking process. The basic structural attribute of a subgovernment was that it was relatively bounded with a stable set of participants. Even if there was some conflict in that subgovernment, there were predictable divisions and relatively clear expectations of what kind of conciliation between interest groups was possible. In contrast, issue networks seem like free-for-alls. In the health care field alone, 741 organizations have offices in Washington or employ a representative there.[12] Where subgovernments suggested control over public policy by a limited number of participants, issue networks suggest no control whatsoever. Citizen groups make policymaking all the more difficult because they frequently sharpen the ideological debate; they have different organizational incentive systems from those of the corporations and trade groups with which they are often in conflict; and they place little emphasis on the need for economic growth, an assumption shared by most other actors.

This picture of contemporary interest group politics may make it seem impossible to accomplish anything in Washington. Indeed, it is a popular perception that Congress has become unproductive and that

11. Bruce Stokes, "Greens Talk Trade," *National Journal*, 13 Apr. 1991, pp. 862-66.

12. Robert Pear, "Conflicting Aims in Booming Health Care Field," *New York Times*, 18 Mar. 1992.

we are subject to some sort of national gridlock. Yet the policymaking system is adaptable, and the relationship between citizen groups and other actors in issue networks suggests that there are a number of productive paths for resolving complicated policy issues.

COMPLEX POLICYMAKING

The growth of issue networks is not, of course, the only reason why the policymaking process has become more complex. The increasingly technical nature of policy problems has obviously put an ever higher premium on expertise. Structural changes are critical, too. The decentralization of the House of Representatives that took place in the mid-1970s dispersed power and reduced the autonomy of leaders. Today, in the House, jurisdictions between committees frequently overlap and multiple referrals of bills are common. When an omnibus trade bill passed by both houses in 1987 was sent to conference, the House and the Senate appointed 200 conferees, who broke up into 17 subconferences.[13] The growth of the executive branch has produced a similar problem of overlapping jurisdictions. In recent deliberations on proposed changes in wetlands policy, executive branch participants included the Soil Conservation Service in the Agriculture Department, the Fish and Wildlife Service in Interior, the Army Corps of Engineers, the Environmental Protection Agency (EPA), the Office of Management and Budget, the Council on Competitiveness, and the President's Domestic Policy Council.[14]

Nevertheless, even though the roots of complex policymaking are multifaceted, the rise of citizen groups has been a critical factor in forcing the Congress and the executive branch to focus more closely on developing procedures to negotiate settlements of policy disputes. The quiet bargaining of traditional subgovernment politics was not an adequate mechanism for handling negotiations between scores of interest groups, congressional committees, and executive branch agencies.

Citizen groups have been particularly important in prompting more structured negotiations for a number of reasons. First, in many policy areas, citizen groups upset long-standing working arrangements between policymakers and other interest groups. Citizen groups were often the reason subgovernments crumbled; under pressure from congressional allies and public opinion, they were included in the bargaining and negotiating at some stage in the policymaking process.

Second, citizen groups could not be easily accommodated in basic negotiating patterns. It was not a matter of simply placing a few more chairs at the table. These groups' entrance into a policymaking community usually created a new dividing line between participants. The basic ideological cleavage that exists between consumer and environmental interests and business is not easy to bridge, and, consequently, considerable effort has been

13. Lawrence D. Longley and Walter J. Oleszek, *Bicameral Politics* (New Haven, CT: Yale University Press, 1989), p. 67.

14. Margaret E. Kriz, "Swamp Fighting," *National Journal*, 3 Aug. 1991, pp. 1919-23.

expended to devise ways of getting mutual antagonists to negotiate over an extended period. As argued above, once accepted at the bargaining table, citizen groups could be attractive coalition partners for business organizations.

Third, as also noted earlier, citizen groups typically have a great deal of credibility with the press. Thus, in negotiating, they often have had more to gain by going public to gain leverage with other bargainers. This adds increased uncertainty and instability to the structure of negotiations.

Fourth, citizen groups are often more unified than their business adversaries. The business interests in an issue network may consist of large producers, small producers, foreign producers, and companies from other industries trying to expand into new markets. All these business interests may be fiercely divided as each tries to defend or encroach upon established market patterns. The environmentalists in the same network, while each may have its own niche in terms of issue specialization, are likely to present a united front on major policy disputes. In a perverse way, then, the position of citizen groups has been aided by the proliferation of business groups. (Even without the intrusion of citizen lobbies, this sharp rise in the number of business groups would have irretrievably changed the nature of subgovernments.)

Institutional changes have been made in both the legislative and executive branches to overcome the fragmentation of policymaking among so many different private and governmental actors. In the House of Representatives, for example, strength-ened leadership, the Democratic party caucus, and special rules have all worked to make policymaking more coherent and expeditious.[15] The White House has used regulatory review by the Office of Management and Budget to centralize policymaking and enhance White House control. The Reagan administration's greater emphasis on the ideology of appointees to the executive branch was another means of enhancing centralized control.

Although these are generalized responses to the growing complexity of issue networks, there are developments that are specifically related to the difficulty of formulating policy when there is conflict between citizen groups and business interests. A significant movement in this direction was the passage of the Negotiated Rulemaking Act of 1990.[16] This law actually gave a statutory basis to some agencies' practice of turning regulation writing over to representatives of interest groups. EPA and the Occupational Safety and Health Administration were two agencies already making use of negotiated regulations, or reg-negs, to try to put closure on issues and end the chronic conflict that often existed between competing lobbies. As EPA Administrator William Reilly said, "Four of every five decisions I make are contested in court."[17] Negotiated rule

15. David W. Rohde, *Parties and Leaders in the Postreform House* (Chicago: University of Chicago Press, 1991).

16. Pub. L. 101-648.

17. Matthew L. Wald, "U.S. Agencies Use Negotiations to Preempt Lawsuits over Rules," *New York Times*, 23 Sept. 1991. Copyright © 1991 by The New York Times Company. Reprinted by permission.

making is a way of putting an end to time-consuming and expensive litigation since negotiated rules require consensus on the part of all those participating in the deliberations. The law requires that the committees formed to negotiate be balanced in viewpoint and include all the interests that "will be significantly affected" by the rule.[18]

Reg-negs are not always feasible, and only some agencies are frequent users of this method. Yet it holds great promise, as it has proven to be an effective way to get perpetual adversaries to agree on a policy. After a reg-neg on the Clean Air Act, one EPA administrator said, " 'We had people at the table who probably wouldn't have returned each other's telephone calls.' "[19] This reg-neg produced rules on reducing pollution by requiring cleaner-burning gasoline in the smoggiest U.S. cities. The parties negotiating the regulations were the Sierra Club, the Natural Resources Defense Council, the American Petroleum Institute, the National Petroleum Refiners Association, and the EPA.[20] Reg-negs are a particularly suitable

tool for complex policymaking because they are designed for multiple-party negotiations and work best when there are many different policy problems to be resolved. (With more issues on the table, there is more to trade off in the bargaining.)[21]

There is no equivalent governmental mechanism for developing legislation. Sometimes opposing interest groups will, however, try to agree on legislation to break an apparent impasse in Congress. The inability of Congress to revise the nation's basic pesticide law eventually led to direct negotiations between environmental groups and chemical manufacturers.[22] The National Coal Policy Project was an elaborate effort to negotiate the differences between environmentalists and the coal industry. Although agreement was reached on many issues, the bargainers were unable to get their organizations to endorse the compromises reached. Moreover, the government was not committed to carrying out any such agreement, and it did not embrace the work of the National Coal Policy Project.[23]

Some government blessing of negotiations seems critical to the success of bargaining between sets of organizations. In the wake of the stalemate between Congress and the Bush White House over civil rights legislation, representatives of major

18. *Negotiated Rulemaking Act of 1989*, 101st Cong., 1st sess., 1989, S. Rept. 101-97, p. 16.

19. Wald, "U.S. Agencies Use Negotiations." Steven Kelman argues that procedures promoting direct negotiation between opposing interest groups nurture more publicly spirited decisions by participants. See his "Adversary and Cooperationist Institutions for Conflict Resolution in Public Policymaking," *Journal of Policy Analysis and Management*, 11:178-206 (1992). See also, Thomas R. Rochon and Daniel A. Mazmanian, "Social Movements and the Policy Process," this issue of *The Annals* of the American Academy of Political and Social Science.

20. Michael Weisskopf, "Cleaner Gasoline for Smoggy Cities," *San Francisco Chronicle*, 16 Aug. 1991.

21. *Negotiated Rulemaking Act of 1989*, p. 6.

22. Christopher J. Bosso, *Pesticides and Politics* (Pittsburgh: University of Pittsburgh Press, 1987), pp. 225-32.

23. Andrew S. McFarland, "Groups without Government: The Politics of Mediation," in *Interest Group Politics*, 2d ed. (Washington, DC: Congressional Quarterly, 1986), pp. 289-302.

corporations and civil rights groups opened up direct negotiations. Promising as this was, the Bush administration asked business leaders to drop out of the bargaining, thus dooming it. Presumably, the White House was not ready to have the issue settled because the President was getting a great deal of political mileage out of his denunciations of racial quotas, which, he alleged, were protected by the proposed legislation.[24] Private settlements between interest groups may be easiest to achieve when there are just two sides, such as in an environmental-business dispute. Conflicts with multiple sides may be better suited to the direct involvement of a committee chair or agency administrator since the bargaining becomes more complicated and, again, the trading possibilities increase.

Such multiparty negotiations are, of course, traditional staples of legislative and agency politics and demand the same leadership skills that have always been valued in pluralistic political systems. What is different today is the increased number of interests represented. What has also changed is the increasing prominence of citizen groups in the bargaining that ensues. As subgovernment politics crumbled, citizen groups made it difficult for brokered solutions to exclude them. Since the vast majority of citizen groups that are directly active in legislative and administrative lobbying are liberal

24. Timothy Noah, "Lawsuits by Women, Disabled Are Likely to Be the Main Result of Compromise Civil Rights Bill," *Wall Street Journal*, 28 Oct. 1991.

in their political orientation, their participation has also strengthened the hand of liberal policymakers. At a time when liberalism was supposedly on the wane, consumer, environmental, and other citizen groups invigorated the Left with their persistent and resourceful advocacy.

CONCLUSION

Citizen groups have changed the policymaking process in valuable and enduring ways. Most important, they have broadened representation in our political system. Many previously unrepresented or underrepresented constituencies now have a powerful voice in Washington politics. The expanding numbers of liberal citizen groups and their apparent success helped to stimulate a broad mobilization on the part of business. The skyrocketing increase in the numbers of interest groups worked to break down subgovernments and led to the rise of issue networks.

Issue networks are more fragmented, less predictable policymaking environments. Both Congress and the executive branch have taken steps to bring about greater centralized control and coherence to policymaking. Some of these institutional changes seem aimed directly at citizen groups. Negotiated regulations, for example, are seen as a way of getting around the impasse that often develops between liberal citizen groups and business organizations. Centralized regulatory review has been used by Republican administrations as a means of ensuring that business interests are given primacy;

regulators are seen as too sympathetic to the citizen groups that are clients of their agencies.

Although government has established these and other institutional mechanisms for coping with complex policymaking environments, the American public does not seem to feel that the government copes very well at all. Congress has been portrayed as unproductive and spineless, unwilling to tackle the tough problems that require discipline or sacrifice. At the core of this criticism is that interest groups are the culprit. Washington lobbies, representing every conceivable interest and showering legislators with the political action committee donations they crave, are said to be responsible for this country's inability to solve its problems.

Although it is counterintuitive, it may be that the increasing number of interest groups coupled with the rise of citizen groups has actually improved the policymaking system in some important ways. More specifically, our policymaking process may be more democratic today because of these developments. Expanded interest group participation has helped to make the policymaking process more open and visible. The closed nature of subgovernment politics meant not only that participation was restricted but that public scrutiny was minimal. The proliferation of interest groups, Washington media that are more aggressive, and the willingness and ability of citizen groups in particular to go public as part of their advocacy strategy have worked to open up policymaking to the public eye.

The end result of expanded citizen group advocacy is policy communities that are highly participatory and more broadly representative of the public. One can argue that this more democratic policymaking process is also one that is less capable of concerted action; yet there is no reliable evidence that American government is any more or less responsive to pressing policy problems than it has ever been. There are, of course, difficult problems that remain unresolved, but that is surely true of every era. Democracy requires adequate representation of interests as well as institutions capable of addressing difficult policy problems. For policymakers who must balance the demand for representation with the need for results, the key is thinking creatively about how to build coalitions and structure negotiations between large groups of actors.

Citizen Movements and Technological Policymaking in Germany

By CAROL HAGER

ABSTRACT: In Germany, the mobilization of grass-roots citizen groups in the past two decades has posed a fundamental challenge to institutional politics. One important aspect of this challenge, which is often overlooked, is the relationship of democratizing movements to technology. Grass-roots protest arose mainly in reaction to large, state-sponsored technological projects. Citizen movements reopened the question of the citizen's proper role in technological decision making, which had long been part of theoretical discourse. Grass-roots activists challenged not only policy decisions but also the legitimacy of the bureaucratic institutions that produced those decisions. Informed political participation has raised the technical competence of policy in Germany while eroding the legitimacy of traditional policymaking institutions. Citizen groups have since directed their efforts toward developing alternative political forms that will reconcile technical competence and participatory democracy. The theories of Claus Offe and Jürgen Habermas illuminate the legitimation problems that lead to citizen protest. A comparative analysis of grass-roots movements in several issue areas explores the various forms of citizen activism and their impact on German politics.

Carol Hager has, since 1989, been a member of the faculty of Bryn Mawr College as assistant professor of political science, with specializations in European and environmental politics. She is the author of Technological Democracy: Bureaucracy and Citizenry in the West German Energy Debate *(forthcoming) as well as several articles. She is currently conducting field research on social movements in eastern and western Germany, courtesy of a fellowship from the Social Science Research Council and the Free University of Berlin.*

IN the early 1970s, the West German postwar economic and social consensus was shaken by increasingly large and widespread citizen protest movements. Protest arose mainly in opposition to large state-sponsored industrial projects, from airport runways to nuclear power plants. In many cases, the aims of these groups evolved from protecting the immediate area from environmental destruction to the democratization of decision making in general. Protesters challenged not only the projects themselves but also the legitimacy of the bureaucratic institutions that had produced them.[1] Finding themselves unable to participate effectively through parliamentary channels, grass-roots "citizen initiatives" organized outside the political system. They sought to influence policymaking through mass mobilization and the courts. Their presence politicized questions of technological change that had traditionally been considered purely technical.

Bureaucratic authorities had justified their dominance of policymaking by invoking their expert credentials. Empirical evidence reveals, however, that grass-roots groups held their own in technical debates, often proposing innovative solutions to technological problems. For some

participants, fighting the technical battles was a two-edged sword. On the one hand, they wanted to stop construction of large technological projects in their area. On the other hand, they wanted to avoid becoming an elite of counterexperts and instead wanted to create a political discourse between policymakers and citizens through which the goals of society could be set collectively. Only such a democratic decision-making process, they argued, could restore the legitimacy of political institutions. To this end, many protest groups developed new, grass-roots democratic forms of decision making within their own organizations, which they later tried to transfer to the political system at large.

The legacy of grass-roots protest in Germany is twofold. First, it produced major substantive changes in public policy. Informed citizen pressure was largely responsible for the introduction of new pollution-control technologies, the stagnation of the government's nuclear power program, and the introduction of stricter environmental regulations. Second, informed citizen protest delegitimized the technocratic form of policymaking that had excluded citizens from decisions that affected their lives. The challenge in the years since has been to develop new forms that are compatible with both technological development and citizens' environmental and democratizing concerns. Despite the advent of green and alternative political parties, this policy debate has taken place largely outside the established political institutions. Thus the legitimation issue remains unresolved. An accept-

1. Michael Bühnemann, et al., eds., *Die Alternative Liste Berlin: Entstehung, Entwicklung, Positionen* (Berlin: LitPol Verlagsgesellschaft mbH, 1984), p. 52. See also Roland Roth, "Neue soziale Bewegungen in der politischen Kultur der Bundesrepublik—eine vorläufige Skizze," in *Neue Soziale Bewegungen in Westeuropa und den USA*, ed. K. W. Brand (Frankfurt am Main: Campus Verlag, 1985); Bernd Guggenberger and Udo Kempf, eds., *Bürgerinitiativen und repräsentatives System*, rev. ed. (Opladen: Westdeutscher Verlag, 1984).

able permanent forum for citizen-state dialogue has not been found. Nevertheless, grass-roots participation has raised possibilities for reconciling technological development and democracy.

This article gives a brief overview of several major conflicts involving grass-roots citizen movements in the past 25 years. Policy aspects of these conflicts are analyzed elsewhere; here I am interested in exploring the legitimation problem, that is, how protest over a particular facility became a challenge to the political system as a whole and what effects this challenge has had on German politics. The following sections will analyze the rise of citizen initiatives in Germany, their goals and forms of protest, and the impact of their actions on the relationship between citizen and state in the technological society.

LEGITIMATION PROBLEM: THE ROOTS OF CITIZEN ACTIVISM

Max Weber exposes the roots of the legitimation problem in his discussion of the problems of modernity. Weber describes the historical decoupling of bureaucracy and politics and the contraction of the substantive realm of politics.[2] In modern democracies, as governing becomes more complex, an increasing number of functions are given to bureaucracies on the grounds that bureaucratic decision making is more objective,

faster, and technically more competent than parliamentary politics. Bureaucratization also, however, severs the political link between state and society. Problems arise when societal goals no longer correspond to the goals pursued by those bureaucratic experts. When citizens then try to claim their democratic mandate, they find that they have no institutional link to the centers of power. In Germany today, the decline of politics seems particularly clear in the controversies over large technological projects, which illuminate the stark contrast between the ecological concerns of a local populace and the economic or technical concerns of government and industry. Fundamental preliminary decisions are made behind closed doors between administrators and industry representatives. Thus it is no surprise that grass-roots protest arose largely around such projects.

Parliaments, whose function is to link government and citizenry, are increasingly viewed as irrelevant to decision making for technology-related programs. Claus Offe notes that both bureaucrats and lay citizens avoid the parliamentary institutions that are supposed to connect them.[3] State authorities seek to bureaucratize particularly those areas of decision making that involve technological choices, so that experts can make policy unencumbered by outside interests. Citizens, noting the irrelevance of parliaments to decision making in these areas, form extraparliamentary citizen initiative groups to confront bureaucratic poli-

2. H. H. Gerth and C. Wright Mills, *From Max Weber: Essays in Sociology* (New York: Oxford University Press, 1946), esp. pp. 196-244.

3. Claus Offe, *Contradictions of the Welfare State* (Cambridge: MIT Press, 1984), p. 168.

cymakers directly. By 1975, professed membership in environmental citizen initiatives alone exceeded membership in all West German political parties combined. In turn, the more these extraparliamentary groups challenge bureaucratic policymakers, the more the latter attempt to withdraw from politics by invoking their own expertise—for example, by forming expert commissions. The result is a widening chasm between citizen and state, which occurs not as an open challenge to parties and parliaments but as "an *inconspicuous loss of function and relevance* of these institutions which are increasingly bypassed rather than destroyed by both sides."[4]

This phenomenon is widely evident in conflicts over technological projects in Germany. Disgruntled citizens either avoid the parliamentary route for expressing their grievances altogether, or they first try it and, disappointed when it fails to offer them the kind of voice they want, angrily reject it. Grass-roots activists and bureaucratic policymakers meet only at demonstrations and in administrative courts, a distorted form of participation at best.

The problem is deeper than a lack of access to decision making. Many protest groups consider environmental destruction to be linked to the basic goals of the postwar German state. Thus, as Suzanne Berger has noted, the state itself comes under their attack.[5] Jürgen Habermas explores this problem.[6] He notes that the welfare state compromise was designed to promote economic growth while compensating disadvantaged groups. During the economic-miracle years, this growth was associated positively with democracy. Now pursuit of the economic goal has proved detrimental to the environmental quality of life, and the welfare state no longer seems as benevolent.

Citizen activists now want to claim their democratic mandate by exercising a voice in reformulating fundamental societal goals. Habermas argues that the bureaucratized welfare state system not only prevents them from achieving this voice; it actually breaks down their political efficacy. The bureaucratic form of decision making limits discussion to procedural and technical points: the system allows a discussion of means but not ends. As the welfare state expands into ever more areas of life, it begins to appear as a threat: "the social-welfare guarantees are supposed to serve the ends of social integration and yet they foster the disintegration of those life contexts."[7] That is, by substituting technical procedure for more familiar forms, the state devalues ordinary political discussions of what should be done.

According to this view, the state gives material rewards but takes away personal autonomy and political efficacy. For Habermas and Offe, it guarantees its subjects some freedom from economic want, while citi-

4. Ibid., p. 170.

5. Suzanne Berger, "Politics and Anti-Politics in Western Europe in the Seventies," *Daedalus*, 108(1):27-49 (Winter 1979).

6. Jürgen Habermas, *The Theory of Communicative Action*, vols. 1 and 2, trans. Thomas McCarthy (Boston: Beacon Press, 1981 and 1987).

7. Ibid., 1:xxxiv-xxxv.

zens desire freedom to shape their collective destiny. While the state guarantees the role of client, society strives to develop the role of citizen. The legitimation problem, claims Habermas, "is not primarily a question of compensations that the social-welfare state can provide, but of protecting and restoring endangered ways of life or of establishing reformed ways of life."[8]

Although grass-roots groups challenge the legitimacy of technical experts, they do not oppose technological development per se. Most do not advocate a return to a romanticized past; their demands for an open political discussion of societal goals fit squarely into the project of modernity. The new citizen aims do, however, require the development of new organizational forms. They can be served neither by bureaucratic decision procedures nor by a new pluralism that would substitute market forces for state control, since pluralist bargaining requires neither open discussion nor consensus on goals. One of the contributions of grass-roots groups has been their attempt to develop alternatives to state and market organization, drawing on their own experiences with organizations from private life, such as family, church groups, neighborhood associations, and other informal groups.[9]

The twin goals of stopping technological projects and democratizing policymaking produce a tension in

citizen action that has never been resolved. As Habermas notes, much of the effort of grass-roots groups has been devoted to defending local communities against further encroachment, in the form of technological development, by state and industry. The effort to stop industrial expansion leads activists into legal battles with government and industry experts as well as mass actions such as site occupations and demonstrations. These often work against the long-term goal of developing an open political dialogue between all interested participants.

Some grass-roots groups have attempted to overcome their defensive posture not by dropping out of the political system but by reentering it in the form of green and alternative parties. These parties operate as a critical force, participating in institutionalized politics while proposing alternatives based upon their own experience with grass-roots organizations. As internally divisive as these experiments have been, it is significant that the groups have worked toward creating a political discourse that, while technical, is democratic and that they have partially revived parliamentary politics as an instrument for democratic change.

FORMS OF CITIZEN ACTION

The upsurge in citizen protest began as West Germany's economic miracle began to wane in the late 1960s. At the same time, information on the harmful effects of air and water pollution was becoming more widely available. Many local populations began to question government's con-

8. Habermas, *Theory of Communicative Action*, 2:392.

9. John Keane, ed., *Civil Society and the State* (London: Verso, 1988), introduction; E. J. Dionne, Jr., "Fresh Ideas Awaited in the Democracies," *International Herald Tribune*, 13 July 1992.

tinued support of industrial growth at the expense of the natural environment, a phenomenon often referred to as the "economy-ecology trade-off."

A variety of large-scale industrial projects stimulated public protests. In the mid-1960s, for example, a large West German utility (Steinkohlen-Elektrizitäts-AG, or STEAG) announced its plans to build a 1200-megawatt coal-fired power plant near the town of Voerde at the edge of the heavily populated industrial area of North Rhine-Westphalia. Another large company soon followed with a planned oil refinery complex not far away. Some 2000 people would have to be removed from the area because of deadly fumes from the facilities.[10] In Frankfurt, plans to build a new runway to expand the capacity of the international airport were also under way. The construction would require denuding a sizable tract of forest that had served as a recreational area for the surrounding communities. The federal government announced its support for the construction of numerous nuclear facilities during the 1960s, 1970s, and 1980s, including reactors at Wyhl, Brokdorf, Grohnde, and Kalkar and recycling facilities at Gorleben and later Wackersdorf. These public announcements came only after preliminary planning decisions had been reached. Against the backdrop of increased environmental awareness, the economy-ecology trade-off became a political issue of explosive proportions.

In Germany, early planning decisions on projects such as these are typically made behind closed doors by industry and government experts. Governments have traditionally considered planning a technical rather than a political matter. Moreover, important industries, particularly utilities, enjoy a symbiotic relationship with government. Although these companies are structured as private joint-stock corporations, state (*Land*) and local governments tend to hold all but a handful of the shares. In the Frankfurt runway example, the state of Hesse owned 45 percent, the city of Frankfurt 28.9 percent, and the federal government 25.9 percent of the Airport Corporation (Flughafen AG) commissioned to build the runway.[11] Also, members of local and state governments often sit on utility boards of directors. In effect, state and local governments serve as both owners and regulators of polluting industries.

The structure of West German planning in the 1960s thus fit the theoretical model of a bureaucratized system with heavy ties to industry in which political participation was severely restricted. National and/or local legislative bodies had oversight responsibilities but typically possessed no sources of information independent of industry and bureaucracy and were not consulted in the early stages of planning. The previously mentioned projects, designed to promote German industrial development, raised the ire of local populations, which began to mobilize against them. Large grass-roots resistance groups developed nationwide,

10. Günter Wallraff and Jens Hagen, *Was wollt ihr denn, ihr lebt ja noch* (Munich: Wilhelm Heyne Verlag, 1985), p. 56.

11. Gottfried Orth and Adalbert Podlech, eds., *Testfall Startbahn West* (Wuppertal: Jugenddienst-Verlag, 1982), p. 10.

involving hundreds of thousands of people and producing "civil war-like" confrontations with authorities.[12]

The political system offered two institutional routes for citizen participation: parliaments and administrative courts. The obvious route was parliament, the official overseer of planning and the institutional link between citizen and state. Many citizen groups rejected the parliamentary route altogether, however. At best, they argued, parliaments were irrelevant to planning, and at worst they masked the domination of policymaking by unelected bureaucratic and industry experts. A West Berlin group explained,

The elected officials . . . could equally well head the school or construction administrations, their own companies or the environmental agency, because the substantive decisions that would require expertise are made in any case by officials who are not popularly elected and thus not in any way controllable by the citizen.[13]

Some movements, such as the Frankfurt runway opponents, first tried the parliamentary and legal routes and increased their efforts at mass mobilization later, when these did not provide the kind of public forum they sought.

Certain legal guarantees existed. Federal construction and, after 1974, air pollution laws required companies to obtain permits before beginning construction.[14] Both laws pro-

vided for citizen participation in the form of public hearings and written inquiries, although citizens were still barred from participating in early planning decisions and policymakers were not required to incorporate public suggestions into their plans. Citizens could also file appeals in administrative court against construction permits. Once a site had been cleared, however, there often remained little to defend.

Prior to the late 1960s, new industrial facilities had generally not provoked such mass opposition. A participant in the Frankfurt airport conflict explained the rather sudden rise of citizen protest in much the same terms as Habermas, claiming that citizens feared losing control of policies that affected their lives and found themselves defending their communities against an alien and encroaching political-economic system. He blamed a "threatening economic and political concentration" of power: critical decisions were made from afar by anonymous officials, while the people immediately affected were barred from participation. The decision process itself was impenetrable.

12. Dieter Rucht, *Von Wyhl nach Gorleben* (Munich: C. H. Beck, 1980), p. 89.

13. Bürgerinitiative Kraftwerk Oberhavel, Infoblatt nr. 23, Oct. 1976. All translations are mine.

14. The Law for Protection from Harmful Effects from Air Pollution, Noise, Vibrations and Similar Incidents, or the Federal Immission Control Law (Bundesimmissionsschutzgesetz), was passed in 1974, partly in response to public pressure on the national government to do something about the environment. "Immission" is synonymous with "ambient air quality." Accompanying this law were the Technical Instructions for Air Quality (TA-Luft), which set the specific ambient air-quality standards and instructions for their measurement. This law, as well as changes made in 1977 to the federal Administrative Code and the Federal Construction Law, expanded opportunities for citizens to voice complaints against projects. Authorities were required to respond in writing or by public hearing.

Most of all, the increasing concentration of power in the hands of a few choked off the discussion of alternatives.[15] Many activists complained that no route existed by which alternatives could be raised and discussed within the system.

Activists blamed this concentration of power for the apparent inability of government to coordinate various planning decisions. In the Frankfurt airport example, no one had developed a traffic plan for all airports in the region. Licensing authorities relied for their planning concept on the Airport Corporation itself, whose interests were better served by recommending an expensive new runway for Frankfurt than a solution that would prevent overcrowding by distributing traffic among area airports and making better use of rail lines. Because government-industry dominance precludes the consideration of alternatives that might arise from a more open structure, protesters argued, instead of enhancing the ability to consider the broader picture in planning, this structure restricts it. The solution, according to many activists, would be a participatory, democratic planning structure.

Protesters first raised objections to proposed power plants, nuclear waste facilities, and other large industrial projects that affected them immediately. As they delved into the decision process behind the projects, many began to question the legitimacy of the system in which technical experts make such "ruinous" decisions. As one activist explained, they started with a critique of a specific

project and arrived at *Systemkritik*.[16] Fanned by publications such as the Club of Rome's report "The Limits to Growth," the view spread among activists that the crisis phenomena were not merely a passing phase but indicated instead "a long-term structural crisis, whose cause lies in the industrial-technocratic growth society itself."[17]

Having diagnosed the existing political structure as part of the problem, activists organized outside of it and tried to structure their own groups democratically. A variety of new local and national environmental groups formed to inform and mobilize public opinion on environmental issues. During the heyday of grass-roots action in the 1970s and 1980s, their palette of activities included petition campaigns, nature walks through affected areas, information booths, demonstrations, and festivals. These groups considered public information their primary weapon against the encroachment of government and industry.

Administrative officials attempted in various ways to depoliticize the issue. Some continued to insist that planning was a technical matter in which parliaments and lay citizens could play no useful role. In West Berlin, state officials attempted to dampen protest against a proposed power plant by declaring a state of "planning emergency," thereby allowing the bureaucracy to circumvent the citizen participation provisions of the licensing process in order

15. Orth and Podlech, *Testfall Startbahn West*, p. 116.

16. Interview with Egbert Herrmann, supporter of Bürgerinitiative Kraftwerk Oberhavel, 7 July 1986.

17. Bühnemann, ed., *Die Alternative Liste Berlin*, p. 52.

to expedite the construction.[18] More often than not, bureaucrats' attempts to depoliticize the issue only strengthened the protesters' argument that the process was undemocratic and thus had the unintended effect of bringing the legitimation problem to the fore.

As Offe argued, both government and disgruntled citizens avoided the parliamentary institutions that were supposed to connect them. Governments sought to avoid political interaction wherever possible, while protesters sought to achieve it. Where their methods failed to dampen protest, bureaucrats and industry representatives began to argue that industrial projects would bring prosperity to local communities in the form of jobs. Such arguments found a certain resonance in depressed rural villages. The projects thus pitted neighbor against neighbor and complicated the citizen initiatives' task of uniting the community.

The activists included a broad cross section of the population. Students and professors from local universities often helped out, as did senior citizens, younger urban radicals, and otherwise socially conservative citizens who objected to the destruction of the natural environment.[19]

Farmers were an important part of the protest in rural areas such as Wyhl, the site of a planned nuclear power plant. The diversity of citizen groups proved to be both a strength and a weakness. The participation of farmers' organizations, for example, gave the protest a certain legitimacy among the general populace. It would be difficult for government officials to brand stalwart local farmers as leftwing radicals and rowdies. At the same time, farmers' organizations were often more concerned with the possibility of collecting indemnities than with changing the nature of politics.[20]

In the mid-1970s, site occupations were another favored protest strategy. Companies would often try to begin construction before receiving permits. Once a site was cleared, the company was unlikely to abandon its project, and courts were unlikely to rule against it. Protesters had to delay construction long enough to allow their legal challenges to be heard. This strategy worked well in Wyhl, for example, where antinuclear groups occupied the proposed plant site for almost nine months in 1975 and subsequently kept a watch there until the courts voided the partial construction permit in 1977. Wyhl was a turning point in citizen protest; after 1975, tent cities sprang up at other

18. The Federal Construction Law (Par. 31 Abs. 2: 2. Alternative) contains a clause allowing exemptions from requirements for the Land Use Plan and Construction Plan in emergency situations where the deviation can be justified on grounds of city planning and where the essential aspects of planning are not affected.

19. See, for example, Christoph Butterwegge, et al., eds., *Friedensbewegung—Was nun?* (Hamburg: VSA-Verlag, 1983), pp. 148, 149. Also interviews with Bürgerinitiative Kraftwerk Oberhavel/Oberjägerweg supporters Gudrun Strehmann, on 31 July 1986, and Egbert Herrmann, on 7 July 1986.

20. Joachim Schritt, *Bauern gegen Atomanlagen oder wi wüllt den schiet nich hebben* (Stuttgart: Plakat-Bauernverlag, 1977), pp. 44, 45. Schritt claims that farmers' concerns also broadened during the course of the conflicts. Whereas at first they were worried about defending their own economic existence, eventually many wanted to put a stop to the entire nuclear power program. Ibid., p. 60.

sites nationwide. The sense of community among participants in these occupations helped reinforce the efforts to develop new forms of organization and action. Site occupations eventually lost some of their effectiveness, however. Violent clashes between protesters and police at the nuclear power plant sites at Brokdorf and Grohnde in 1977 dampened the general public's support for this form of action. Further, mass mobilization was difficult to sustain over long periods of time.

In addition to their efforts to inform and mobilize the public, protest groups often tried to stop industrial projects through the courts. The permit processes offered opportunities to raise objections on procedural or technical grounds. Opponents could attack the project during the public hearing stage before permits were issued on the grounds that it would violate environmental or construction law. Where permits had already been issued, they could try to show that permit procedures had been violated. The legal strategy required a great deal of technical expertise, but many activists considered it their only real chance to halt the offending construction.[21]

The legal strategy worked well for protesters. Citizen groups hired their own experts or familiarized themselves with the technical data needed to participate in hearings and file objections. At Voerde, Hans Baßfeld, a local engineer, set up his own measuring equipment to record air pollu-tion levels in his neighborhood after a new coal-fired power plant opened nearby. These levels often far exceeded legal limits. Presenting his own evidence in court, Baßfeld is credited with single-handedly delaying the expansion of this plant for several years.[22] In West Berlin, protesters ultimately lost their legal battle against construction of a coal-fired plant, but through their myriad technical objections they ensured that the new plant was scaled down, moved, and equipped with more sophisticated pollution-control equipment than the original plan had proposed. Legal objections contributed to the demise of numerous nuclear projects, such as those at Wyhl, Gorleben, and Wackersdorf.

This legally oriented strategy also helped break down the legitimacy of bureaucratic policymaking. The legal challenge forced planners for the first time to justify publicly their technological choices. They often found themselves without sufficient data to answer the objections. Bureaucratic authorities had long legitimated their policymaking dominance on the basis of their superior technical expertise. The permit hearings produced the surprising result that the protesters often "out-experted the experts"; their technical challenge revealed government and industry authorities to be less informed than the protesters themselves. The legal strategy thus undermined the legitimacy of the technocrats on their own grounds.

Technical court battles did little to resolve the legitimation issue, how-

---

21. Roman Arens, Beate Seitz, and Joachim Wille, *Wackersdorf: Der Atomstaat und die Bürger* (Essen: Klartext Verlag, 1987), p. 98.

22. Wallraff and Hagen, *Was wollt ihr denn*, p. 191.

ever. The strategy of legal or technical challenge might delay or even prevent plant construction, but it would not by itself accomplish the broader goal of democratization. Administrative courts merely evaluate whether an applicant has followed legally required permit procedures. Many activists wanted to challenge the right of nonpolitical authorities to make these decisions in the first place, maintaining that the entire populace should decide the future. Moreover, the permit process allowed only a narrow discussion of technical points. It excluded the discussion of goals in favor of an argument about means. Acquiescing in bureaucratic form did not help the activists counter the Weberian problem of the displacement of politics by bureaucracy.

A member of Robin Wood, an activist ecologist group, wondered aloud whether the technical protest merely served to make the nuclear power plants safer, the chemical works more carefully planned, and the group's industrial adversaries more sophisticated in their methods. The problem with this outcome, he asserted, was that environmentalists wanted "something completely different: a world without nuclear power plants, without the crazy overuse of automobiles and energy and with nature intact."[23]

Citizens had proved they could contribute to a substantive policy discussion. With this experience, some activists turned to the parliamentary arena as a possible forum for dialogue. Parliaments had been conspicuously absent as relevant policymakers on technology-related policy up to

this point. If they could be reshaped and activated, citizens would have a forum in which the broad questions of policymaking goals and form could be addressed. None of the established political parties could offer an alternative program, however. Thus local activists met to discuss forming their own voting lists.

Green or alternative parties and voting lists sprang up nationwide in the late 1970s and by the early 1980s began to win seats in local assemblies. In the Frankfurt case, opposition to the runway ensured that all three of the established parties lost votes in local elections, while the newly organized greens won representation in every race they contested, polling as much as 25 percent in some districts.[24] The local mayor, a Social Democrat and avid opponent of the project, could not prevent his party's loss of credibility.

The new green parties and voting lists saw themselves not as conventional parties but as the parliamentary arm of the citizen initiative movement. One member of the West Berlin Alternative List explained, "The starting point for alternative electoral participation was simply the notion of achieving a greater audience for [our] own ideas and thus to work in support of the extraparliamentary movements and initiatives."[25] In keeping with this notion, the Alternative List tried to avoid developing structures and functions autonomous from the citizen initiative movement. Members adhered to a list of princi-

23. Reiner Scholz, *Betrifft: Robin Wood* (Munich: C. H. Beck, 1989), p. 110.

24. Orth and Podlech, eds., *Testfall Startbahn West*, p. 13.

25. Bühnemann, ed., *Die Alternative Liste Berlin*, p. 185.

ples, such as rotation and the imperative mandate, designed to keep parliamentarians attached to the grass roots. Although their insistence on grass-roots democracy resulted in interminable heated discussions, the participants recognized the importance of avoiding succumbing to the same bureaucratic forms they wished to challenge. Some argued that the proper role of citizen initiative groups was not to represent the public in government but to mobilize other citizens to participate directly in politics themselves; self-determination was the aim of their activity.

Although the fortunes of the national-level greens have waxed and waned, local and regional green parties have tended to retain a core of their support even after the catalyzing issue, the offending project or policy, is resolved.[26] In parliament, these groups push for much the same things the citizen initiative groups pushed for outside of parliament: greater public information, a more democratic and open decision process, and a discussion of broad societal goals. By keeping one foot outside of parliaments, they retain their critical perspective even as they participate in institutionalized policymaking. By proposing alternative policies, they force bureaucratic authorities to justify their choices publicly. They thus help remedy the citizen complaint that the bureaucratized

German system cannot raise and consider alternative points of view. And in submitting proposals for more small-scale, environmentally friendly development, they serve as technological innovators.

CONCLUSION: RESULTS OF GRASS-ROOTS ACTIVITY

With the rise of citizen initiatives in the 1970s, German politics began to develop in the direction Claus Offe described, with bureaucrats and protesters avoiding the parliamentary channels through which they should interact. As Jürgen Habermas explained, underlying the objections to particular projects was a reaction against the administrative and economic system in general. The citizen groups themselves, however, have to a degree reversed the slide into irrelevance of parliamentary politics. By critiquing the system from without in the form of grass-roots protest movements, citizens have forced a political discussion of issues that had previously been the territory of bureaucratic experts. By reentering parliaments in the form of alternative parties and voting lists, they have attempted to establish an institutional forum for this discussion. Some claim that their challenge to the parliamentary system has in fact helped restore its legitimacy.[27]

Strengthening the parliamentary system is not a desirable outcome for all activists. Many remain skeptical that political institutions can offer the kind of substantive participation that grass-roots groups want. The

26. See Herbert Kitschelt, "Social Movements, Political Parties, and Democratic Theory," this issue of *The Annals* of the American Academy of Political and Social Science; also Dieter Rucht, "Environmental Movement Organizations in West Germany and France," in *Organizing for Change*, ed. Bert Klandermans (Greenwich, CT: JAI Press, 1989).

27. Orth and Podlech, eds., *Testfall Startbahn West*, p. 140.

constant tension between institutionalized politics and grass-roots action was evident in the recent internal debate between fundamentalist and realist wings of the greens. *Fundis* wanted to keep a firm footing outside the realm of institutionalized politics. They refused to bargain with the more established parties or to join coalition governments. *Realos* favored participating in institutionalized politics while pressing their grass-roots agenda. Only this way, they claimed, would they have a chance to implement at least some parts of their program. The two factions never reached agreement, although the *Realo* position tended to prevail in individual cases.[28]

The twin goals of stopping environmentally destructive technological projects and democratizing policymaking produce a further tension in citizen action that has not been resolved. Grass-roots groups have enjoyed some success in achieving the former goal. Activists often won court decisions in favor of environmental protection, at times proving to be more informed than bureaucratic experts themselves and thus demonstrating that grass-roots groups, far from impeding technological advancement, could actually serve as technological innovators. Moreover, citizen expertise helped challenge the legitimacy of technocratic policymaking. By demonstrating the fallibility of the technical arguments, activists forced authorities to acknowledge that energy demand, for example, was a political variable, whose value at any one point was as much influenced by the choices of policymakers as by independent technical criteria.

As Habermas and Offe note, however, the technical language of policymaking tends to limit broader participation and thus works against the long-term goal of democratization. The large-scale mobilization that helped citizen groups in the 1970s and 1980s has waned, although it flares again periodically in individual cases. Those wishing to participate in technological politics on a long-term basis have had to accede to the language of bureaucratic discussion, if not the legitimacy of bureaucratic authorities. Citizen groups have not yet offered a viable long-term alternative to bureaucracy. At the very least, however, they have raised the possibility of a dialogue that is both technically sophisticated and democratic.

It is difficult to assess the long-term impact of citizen activism on German politics, indeed on democratic politics in general. Some of the less immediately visible results may be the most important in the long run. As Alberto Melucci explains, social movements, besides acting on the broader political system, also act on a prepolitical, or private, level, connecting people through group activities. The new social movements integrate these two dimensions of collective action: they "express the complementarity, continuity between private life, where new meanings are produced and experienced, and publicly expressed commitments."[29] These

---

28. See Hubert Kleinert, *Aufstieg und Fall der Grünen: Analyse einer alternativen Partei* (Bonn: Dietz, 1992).

29. Alberto Melucci, *Nomads of the Present*, ed. John Keane and Paul Mier (Philadelphia: Temple University Press, 1989), p. 206.

groups are a testing ground for new forms of communication and interaction. They provide the basis for overt political action and make such action possible.

By the same token, the results of new social movement action are in large part subterranean; they involve subtle changes in the way citizens think of their role in democratic politics. The impact of the movements, argues Melucci, cannot therefore be judged by normal criteria of efficacy or success. These groups offer "a different way of perceiving and naming the world."[30] They demonstrate that alternatives are possible, and they expand the communicative, as opposed to the bureaucratic or market, realms of societal activity. People win a sense of identity through their participation. A Wackersdorf activist says the sense of contributing to society is most important; through her activities, "life for [her] has become more interesting, more purposeful, richer."[31]

Some participants express regret that their trust in the state has diminished. The battles over industrial projects also split communities, leaving behind a populace less trusting of neighbors. In encouraging citizens to take an active, critical role in their own governance, however, the contribution of grass-roots environmental groups has been significant. Thomas Rochon notes, for example, that although the West German peace movement's impact on policy was negligible, its effect on the public discussion of security issues has been tremendous.[32] In general, one sees in Germany today increased citizen interest in areas formerly left to technical experts. Citizens have formed nationwide associations of environmental and other grass-roots groups as well as alternative and green parties at all levels of government. The level of technical competence within these groups is generally quite high, and their participation, especially in local politics, has raised the awareness and engagement of the general populace noticeably. The attempts of the established political parties to co-opt green issues have met with limited success. Even green parties themselves have not tapped the full potential of public support for these issues. The continued questioning of the legitimacy of traditional authorities, along with the growth of a culture of informed political activism, will ensure that the search continues for a space for participatory democracy in modern technological society.

30. Alberto Melucci, "Social Movements and the Democratization of Everyday Life," in *Civil Society and the State*, ed. Keane, p. 248.

31. Arens, Seitz, and Wille, *Wackersdorf*, p. 57.

32. Thomas Rochon, *Mobilizing for Peace* (Princeton, NJ: Princeton University Press, 1988), p. 208.

The Cross-National Diffusion
of Movement Ideas

By DOUG McADAM and DIETER RUCHT

ABSTRACT: Current theory and research on social movements continue to treat these movements as discrete entities, rather than to focus on the ways in which activists in one struggle borrow elements from other similar groups. With its emphasis on the spread of information or other cultural elements, the diffusion literature represents a potentially fruitful starting point for theorizing about the transfer of ideas or tactics from one movement to another. Drawing on this literature, the authors sketch a model of the cross-national diffusion of movement ideas that emphasizes (1) the role of direct relational ties in encouraging an initial identification of activist-adopters in one country with activist-transmitters in another and (2) the role of nonrelational channels as the principal means of information transmission once this initial identification is established. The authors then use the case of the American and German New Left to illustrate the utility of the approach for the study of cross-national diffusion.

Doug McAdam is professor of sociology at the University of Arizona. He was the recipient of a Guggenhiem Fellowship in support of his follow-up study of the 1964 Mississippi Freedom Summer Project. His book, Freedom Summer, *summarizes the results of that research.*

Dieter Rucht is research associate in the research group Public Sphere and Social Movements at the Wissenschaftszentrum Berlin. His current research focuses on the environmental movements in the United States and Germany and the public discourse on abortion in the same two countries.

THE group named itself the Clamshell Alliance, wrote a Founding Statement, and made plans for education and protests against the plant. Inspired by the citizen occupation that had blocked construction in Wyhl, West Germany, the Clams planned a first civil disobedience action for 1 August."[1] The event took place as scheduled in 1976. Eighteen activists walked down the railroad tracks onto the nuclear site of Seabrook and were arrested, while 600 people rallied in support. Three weeks later, 180 people went onto the site. All except one were arrested. During the support rally that attracted 1200 people, Jo Leinen, a leader of a German antinuclear coalition, brought greetings from Wyhl. Obviously, the Wyhl event was an important reference point for the antinuclear activists of the Clamshell Alliance. Therefore, let us take a closer look at these actions on the other side of the Atlantic that preceded and inspired the Clams in New England.

Indeed, the Wyhl event was remarkable. On 23 February 1974, 28,000 people demonstrated against the construction of a nuclear plant in Wyhl. Among the demonstrators were people from France and Switzerland. During the demonstration, several thousand people invaded the site. Two thousand of them stayed overnight, thus marking the beginning of a spectacular site occupation. Because of the strong backing of the antinuclear activists by the local population, the state government did not dare use force in order to break the

occupation. Only in November, after a series of negotiations that ended in a kind of treaty between the government and citizen initiatives, was the occupation called off by the activists.

But this successful act of civil disobedience was not the first of its kind. The Wyhl action was directly inspired by the 1974 occupation of an industrial site in Marckolsheim, France, only a dozen miles away from Wyhl. The Marckolsheim occupation, in which many citizen groups from Germany—including the Wyhl area— took part, ended in February 1975, after the French government canceled plans for industrial lead production at this site.

Nor does our story begin in Marckolsheim. This occupation was itself preceded by an act of civil disobedience at Kaiseraugst in Switzerland. A dozen members from a nonviolent action group symbolically occupied the site on which a nuclear power plant was to be constructed. This group, in turn, was influenced by a 1971 conflict at Larsac in southern France. In this conflict a coalition of pacifist groups, nonviolent action committees, and regional and local peasant movements used civil disobedience to prevent the extension of a military training area. The people involved in this conflict were inspired by Lanza del Vasto, a charismatic leader who had founded a spiritual community close to Larsac in 1948. Six years later, del Vasto initiated the first nonviolent blockade at Marcoule, France, where the French nuclear bombs were constructed. Del Vasto, however, had not invented this kind of activity. In 1937 he had traveled to India to stay with Gandhi for

1. Anna Gyorgy et al., *No Nukes: Everyone's Guide to Nuclear Power* (Boston: South End Press, 1979), p. 396.

a year to learn about the philosophy and tactics of nonviolence.[2]

What is the lesson to be learned from these stories? Protest makers do not have to reinvent the wheel at each place and in each conflict. As the preceding articles have already shown, they often find inspiration elsewhere in the ideas and tactics espoused and practiced by other activists. In short, they play the role of adopters in the cross-national diffusion of movement ideas and tactics.

Diffusion processes have been studied in many areas, such as the spread of language, consumer goods, industrial technology, and medical techniques.[3] So far, however, diffusion has been largely neglected in the field of social movements. Although a few scholars have alluded to the role of diffusion in the growth and spread of collective action, no systematic attempt has been made to apply diffusion theory to social movements and to distinguish diffusion within and between social movements. As in other fields in which diffusion has

been analyzed, the real challenge is not so much in demonstrating the mere fact of diffusion—as we did in our introductory example—but to investigate systematically the conditions under which diffusion is likely to occur and the means by which it does.

Given the relative lack of conceptual attention to diffusion processes in the social movement literature, it would be premature to offer an article based on systematic empirical research. The central aim of our article is more modest. We want to draw attention to a neglected field of study and to outline some ideas and hypotheses that can guide future research. More concretely, we will (1) review the general tenets of diffusion theory, (2) parse the social movement literature for work that implicitly or explicitly touches on diffusion, and (3) outline a suggestive account of a single case of cross-national diffusion: the nearly contemporaneous rise of the so-called New Left in the United States and West Germany.[4] With this example, we hope to demonstrate the usefulness of diffusion theory to our field of study. It is our contention that neither the empirical literatures on the rise of the New Left in both countries nor the dominant theoretical perspectives available to movement scholars—resource mobilization and political process in the

2. This chain of events from Gandhi's acts of civil disobedience to those of the Clamshell Alliance could be easily extended in both chronological directions, but also broadened into a more complex web that covers other areas and conflicts: for example, the influence of Gandhi on the U.S. civil rights movement in the 1950s and 1960s and from there to the Californian farm workers movement as well as to activities of the nuclear freeze movement in the United States; the support of the Larsac activists for antinuclearists in Plogoff, Brittany, in the late 1970s; the blockade of housewives in Port Tenant, England, that opposed the construction of a polluting industrial plant in 1972, which, besides the Larsac conflict, was the second source of inspiration for the Kaiseraugst activists.

3. Everett M. Rogers, *Diffusion of Innovations* (London: Collier Macmillan, 1983).

4. Some of the general similarities in the protest experiences in each nation have already been highlighted in preceding articles in the present volume; see Jeffrey M. Berry, "Citizen Groups and the Changing Nature of Interest Group Politics in America"; Carol Hager, "Citizen Movements and Technological Policymaking in Germany," this issue of *The Annals* of the American Academy of Political and Social Science.

United States and new social movements in Europe—adequately acknowledge the important role that intra- and intermovement links and diffusion play in the emergence and spread of collective action. We hope our article will help focus attention on this neglected aspect of collective action and help stimulate systematic research on the topic.

DIFFUSION THEORY

The strength of diffusion theory lies in the explanation it provides for how new ideas and practices spread. But unlike many diffusion theorists who define diffusion as the spread of innovation, we prefer a more general concept. "Diffusion . . . [is] defined as the acceptance of some specific item, over time, by adopting units—individuals, groups, communities—that are linked both to external channels of communication and to each other by means of both a structure of social relations and a system of values, or culture."[5] Hence diffusion involves the following elements: (1) a person, group, or organization that serves as the emitter or transmitter; (2) a person, group, or organization that is the adopter; (3) the item that is diffused, such as material goods, information, skills, and the like; and (4) a channel of diffusion that may consist of persons or media that link the transmitter and the adopter.

Turning to this last dimension, we distinguish between two models of diffusion, each emphasizing a very different channel of diffusion. The traditional perspective might be termed the relational model of diffusion, in which direct, interpersonal contact between transmitters and adopters is presumed to mediate the diffusion process. Besides the relational model, scholars have also emphasized diffusion based on nonrelational channels, such as the mass media.[6] Taking this as their starting point, the sociologists David Strang and John Meyer have sought to understand the cross-national diffusion of policy or other organizational innovations.[7] They start with an empirical observation: there is a uniformity to policy practices worldwide that would be hard to explain on the basis of direct interpersonal contact. Clearly, some kind of mimetic process is taking place but apparently not mediated by direct, relational ties. The authors contend that cross-national diffusion can occur in the absence of high levels of direct contact, provided nonrelational channels of information are available to a group of potential adopters who define themselves as similar to the transmitters and the idea or item in question as relevant to their situation. The image, then, is of a much more amorphous process, depending more on information and a certain similarity or even identification of

6. See, for example, Everett M. Rogers with John Dudley Eveland, "Diffusion of Innovation Perspectives on National R&D Assessment: Communication and Innovation in Organization," in *Technological Innovation: A Critical Review of Current Knowledge*, ed. Patrick Kelly and Melvin Kranzberg (San Francisco: San Francisco Press, 1981), p. 271.

7. David Strang and John W. Meyer, "Institutional Conditions for Diffusion" (Paper delivered at the Workshop on New Institutional Theory, Ithaca, NY, Nov. 1991).

5. Elihu Katz, "Diffusion (Interpersonal Influence)," in *International Encyclopedia of the Social Sciences*, ed. David L. Shils (London: Macmillan and Free Press, 1968), 4:78-85.

adopters with transmitters than on direct interpersonal contact. Most of the examples noted by Strang and Meyer—free trade policies, Keynesian economic planning, and so on—involve the diffusion of policy innovations among structurally similar, or otherwise institutionally equivalent, actors.

We think that Strang and Meyer point in an interesting direction. We find their emphases on institutional equivalence and the social construction of similarity to be useful points of departure for our own work. At the same time, we think that Strang and Meyer have drawn too sharp a distinction between the classic relational model and the kinds of diffusion in which they are interested. In building on their approach, we will want to soften two assumptions they seem to make. First, we believe that the social construction of similarity is not peculiar to instances of nonrelational diffusion. All instances of diffusion depend on a minimal identification of adopter with transmitter. It is just that direct interpersonal contacts—and the kinds of preexisting ties they imply—make this attribution of similarity much more likely than in cases of nonrelational diffusion. Second, we think that Strang and Meyer exaggerate the extent to which nonrelational diffusion is characterized by the absence of direct relational ties. Instead of two distinct types of diffusion, we see virtually all such processes making use of a mix of relational and nonrelational channels. It is simply the distribution and relative importance of these two channels that shift as we move from geographically proximate to geographically distant groups of actors. Even in

the case of cross-national diffusion, therefore, we expect direct interpersonal contacts to play a role. Specifically, we see such ties as especially critical at the outset of the process in helping to encourage the identification of adopters with transmitters.

DIFFUSION THEORY
AND THE STUDY OF
SOCIAL MOVEMENTS

The relevance of the diffusion literature to the study of movement emergence would seem to be obvious. At one level, social movements are nothing more than clusters of new cultural items—new cognitive frames, behavioral routines, organizational forms, tactical repertoires, and so on —subject to the same diffusion dynamics as in other fields. Yet the movement literature has been distinguished by the virtual absence of any explicit application of diffusion theory.

To be sure, early theorizing emphasized the role of contagion regarding crowds, fads, cults, and other forms of collective behavior.[8] Later, work in the collective behavior tradition suggested various mechanisms for the spread of collective behavior such as suggestibility, circular reasoning, identification, and imitation.[9] More recent research on "protest cycles" and "repertoires of action" rests on an implicit acknowledgment of diffusion dynamics.[10] To our knowledge,

8. Gabriel Tarde, *The Laws of Imitation*, trans. Elsie Clews Parsons (New York: Holt, 1903).

9. Ralph Turner and Lewis Killian, *Collective Behavior*, 3d ed. (Englewood Cliffs, NJ: Prentice-Hall, 1986).

10. James Rosenau, *Turbulence in World Politics: A Theory of Change and Continuity*

however, only Pinard and McAdam have explicitly applied the empirical insights from the diffusion literature to the study of social movements.[11] But even they did so in only the most general way, without distinguishing between diffusion within movements and diffusion between them.

Intramovement links

Despite the lack of explicit attention to the diffusion literature, much of the recent empirical work on the emergence and spread of collective action can be readily interpreted in terms of diffusion theory. The oft noted role of preexisting organizations or associational networks in the initial emergence of collective action is entirely consistent with the stress in the diffusion literature on the importance of strong, established networks of communication as a precondition for diffusion.[12] Empirical ac-

counts of the growth of various movements also fit with the importance attributed to "weak bridging ties" in the diffusion literature. Numerous studies have shown that movements typically spread by means of diffuse networks of weak bridging ties or die for lack of such ties.[13]

*Intermovement links
within the same country*

In recent years, the emphasis on linkages between geographically or temporally proximate movements has been growing, as reflected in a number of diverse theoretical or empirical strands in the movement literature. Perhaps the earliest theoretical acknowledgment of links is to be found in Zald and Ash's discussion, and McCarthy and Zald's later elaboration, of the concept of "movement sector."[14]

(Princeton, NJ: Princeton University Press, 1990); Sidney Tarrow, *Democracy and Disorder* (New York: Oxford University Press, Clarendon Press, 1989); Charles Tilly, *From Mobilization to Revolution* (Reading, MA: Addison-Wesley, 1978).

11. Doug McAdam, *Political Process and the Development of Black Insurgency, 1930-1970* (Chicago: University of Chicago Press, 1982); Maurice Pinard, *The Rise of a Third Party: A Study in Crisis Politics* (Englewood Cliffs, NJ: Prentice-Hall, 1971).

12. Those stressing the role of preexisting organizations or associational networks in movement emergence include Jo Freeman, "The Origins of the Women's Liberation Movement," *American Journal of Sociology*, 78:792-811 (1973); Bert Klandermans, "Linking the 'Old' and 'New': Movement Networks in the Netherlands," in *Challenging the Political Order: New Social Movements in Western Democracies*, ed. Russell J. Dalton and Manfred Kuechler (Oxford: Polity Press, 1990), pp. 122-

36; Hanspeter Kriesi, "Local Mobilization for the People's Petition of the Dutch Peace Movement," in *From Structure to Action: Comparing Social Movement Research Across Cultures*, ed. Bert Klandermans, Hanspeter Kriesi, and Sidney Tarrow (Greenwich, CT: JAI Press, 1988); McAdam, *Political Process and the Development of Black Insurgency*; Aldon Morris, *The Origins of the Civil Rights Movement* (New York: Free Press, 1984); Louis A. Zurcher and R. George Kirkpatrick, *Citizens for Decency: Antipornography Crusades as Status Defense* (Austin: University of Texas Press, 1976).

13. For a rich account of the role of such ties in the initial spread of collective action, see Martin Oppenheimer, *The Sit-in Movement of 1960* (Brooklyn, NY: Carlson, 1989). For a case where the absence of such ties appears to have doomed the movement from the outset, see Maurice Jackson et al., "The Failure of an Incipient Social Movement," *Pacific Sociological Review*, 31:35-40 (1960).

14. Mayer N. Zald and Roberta Ash, "Social Movement Organizations: Growth, Decay, and Change," *Social Forces*, 44:327-41 (1966); John D. McCarthy and Mayer N. Zald, *The Trend of*

Implicit in their use of the term was the image of a loose cluster of social movement organizations tied to each other in some fashion. But still their treatment of the linkage phenomenon was tangential to their central concerns and, as such, only implicit in the work.

More explicit theoretical treatments of the issue of linkages are to be found in Tarrow's work on "cycles of protest."[15] At the heart of Tarrow's perspective on cycles is an interest in understanding the role of political opportunities in stimulating mobilization and the influence of pioneering movements in providing other insurgent groups with tactical, organizational, and ideological models for action. Della Porta and Rucht take this imagery one step further and dub the broad cluster of ideologically similar movements that tend to develop during a cycle of protest a "movement family."[16] This concept, by definition, stresses links between movements akin to each other.

One movement family that has received a great deal of empirical attention in recent years is the so-called new social movements that developed in various European countries during the late 1960s and 1970s.

While often studied separately, these movements are clearly related to each other culturally as well as politically. Indeed, it was their ideological, organizational, and tactical similarities that marked them as new compared to the older family of class-based labor movements. But despite these similarities, no one has explicitly sought to analyze the mix of relational and nonrelational channels responsible for the many borrowings across the new movements.

To be sure, some scholars have acknowledged the role of direct ties in linking movements within the same country, though again without explicitly framing their efforts in terms of diffusion theory. For example, Sara Evans, in her study of the origins of the women's liberation movement, stresses the critical role played by interpersonal networks forged between women active in the southern civil rights struggle as well as the American student and antiwar movements.[17] In the language of diffusion theory, these networks served as the relational bridges by which the ideologies, tactics, and organizational structures of the civil rights movement—and the Student Nonviolent Coordinating Committee in particular—were brought to the burgeoning women's movement. McAdam has made much the same argument in his study of the 1964 Mississippi Freedom Summer Project.[18] He argues that the returning project volunteers served as a critically important vehicle by which the lessons—tactical,

Social Movements in America: Professionalization and Resource Mobilization (Morristown, NJ: General Learning Press, 1973); John D. McCarthy and Mayer N. Zald, "Resource Mobilization and Social Movements: A Partial Theory," American Journal of Sociology, 82:1212-41 (1977).

15. Tarrow, Democracy and Disorder.

16. Donatella della Porta and Dieter Rucht, "Left-Libertarian Movements in Context: A Comparison of Italy and West Germany, 1965-1990" (Discussion paper FS III, 91-103, Wissenschaftszentrum Berlin, 1991).

17. Sara Evans, Personal Politics (New York: Vintage Books, 1980).

18. Doug McAdam, Freedom Summer (New York: Oxford University Press, 1988).

ideological, organizational—of the southern civil rights struggle were diffused to the college campuses of the north and west and, from there, to the emerging student, antiwar, and women's liberation movements. Finally, Gerhards and Rucht, in their study of two major protest campaigns in West Germany, stressed the role of intermovement links in facilitating the process of "frame bridging" that allowed heterogeneous groups to work together in the campaign.[19]

Cross-national links
between movements

All of the examples that have been cited concern ideologically similar movements within a single country or even a single locality; the classic relational model of diffusion appears to hold for them. But what happens when we shift our focus to the cross-national diffusion of movement ideas and tactics? Are we really comfortable in positing that such transfers are mediated entirely by the kinds of direct relational ties emphasized in the diffusion literature? Given the relative paucity of such ties between, as opposed to within, countries, this would seem to be a dubious assumption. The assumption gets even harder to sustain in the case of countries separated by considerable geographic distance. For example, take the case of the nearly simultaneous student protests that took place in 1968 in, among other places, Berlin, Paris, Madrid, Prague, New York, Mex-

ico City, and Tokyo, or the revolutions of 1848 in various European cities. Do we really believe that the demonstrable similarities in these cases were the product of direct ties between activists in the various countries? If the answer is no, are we then left to conclude that diffusion did not, in fact, occur; that the similarities were generated independently? Neither of these conceptual options strikes us as satisfactory.

What, then, is our conception of diffusion in such cases? How can we account for such similarities in the absence of extensive relational ties? Building on the work of Strang and Meyer, we want to sketch a model of cross-national diffusion that emphasizes the complementary role of relational and nonrelational channels in the adoption of movement ideas. We begin with the general idea of the attribution of similarity. Consistent with the general thrust of diffusion theory, adopters must identify at some minimal level with transmitters if diffusion is to occur. This identification need not be all that extensive. In the case of social movements, it may involve only a shared identification with the role of activist. Activists in one movement may thereby borrow tactics from their ideological opponents in another.

To us, however, the most interesting case involves a more thoroughgoing identification of adopters with transmitters. The greater this identification, the more extensive the adoption of elements from the transmitter movement. What processes or factors make for this more fundamental attribution of similarity? One factor encouraging identification is Strang

19. Jürgen Gerhards and Dieter Rucht, "Mesomobilization: Organizing and Framing in Two Protest Campaigns in West Germany," *American Journal of Sociology* (in press).

and Meyer's concept of institutional equivalence. Again they use the concept to highlight the tendency of organizationally embedded policymakers to identify with their counterparts in other countries. As regards social movements, other forms of institutional equivalence are likely to facilitate cross-national diffusion. By this reasoning, labor unions tend to regard their counterparts in other countries as potential models for their own actions. In addition, more heterogeneous populations such as college students, environmentalists, or feminists may come to regard their counterparts in other countries as salient reference groups.

Even in cases of clear institutional equivalence, however, the attribution of similarity must be viewed as an accomplishment, as a product of social construction rather than automatic identification. The practical suggestion in this is that the study of cross-national diffusion has much to learn not only from the diffusion literature but also from the recent revival of interest among movement scholars in the more cognitive or cultural dynamics of collective action. In particular, the crucial importance of the attribution of similarity makes the issue of collective identity highly germane to the study of cross-national diffusion. In the kinds of institutional examples cited by Strang and Meyer, the identification of adopters with innovators is less a matter of social construction than a simple reflection of equivalent institutional roles and embeddings. We should not be surprised to find urban planners in one country adopting the innovations proposed by urban planners in another, especially if the country in question has long been seen as a policy leader in that area.

In the case of social movements, however, the whole issue of collective identity tends to be more complicated. Indeed, rather than drawing on stable, institutionally conferred identities, social movements often represent the collective assertion of a new sense of groupness. To their credit, social movement scholars have begun to acknowledge and study the ways in which new collective identities emerge or are consciously constructed in the course of collective action.[20] Clearly, if Strang and Meyer are right about the importance of the attribution of similarity to cross-national diffusion, then researching the ways in which adopter-activists in one country construct or borrow a collective identity similar to that of transmitter-activists in another country is one of the critical challenges facing those who would seek to study the international spread of social movement ideas.

CROSS-NATIONAL DIFFUSION:
THE CASE OF THE GERMAN
AND AMERICAN NEW LEFT

Before we take up the specific case of the German and American New

20. See, for example, Debra Friedman and Doug McAdam, "Identity Incentives and Activism: Networks, Choices and the Life of a Social Movement," in *Frontiers in Social Movement Theory*, ed. Aldon Morris and Carol Mueller (New Haven, CT: Yale University Press, 1992); Alberto Melucci, "The Symbolic Challenge of Contemporary Movements," *Social Research*, 52:789-815 (1985); idem, *Nomads of the Present: Social Movements and Individual Needs in Contemporary Society* (London: Century Hutchinson, 1989); Verta Taylor and Nancy

Left, we need to make clear the limits of our empirical presentation. Our knowledge of the case is based not on any systematic empirical investigation but rather on a thorough reading of the empirical literature on the two cases, combined with a cursory examination of archival materials plus interviews with a handful of pioneering figures in the two movements. Thus we offer the case more suggestively than definitively. In doing so we hope to (1) point up the almost total lack of attention to the issue of links in the empirical literature on the two cases, (2) highlight a number of seemingly obvious shared elements in the two movements, and (3) offer an empirically informed account of the nature of the diffusion processes linking the American and German New Lefts.

In spite of the many seemingly obvious examples of borrowing by the German New Left from its American counterparts, we were struck by the myopic quality of the empirical literatures on both movements. That is, neither literature focused any real attention on links between the two movements. This is perhaps not so surprising as regards the popular and scholarly literature on the American New Left.[21] Given that the American New Left appears to have played the role of transmitter in this case, it is easier to understand the absence of material on the links to its German counterpart. Less understandable is the neglect of the topic by authors exploring the origins and development of the New Left in Germany.[22]

The point is that we tend to think of social movements as discrete entities that arise independently of one another; hence the search for unique causes. But the tendency of movements to cluster in time and space suggests another possibility: that while the development of insurgency is expected to be profoundly shaped by the unique political and cultural context in which it is embedded, it is quite likely that the initial impetus or inspiration for the movement may be imported from elsewhere. This would appear to be the case for the German New Left, whose emergence and development bears the imprint of its U.S. counterpart.[23] Let us explore these connections in more detail.

Whittier, "Collective Identity in Social Movements," in *Frontiers in Social Movement Theory*, ed. Morris and Mueller.

21. Wini Breines, *Community and Organization in the New Left, 1962-1968* (New Brunswick, NJ: Rutgers University Press, 1989); Richard Flacks, *Making History: The Radical Tradition in American Life* (New York: Columbia University Press, 1988); Ronald Fraser et al., *1968: A Student Generation in Revolt* (New York: Pantheon, 1988); Todd Gitlin, *The Sixties: Years of Hope, Days of Rage* (New York: Bantam Books, 1987); Maurice Isserman, *If I Had a Hammer: The Death of the Old Left and the Birth of the New Left* (New York: Basic Books, 1987); James Miller, *"Democracy Is in the Streets": From Port Huron to the Siege of Chicago* (New York: Simon & Schuster, 1987).

22. Hans Manfred Bock, *Geschichte des 'linken Radikalismus' in Deutschland* (Frankfurt am Main: Suhrkamp, 1976); Peter Mosler, *Was wir wollten, was wir wurden: Zeugnisse der Studentenrevolte* (Reinbek: Rowohlt, 1988).

23. In highlighting the American influence on the German New Left, we are nonetheless mindful of the central role of the British intellectual Left in shaping the thinking of New Leftists in both Germany and the United States in this period. Indeed, at the beginning of the decade, it is clear that young leftists in both countries were far more attuned to ideo-

In thinking about diffusion, it strikes us that one must be able to establish three facts if a persuasive case is to be made for its occurrence in any given instance. First, one must be able to show that the temporal patterning of collective action in the two movements is consistent with the notion of diffusion. More specifically, one must be able to show that the timing and pace of action by the adopter movement lagged behind those of the transmitter. Second, one needs to demonstrate that, in fact, the two struggles share specifiable common elements. These shared elements may be highly variable from case to case, involving common ideological themes, tactics, organizational forms, material cultural items, slogans, and the like. Far and away the most important of these shared elements, however, is a fundamental attribution of similarity on the part of the adopter. This collective attribution will likely feature both an identity component and a problem-definition component. That is, as already stated, thoroughgoing diffusion is most likely to occur in cases where activists in the adopter movement borrow and adapt both the collective identity and the problem definition of the transmitter. Indeed, this attribution of similarity is really the key to diffusion, motivating, as it does, the adopter's use of certain elements of the transmitter movement as a model for its own program. Finally, one must be able to specify and em-

pirically document the means by which these shared elements are diffused from one movement to the other. In practice, this means being able to specify those relational or nonrelational links—or combination of the two—that tie the two movements together and shape the diffusion process. In the next three sections, we will briefly address each of these dimensions of diffusion in relation to the case at hand.

Temporal sequence

Of the three dimensions of diffusion just noted, the temporal sequencing of activism is perhaps the easiest to establish as regards the American and German New Left. The various histories of the two movements—popular and scholarly alike—tell a consistent story. The American New Left began its rise from the ashes of the Old Left as the 1960s dawned, revived at least in part by the example of the black student sit-in movement in the spring of 1960. At the forefront of this resurgence was the Students for a Democratic Society. This organization began the decade with but three chapters and no more than a few hundred members but by the spring of 1964 had grown to 29 chapters and better than a thousand members.[24] By the end of that same year, the number of chapters and members had nearly doubled. At the organization's peak, in 1968, there were perhaps 350 and 100,000, respectively. This trajectory nicely captures the growth of the American New Left generally. From

logical and intellectual developments in Great Britain than to each other. In their interviews, Todd Gitlin and Michael Vester confirmed this impression for both the U.S. and German New Left.

24. Kirkpatrick Sale, *SDS* (New York: Random House, 1973), pp. 15, 122-23.

its very low-level beginnings in 1960, the New Left grew slowly through the summer of 1964; however, the rate of growth increased markedly during the fall of that year. The increase is largely attributable to two related influences. The obvious one is the rise of the Free Speech Movement (FSM) at the University of California at Berkeley. The significance of the FSM in the development of the American New Left has long been recognized. The second influence is rarely, if ever, noted in accounts of the New Left but is arguably more important. That would be the 1964 Mississippi Freedom Summer Project, which brought 1000 primarily white, northern college students to Mississippi for part or all of the summer of 1964 to aid the civil rights movement in the state. The project served to stimulate growth in the New Left in two ways. First, it served as a kind of activist basic training for most of those who took part in the project.[25] When they returned to their home universities in the fall of 1964, the volunteers brought with them the ideological and tactical lessons of Mississippi as well as the resolve to act on them. This group included the majority of those volunteers who returned to Berkeley for the fall term. By inspiring many of the key figures in the FSM and thus setting in motion the events at Berkeley, the summer project fueled the rise of the New Left in a second, more direct way.[26]

In the wake of the summer project and the FSM, the New Left ex-panded rapidly, peaking in the years 1967-69. Thereafter, crippled by internal divisions and an increasingly hostile political establishment, the American New Left declined fairly rapidly, surviving for a time as a cluster of radical splinter groups, including a loose network of underground terrorists.

Overall, the course of the New Left in West Germany bears a striking similarity to that of the U.S. movement. The German New Left also began in the early 1960s, but the movement's takeoff as an important political phenomenon and, in a later phase, as a mass rebellion occurred later than in the United States. Again, there is a student organization, the Sozialistischer Deutscher Studentenbund (SDS), at the very core of the movement in statu nascendi. After being expelled from the Social Democratic Party in 1960, the SDS became more and more radical. Though it was not the only organizational body within the emerging movement, it kept a dominant position in both theory and political practice within the New Left until the late 1960s. By the mid-1960s, the movement was composed of various wings or segments. Beyond the intellectual wing of the movement, which emerged in the universities, important segments were also centered in the peace movement, the movement against the passing of the Emergency Acts, and the burgeoning counterculture rooted in the Situationist International.[27] These elements merged to form one broad movement, which

25. McAdam, *Freedom Summer*; idem, "The Biographical Consequences of Activism," *American Sociological Review*, 54:744-60 (1989).

26. McAdam, *Freedom Summer*, pp. 162-71.

27. Passed in 1965, the Emergency Acts granted state authorities enormous discretion in the handling of internal conflicts.

peaked between 1967 and 1968, attracting tens of thousands of demonstrators and directly challenging those in power. But thereafter, as in the United States, the movement declined rapidly. Indicative of this decline was the dissolution of the SDS in March 1970. Also like the U.S. New Left, the decline of the movement was marked by severe ideological conflicts, sectarian splits, and the rise of an underground.

Common elements

It would be impossible to enumerate all of the elements that would appear to have been shared by the American and German New Lefts. Instead, in what follows, we want merely to highlight the extent of the apparent borrowings by the German New Leftists from their American counterparts.

We argued earlier that the most important elements that any two movements can share concern the collective identity of adherents and the problem definition underlying movement action. Indeed, in practice, it is hard to separate these dimensions, with movement adherents drawing much of their sense of identity from the problems they seek to address. The American and German New Lefts were characterized by considerable convergence on both of these dimensions. What were the defining issues around which the American New Left crystallized? At the risk of oversimplification, it strikes us that four issues were granted special significance by the early New Leftists. These were racial discrimi-

nation, American militarism, the dehumanizing effect of the university, and the general amorality of a society that prized profits over justice and equality. All of these themes received explicit expression in that most important formulation of New Left thought, the Port Huron Statement. Drafted in June of 1962, the statement also proposed the concept and practice of "participatory democracy" as the essential remedy for these various ills. This early definition of both problem and solution had the effect of shaping the ideological agenda of the movement for years to come. To the four issues that have been named Vietnam would, of course, soon be added. But the power of this initial framing can be seen in the way that it helped shape the New Left's understanding and critique of the Vietnam war. Indeed, that critique drew heavily on the themes elaborated earlier. So, for example, the war came to be seen as simply another example of the kind of racial oppression practiced in the American South. Similarly, university involvement in the war effort—as reflected in Department of Defense research, Reserve Officers' Training Corps programs, and so on—was interpreted as a further expression of the modern "multiversity," which treated students as products and coveted research dollars, regardless of where they came from or the aims of the funding source.

The New Left, then, defined itself as a progressive—later, revolutionary—force seeking to address these issues by fostering a participatory revolution among students, the poor, the working class, and so forth. By empowering others—both by the force of their example and by their skills as organizers—the activists hoped to forge a new society born of the active participation of the people in the decisions that affected their lives. In this sense, the New Left conceived of itself as a cadre, but not a cadre of leaders so much as midwives to a nonviolent revolution that would, through the force of collective action, create new humane institutions to replace those that currently enslaved and degraded the majority of the populace.

The American New Left's vision of itself, the problem, and its mission had a considerable impact on the thinking of the embryonic German New Left. Although the flow of ideas from the British intellectual Left was very important in the early 1960s, over time the German Left came to be more strongly influenced by the ideological themes and cultural symbols of the U.S. New Left. The only important theme that was missing in the German case was the emphasis on civil rights, racial discrimination, and the prominent role of civil disobedience that grew out of these conflicts.

This fundamental attribution of similarity on the part of the German New Left encouraged a more general receptivity to all manner of movement-related innovations emanating from the United States. These included tactics such as the sit-in, go-in, teach-in, polit-happening, and the like; styles of dress and appearance; and even specific sayings or slogans. For example, the sardonic statement,

"We are the people our parents warned us about," made by J. J. Jacobs at the height of the Columbia University strike in April 1968, quickly spread among German Left and countercultural groups. In similar fashion, the defiant cry of "Burn, baby, burn," first voiced by black radicals in the mid-1960s, was recast in 1967 as "Burn, warehouse, burn" by activists in Berlin and, indeed, later helped to inspire the firebombing of warehouses and other symbols of capitalism in Germany. This list of specific borrowings could be added to indefinitely, but the point should already be clear: fueled by their adoption of many of the central elements of the collective identity and problem definition of their American counterparts, the German New Left came, as well, to appropriate and adapt many other specific elements of the U.S. movement.

Channels of diffusion

Of the three dimensions of diffusion we are interested in, it is the channels or means of diffusion that are the hardest to specify in the absence of systematic empirical research. What follows, then, is a suggestive account of the way we think diffusion worked in this case. At first glance, the relative absence of references to direct relational ties in the empirical literature on the two movements might lead one to conclude that the transfer of elements from the American to the German New Left turned exclusively on the kind of nonrelational processes emphasized by Strang and Meyer. Information from our interviews with pioneering activists in the German New Left, however, clearly shows that relational contacts played a far greater role than their numeric incidence would suggest.

From our interviews we learned that at least three important figures of the German SDS—Michael Vester, Günter Amendt, and Karl-Dietrich Wolff—gained firsthand experience of the American New Left during extended visits to the United States. Vester spent an academic year in this country in 1960-61 on a Fulbright scholarship; Amendt was his successor the following year; and Wolff was an exchange student in the United States in 1959-60. During his stay, Vester, who was also strongly influenced by the British New Left, developed close ties to such leading U.S. activists as Michael Harrington, Al Haber, Dick Flacks, and Tom Hayden. So integrated was he into the New Left orbit in the United States that he attended the 1962 SDS Conference at which the Port Huron Statement was drafted, even helping craft the language of certain sections. Back in West Germany, he became a key figure in the German SDS and, in particular, took responsibility for its international relations. He also published several articles in the SDS journal *Neue Kritik* in which he either expounded favorably on the thinking of various New Left intellectuals or described specific political struggles in the United States.[28]

Wolff's early contacts in the United States were more educational and personal than political. After he joined the German SDS, however, and especially after he became its president in the fall of 1967, he intensified his political contacts with American New Leftists. He sent copies of German New Left publications to contacts in the States. He also invited Americans, most notably, Bernadine Dohrn, to participate in the International Vietnam Congress held in Berlin in 1968. In turn, Wolff was invited by American leftists to make a tour through the United States to report on protests in Germany. On this tour, he visited some 40 cities and raised considerable money to support New Left activities in Germany. Back in Germany, Wolff organized a solidarity demonstration in Frankfurt to collect money for imprisoned Black Panther leader Bobby Seale.[29]

There were also a few Americans politically active in West Germany during the formative years of the German movement. Most of their activities were directed against the Vietnam war, with draft resistance starting in 1964-65. Gretchen Klotz, who later married Rudi Dutschke, the star of the German New Left, was an active member of this network. According to her, "in this early period these people brought many elements from the American SDS to the German SDS."[30]

We have no doubt that as our research goes forward on this case, we will turn up other instances of direct contact between adherents of the American and German New Lefts. The importance of these relational

28. Interview with Michael Vester, 28 June 1992.

29. Interview with Karl-Dietrich Wolff, 3 July 1992.

30. Wilhelm Bittdorf, "Träume im Kopf, Sturm auf den Straßten," *Der Spiegel*, 4 Apr. 1988, p. 101.

ties cannot be discounted. The literature on the effectiveness of various forms of communication is unambiguous on this point: face-to-face ties are superior to any other means of influence. We have no reason to suspect things were otherwise in this case. On the contrary, we think these ties—especially the earliest of them—were critical in personalizing the lessons of the American movement. The ties helped infuse the contacts between the two movements with a sense of immediacy and direct relevance, thereby encouraging the attribution of similarity on the part of the German activists.

There were other factors that may have encouraged this identification as well. We will touch on four of them. The first is the institutional equivalence that Strang and Meyer see as mediating the kinds of diffusion they study. In and of itself, the fact that the American New Left was centered in the universities went a long way toward encouraging identification on the part of German students. Second, the broadly similar social characteristics of the two groups no doubt contributed to this sense of identification. By and large, students in the United States and Germany were drawn from among the same social strata: white, well-educated, middle-class youths. Third, with the exception of Britain, the percentage of German students who spoke or understood English was considerably higher than the comparable percentage among their counterparts in most other European countries. This greater facility with English did two things; first, it aided the flow of information from the United States to

Germany, and, second, it further encouraged identification by creating a kind of linguistic bond on the part of the German students. Finally, and more speculatively, one could argue that the German students were more receptive to influences from abroad owing to a certain lack of fixed national identity. This lack of a deep national identity can be traced to the infancy of the West German state as well as the traumas of the nation's recent past. Defeat in two world wars and the nightmare of national socialism had left the German students with few raw materials out of which to fashion a firm sense of identity. It may also be that a diffuse sense of guilt and shame over the nation's recent Nazi past inclined the students to search for an identity on the political Left.

When combined with the instances of direct relational contact, these four amplifying factors helped to cement the identification of the German with the American New Left. Once established, this identification enabled diffusion to take place via a variety of nonrelational channels. These channels included television, newspapers, and writings of both a scholarly and a radical nature. At least in the second half of the 1960s, television was clearly the most immediate of these nonrelational channels. It provided an intense, albeit distorted, view of movement events, not only in the United States but elsewhere. Via news broadcasts, the German activists were able, from afar, to witness the beginnings of the FSM in 1964, the symbolic war between communists and capitalists in the streets of Stockholm in November 1966, the Days of Rage in Chicago in October 1969, and so on. As Todd Gitlin convincingly argued, "the whole world" was indeed "watching."[31] For activists keen to learn how the revolution was going, and anxious to appropriate the latest tactics, slogans, and the like, television was an important means of diffusion.

The written word was important as well. In fashioning their movement, the German activists drew on selected scholarly and radical writings. The radical writings were drawn, in part, from the American New Left. *Neue Kritik*, the journal of the German SDS, served as an important early conduit for the transmission of radical writings from the United States. For example, in 1965, on the eve of the German student revolt, the journal published an article describing in detail various direct-action tactics utilized by the American student Left.[32] This article was widely discussed within the German SDS. The author, Michael Vester, had drawn his information from the writings of various Americans as well as his own firsthand experiences in the United States. Another article worth mentioning is Günter Amendt's report on the student revolt in Berkeley in the same journal.[33]

The scholarly writings that were singled out for attention came from both sides of the Atlantic and were shared by American and German New Leftists alike. These writings included works by E. P. Thompson, Karl Marx, Wilhelm Reich, and Herbert Marcuse. The latter figure proved especially influential, based, in part, on his numerous appearances at movement events in both the United States and Germany. American scholars exerted an influence on the burgeoning German New Left as well. For example, the work of C. Wright Mills—so important in shaping the early thought of the American New Left—was also appropriated by German students. In a 1963 article in *Neue Kritik*, Michael Vester offered a positive review of Mills's work.[34]

The image, then, is of a German New Left attuned to events in America by virtue of its own socially constructed assertion of similarity. Having defined itself, the issues, and its mission as broadly similar to those of the American New Left, the German student Left was keen to exploit whatever nonrelational channels of diffusion it had at its disposal. The continuous flow of television broadcasts, films, newspapers, journals, books, and the like ensured that the German New Leftists never lacked for information.

CONCLUSION

Activists are well aware of the borrowing—of tactics, organizational forms, slogans, songs, and so on—that goes on between movements. Movement scholars, however, have been slow to acknowledge the phenomenon, owing perhaps to the dom-

31. Todd Gitlin, *The Whole World Is Watching: The Making and the Unmaking of the New Left* (Berkeley: University of California Press, 1980).

32. Michael Vester, "Die Strategie der direkten Aktion," *Neue Kritik*, 30:12-20 (1965).

33. Günter Amendt, "Die Studentenrevolte in Berkeley," *Neue Kritik*, 28:5-7 (1965).

34. Michael Vester, "Schone neue Welt?" *Neue Kritik*, 15:3-8 (1963).

inance of the case study as a model for empirical research. Research has tended to focus on the emergence and development of single movements rather than on the links between movements. With the increase in comparative movement studies in recent years, researchers have begun, at least implicitly, to focus attention on the links between nominally separate movements. Still, virtually no one has sought to theorize about the nature and significance of these links and the dynamics by which they are forged. In our view, the voluminous literature on diffusion represents a useful starting point for just this kind of theorizing.

We start by drawing on the distinction between relational and nonrelational channels of diffusion. Relational diffusion is the spread and adoption of ideas and practices as mediated by direct interpersonal contact. When one reviews the empirical literature on the emergence and spread of a social movement, many examples of relational diffusion are found. Even diffusion between movements within the same country appears quite often to depend on direct relational ties. But when we turn our attention to the cross-national diffusion of movement ideas, it becomes more difficult to account for the phenomenon solely on the basis of relational processes. In their study of the cross-national spread of policy innovation, Strang and Meyer argue that diffusion can occur in the absence of direct relational ties. What is required instead is (1) information on the policy via nonrelational channels and (2) a certain minimal attribution of similarity on the part of adopters

vis-à-vis the transmitters. Having defined themselves as similar to the transmitters, adopters are likely to use the former as models even in the absence of direct interpersonal contact.

With one minor modification, we think the Strang-Meyer perspective affords a useful approach to the study of the cross-national diffusion of movement ideas. The modification concerns the role of relational ties in such cases. We are not as persuaded as Strang and Meyer that such ties are irrelevant to the process. We think this is especially true in the case of social movements, where the critical attribution of similarity may not be facilitated by the kinds of straightforward institutional equivalence emphasized by Strang and Meyer. It may be that urban planners in one country will routinely adopt the policy innovations of their counterparts in another country simply because of some diffuse identification based on their equivalent positions. But rarely does this kind of structural or organizational equivalence undergird collective action. For women —or students or consumers—in one country to identify with their counterparts in another, a nontrivial process of social construction must take place in which adopters fashion an account of themselves as sufficiently similar to that of the transmitters to justify using them as a model for their own actions. In our view, direct relational ties—even if minimal in number—between adopters and transmitters increase dramatically the chances of this process taking place. At least in the case of social movements, we think cross-national diffusion depends more on the interplay of relational and nonrelational channels than on the replacement of the former by the latter. Early relational ties encourage the identification of adopters with transmitters, thereby amplifying the information available through nonrelational channels.

This scenario would appear to fit the single case we have addressed in this article. The marked similarity between the German and American New Left would, indeed, seem to rest on an early identification of the former with the latter. In turn, this identification was certainly encouraged by extended contact between certain key early figures in the German New Left—among them Michael Vester and Günter Amendt—and their counterparts in the American movement. When combined with other amplifying factors—language facility, shared status as students, similar social profiles—these contacts made the many nonrelational channels available to the German students all the more effective as means of communication. Having identified with their American counterparts, the German New Leftists were encouraged to seek information by whatever means were available. In this context, such nonrelational channels as television, the print media, and scholarly and radical writings helped fill the void.

ANNALS, *AAPSS*, **528**, July 1993

Social Movements and the Policy Process

By THOMAS R. ROCHON and DANIEL A. MAZMANIAN

ABSTRACT: Social movements frequently fail to achieve the policy changes they seek, despite impressive demonstrations of widespread support. Yet movement participation has become increasingly popular as a form of political action. The authors seek to resolve this dilemma by distinguishing between three arenas of movement success: changing policy, gaining participation in the policy process, and changing social values. It is suggested that gaining access to the policy process is the most effective path for movement organizations to have an impact on policy outcomes, because authorities are often more willing to offer inclusion in the process than they are to accept movement demands for policy change. The authors' hypotheses are examined in light of the experience of the nuclear freeze movement, which sought and failed to achieve policy change, and the movement to control hazardous wastes, in which environmentalists are having an impact on policy by gaining participation in regulatory and implementation decisions.

Thomas R. Rochon is associate professor and Daniel A. Mazmanian is director and Luther Lee Professor in the Center for Politics and Policy at the Claremont Graduate School. Rochon is the author of Mobilizing for Peace: The Antinuclear Movements in Western Europe *(1988). Mazmanian is the author of* Beyond Superfailure *(with David Morell, 1992);* The Implementation of Public Policy *(with Paul Sabatier, 1989);* Can Regulation Work? *(with Paul Sabatier, 1983);* Can Organizations Change? *(with Jeanne Nienaber, 1979); and* Third Parties in Presidential Elections *(1974).*

PEOPLE join social movements in order to change public policies. This has been demonstrated over the last two decades by the enormous growth of movement activity challenging public policy in defense and foreign affairs; health care policy, pertaining to AIDS and abortion; environmental protection; and the rights of various groups including women, gays, the handicapped, the homeless, and racial and ethnic minorities. Looking back over this period, it is clear that "myriad forms of protest, self help, community building, and insurgency grew and flourished at the grass roots, sending ripples through the entire culture."[1] Yet there is no evidence that social movements are more effective in changing policy than the conventional channels of participation are, and indeed they may well be less effective. We are thus confronted with the question, If the efficacy of mobilizing for policy change through social movements is so problematic, why are so many people doing it?

One answer to the puzzle of why people get involved in social movements is that participation in small groups that engage political issues through protest and direct action is personally rewarding. The testimony from numberless studies of movement activists is that participation opens up the political world in a way that is almost revelatory. Participants in political protest frequently see their involvement as a defining moment in their lives, after which they come to live differently.

1. Harry Boyte, *The Backyard Revolution: Understanding the New Citizen Movement* (Philadelphia: Temple University Press, 1980), p. 2.

We agree that the sense of empowerment is one important explanation for the involvement of so many people in contemporary social movements. Nonetheless, to accept the notion that movement activity results only in the personal empowerment of activists is to suggest that such movements have no impact on the wider political system. "Rewarding for the activist but unable to affect policy" might be the summary judgment of any number of studies of the impact of social movements.

We wish to offer a different perspective on the political impact of social movements by shifting the focus from public policy to the policy process. Traditionally, analysts of the impact of movement protest have focused on success or failure in changing particular policies because that is what movement activists themselves emphasize. But movements that fail to alter particular policies may nonetheless have a significant impact by gaining access to the policy process. Because particular policy decisions are typically isolated moments in a continuous stream of discussion and decision making on a given subject, the emphasis on policy process means taking a longer-term view of the impact of social movements and appreciating the potential influence resulting from incorporation into the ongoing mechanisms of governance.

For reasons we will develop in this article, authorities reluctant to offer immediate policy change to social movements may nonetheless be prepared to concede changes in the policy process that make policy change possible in the future. The route to policy change via inclusion in the policy process means that the impact of social movement activity on policy occurs indirectly and with a time lag. Indeed, the time lag may be such that policies attributable to movement influence are adopted after the movement is no longer active! We believe that this lag in policy response to the activity of social movements has created a substantial underestimation of the policy impact of movement activity.

We will demonstrate in this article that social movements can have a significant effect on policy outcomes by winning access to the policy process. The evidence for this claim takes the form of two contrasting cases. We compare the experience of the nuclear freeze movement, which sought and failed to achieve policy change, with the movement to control hazardous wastes, in which environmentalists are influencing policy by gaining participation in regulatory and implementation decisions.

DEFINING "SUCCESS" IN SOCIAL MOVEMENTS

In his classic study of the determinants of success in protest movements, William Gamson distinguished between two dimensions of success.[2] One form of success is to gain new advantages for the protesting group, a type of success that we label policy change. Gamson's second dimension of success is the acceptance of the protesting group itself as a valid representative for social interests that are newly defined as le-

2. William Gamson, *The Strategy of Social Protest*, 2d ed. (Belmont, CA: Wadsworth, 1990), chap. 3.

gitimate. This is what we call change in the policy process, because the acceptance of new groups as having legitimate interests generally leads to an expansion of the consultation process that precedes the formulation of policy. We are interested in changes in the policy process that involve the inclusion of new groups and interests in the policy discourse. These changes are typically signaled by the creation of new mechanisms for dialogue and collaboration between government and political organizations.

To Gamson's two dimensions of movement success, we would add a third: that of changing social values. Unlike the other two dimensions of change, changing values posits that the society rather than the government is the target of movement activity. By changing social values, movements expand the range of ideas about what is possible. This ultimately has an effect on politics because it changes perceptions of what the most important political problems are. In so doing, movements redefine the political agenda.

Although social change is only an indirect means of changing governmental policy, it is nonetheless a goal in its own right. To change public policy without changing social values can prove to be a Pyrrhic victory, a lesson classically illustrated by the experience of the Temperance Movement in passing the Eighteenth Amendment without diminishing the alcohol consumption of Americans. Thus the success of social movements may be evaluated in terms of policy change, process change, or value change. To be completely successful in gaining the legal and behavioral changes sought by movements, there must be change on all three dimensions: public policy, the policy process, and social values.[3]

A CLOSER LOOK AT PROCESS CHANGE

Of these three movement goals, the one that is most often proclaimed by movement leaders is the goal of influencing policy. In general, movements never have as much policy influence as their activists would like. The specific policy proposals that are made through social movements are rarely enacted into law, at least not as a direct response to movement pressure. That shortfall of policy influence is an important source of the perceptions of movement failure.

By contrast, leaders of movement organizations rarely articulate the goal of changing the policy process, perhaps because they find that activists are more readily mobilized by the desire to change specific policies. Yet movement leaders frequently find that the political establishment, put under pressure by the surge of public interest in an issue area, responds by opening the policy process to incorporate new groups, including the social movement organizations that are leading the protest.

Changes in the policy process involve expansion of the scope of political conflict. This may take a number of forms. One common reform is for

government to require consultation with interested citizens' groups and movement organizations prior to finalizing policy decisions. Alternatively, the government may set up mechanisms to review grievances and to appeal decisions that have already been made. By providing such opportunities for input and review, grievances are channeled into institutionalized means of participation.

A third relevant form of change in the policy process is the decentralization of policy authority. When the domestic surveillance activities of federal intelligence agencies caused concern, for example, one response was to create a congressional oversight committee that effectively decentralized policy authority from the executive alone to an executive-legislative collaboration.[4]

It would be foolish to idealize these forms of policy process change as offering social movements an opportunity to refashion public policy along the lines they advocate. Indeed, the motive of political leaders in conceding process change is frequently to defuse protest with as little substantive change in policy as possible. At the same time, channels of appeal that begin as a symbolic opening of the policy process can develop real policy significance over time. The Equal Employment Opportunity Commission and the Environmental Protection Agency are two examples of bodies created in response to movement protest that were given a narrow focus

3. These dimensions of movement success are similar to the three aspects of transformation described by Raimo Vayrynen: issue transformation, rule transformation, and structural transformation. Raimo Vayrynen, *New Directions in Conflict Theory* (Newbury Park, CA: Sage, 1991).

4. Loch Johnson, "Covert Action and Accountability: Decision-Making for America's Secret Foreign Policy," *International Studies Quarterly*, 33:81-109 (March 1989).

and few enforcement powers when first established. In both instances, the definitions of standing, the scope of valid complaints, and the ability of the agency to define its own priorities have grown over time.[5] Changes in the policy process are thus important concessions to movement pressure, though the substantive significance of these concessions may not be immediately apparent.

Gamson's study of the careers of 53 "challenging groups" shows that 80 percent of them were either successful in both achieving policy change and gaining access to the policy process or failed in both objectives. For only 20 percent of the challenging groups was the outcome one of gaining policy change without acceptance of the group—"preemption," according to Gamson—or of gaining acceptance of the group without policy change, what Gamson called "co-optation."[6] Even in this 20 percent of Gamson's cases, a longer time frame might well have shown that attempted preemption ultimately leads to acceptance of the group as a legitimate voice in the policy process, while attempted co-optation ultimately leads to policy changes responsive to groups newly admitted to the policy process.[7]

One may ask why political authorities would offer inclusion in the policy process when they must often suspect that the eventual outcome will be policy changes that they are currently resisting. We cannot offer definitive answers to this question but can suggest some possibilities. The simplest explanation is that politicians miscalculate when they offer inclusion in the policy process, falsely believing that they can continue to control policy outcomes. Although a parsimonious explanation, it is rendered implausible by the consistent experience that opening the policy process to participation by new groups eventually adds significantly to the power of those groups.

A second possibility is that politicians may want to be responsive to the demands of social movements but fear retribution from their constituencies if they simply give in to movement policy demands. By surrendering control over the policy process to bureaucratic agencies interacting with movement organizations, politicians can avoid responsibility for decisions in such no-win situations as the siting of nuclear power plants. They can also gain credit for involving citizens in the decision-making process, following the American tradition of political inclusion. This is analogous to Roland Vaubel's explanation of international cooperation as a form of collusive behavior meant to shirk responsibility for unpopular decisions while gaining credit for statesmanship.[8]

5. On the strengthening of the Equal Employment Opportunity Commission, see Jo Freeman, *The Politics of Women's Liberation* (New York: Longman, 1975), pp. 181-85; on the Environmental Protection Agency, see *Risk Analysis and the U.S. Environmental Protection Agency*, a special symposium issue of *Environmental Law*, 21(4) (1991).

6. Gamson, *Strategy of Social Protest*, pp. 31-37.

7. Because Gamson ceased to monitor his challenging groups after they gained acceptance, the phenomenon of acceptance followed by policy advantages is beyond the reach of his study. Ibid., p. 31.

8. Roland Vaubel, "A Public Choice Approach to International Organization," *Public Choice*, 51(1):39-57 (1986).

A final reason why politicians may readily open the policy process to new groups is to improve their own oversight capabilities. As McCubbins and Schwartz have pointed out, the way for politicians to get the most credit for solving problems with the least effort is to establish what they call "fire-alarm oversight" mechanisms.[9] Rather than attempting to monitor the activities of bureaucratic agencies themselves, it is more efficient for legislative bodies to design procedures that enable interest groups and movement organizations to monitor the administrative process and to challenge decisions they consider to be improper. "Instead of sniffing for fires, Congress places fire alarm boxes on street corners, builds neighborhood fire houses, and sometimes dispatches its own hook-and-ladder in response to an alarm."[10] In order to motivate interest groups and movement organizations to act as alarm boxes for legislative oversight activities, however, the administrative process must be open to both inspection and appeal by movement organizations.[11]

In sum, political authorities may offer inclusion of challenging groups in the policy process in order to co-opt dissenting organizations, to diffuse responsibility for policy, and to

help politicians monitor bureaucratic performance. Our argument thus far may be summarized in terms of three hypotheses:

H_1. Movement organizations tend to stress policy change goals but typically have a greater long-term policy impact when they focus their attention on gaining access to the policy process.

H_2. Authorities will often accept policy process changes, even while rejecting substantive policy changes.

H_3. Changes in the policy process that offer inclusion to new groups ultimately lead to policy change by introducing new social values to particular policy arenas.

We cannot offer definitive tests of these hypotheses in this article, but we will present here two illustrative case studies of social movements that adopted contrasting strategies for influencing policy. One, the nuclear freeze movement, sought to change legislation but failed to have policy influence. The other, comprising environmental organizations concerned with hazardous waste treatment, adopted the alternative strategy of insinuating themselves into the policy process, with far greater success.

THE NUCLEAR FREEZE MOVEMENT

In the early 1980s, the nuclear freeze movement became the largest social movement in American history. During this period, the idea of the nuclear freeze consistently garnered the support of about 70 percent of the American population. At the height of the movement, there were between 1400 and 2000 local freeze organizations throughout the coun-

9. Matthew McCubbins and Thomas Schwartz, "Congressional Oversight Overlooked: Police Patrols versus Fire Alarms," *American Journal of Political Science*, 28(1):165-79 (Feb. 1984).

10. Ibid., p. 166.

11. For their part, movement leaders may also seek participation in the political process as a way of extending their roles beyond the mobilization phase of movement protest. See Robert Salisbury, "An Exchange Theory of Interest Groups," *Midwest Journal of Political Science*, 13(1):1-32 (Feb. 1969).

try.[12] The freeze was the major force behind the largest demonstration in American history, the assembly of about 750,000 people in Central Park in New York on 12 June 1982. Hundreds of town meetings and city councils went on record in support of the freeze. Referenda held in 1982 demonstrated the popularity of the freeze at the ballot box in 10 states representing 30 percent of the American population, losing only in Arizona.

As with most social movements, the goal of the freeze movement was to influence policy—in this case, by achieving a verifiable, bilateral halt to the development, testing, and deployment of nuclear weapons. The strategy adopted by the movement for doing so was to get Congress to pass a resolution in 1982 that would urge the President to negotiate a freeze with the Soviet Union. This effort, however, quickly became bogged down in congressional politics. Seemingly slight amendments to the wording of the House freeze resolution turned it into a statement supportive of President Reagan's drive to build up the nuclear arsenal to achieve parity with the Soviet Union.

Despite congressional elections in 1982, which produced a wider margin of members claiming to support the freeze, the resolution passed in 1983 was little better. In its final form, the

resolution stated that negotiations for a mutual and verifiable freeze should be undertaken only if the United States and the Soviet Union had "essential equivalence in overall nuclear capabilities," only to the extent that such an agreement would be mutual and verifiable, only to the extent that such an agreement would be compatible with North Atlantic Treaty Organization obligations, only to the extent that the credibility of the American nuclear deterrent would be maintained, and only to the extent that such an agreement would not jeopardize the ability of the United States to preserve freedom. Section 3b of the act states that "nothing in this resolution shall be construed to supercede the treatymaking powers of the President under the Constitution."

In short, the freeze resolution passed by the House offered the President a variety of reasons why its mandate to negotiate a freeze agreement could be refused. Before even introducing the resolution in the House, Representative Markey and his staff agreed that "we should make clear that we are introducing a symbolic measure. . . . We're concerned in this resolution only with making a statement."[13] That President Reagan did not act in accord with the urgings of the freeze resolution could have come as a surprise to no one.

The resolution was so vague that both sides claimed victory. "The freeze still comes first," said Speaker Tip O'Neill. "The priorities [in arms control] have not been altered,"

12. For overviews of the freeze movement, see Adam Garfinkle, *The Politics of the Nuclear Freeze* (Philadelphia: Foreign Policy Research Institute, 1984); Milton Katz, *Ban the Bomb: A History of SANE, the Committee for a Sane Nuclear Policy* (New York: Praeger, 1986); David Meyer, *A Winter of Discontent: The Nuclear Freeze and American Politics* (New York: Praeger, 1990).

13. Douglas Waller, *Congress and the Nuclear Freeze* (Amherst: University of Massachusetts Press, 1987), p. 52.

claimed Minority Leader Robert Michel.[14] Michel's interpretation is supported by the fact that the House followed its freeze resolution with approval of funding for MX and Trident missile development, funding of the first segments of the Strategic Defense Initiative, and approval of deployment of the cruise and Pershing II missiles in Europe. By the time of the 1984 presidential campaign, the meaning of the freeze was so unclear that some Democratic candidates endorsed both the freeze and selected plans for modernization of the strategic nuclear arsenal.

Could the freeze movement have had a greater impact on the arms control policy process had it followed a strategy less reliant on congressional passage of a freeze resolution? In 1982 and 1983, when popular mobilization for the freeze was at its height, the movement was positioned to claim that President Reagan's handling of superpower relations was inadequate to the seriousness of the threat of nuclear war. Popular support for the freeze was less an endorsement of the freeze proposal per se than it was a belief that something had to be done to alter the seeming drift toward military confrontation with the Soviet Union. The survey evidence on support for the freeze strongly suggests that increased fear of nuclear war, more than attraction to the freeze idea it-

self, accounts for the popularity of the proposal.[15]

Under such circumstances, freeze leaders might have argued that arms control policy could not be entrusted solely to the executive office. The decision to use the freeze movement to put pressure on Congress was a sound one, but allowing that pressure to take the form of a symbolic congressional resolution was a mistake. The anger and fear inspired by the bellicose rhetoric and distant relations between President Reagan and the Soviet leadership in the early 1980s might more profitably have been turned into pressure on the Senate to assert itself as a partner in determining the direction of arms control policy. Had the freeze movement demanded changes in the policy process rather than a symbolic freeze resolution, it may have had a greater long-run impact on nuclear arms control policy.

Counterfactual hypotheses, such as the question of what would have happened had the freeze movement sought a greater role for Congress in arms talks with the Soviet Union, are necessarily highly speculative. To launch such a campaign, the freeze would have had to shift all its resources to focusing on the Senate, which, unlike the House of Representatives, is given a constitutional role in the treaty process. The Constitution prohibits Congress from ordering the President to negotiate a particular treaty, but it does not prevent the Senate from expanding its ad-

14. Both citations are from L. Marvin Overby and Sarah Ritchie, "Mobilized Masses and Strategic Opponents: A Resource Mobilization Analysis of the Clean Air and Nuclear Freeze Movements" (Paper delivered at the meeting of the Southern Political Science Association, Atlanta, 1990).

15. Michael Milburn, Paul Watanabe, and Bernard Kramer, "The Nature and Sources of Attitudes toward a Nuclear Freeze," *Political Psychology*, 7(4):661-74 (1986).

vice-and-consent role to establish a more active dialogue with the President on desirable directions in arms control.[16] Having such a dialogue would harken back to the role of the Senate in an earlier period in American history, as, for example, when President Washington sought Senate approval of treaty negotiators as well as Senate advice on their negotiating instructions.[17] Above all, it would press home the argument that arms control policy is too vital to the national interest to be left solely in the hands of the executive branch.

It was just such arguments and concerns that led to other instances of congressional assertiveness in the realm of foreign policy, such as the War Powers Act, which was passed over presidential veto in 1973, and the series of acts passed in the wake of revelations concerning covert intelligence activities abroad, which established greater congressional control over intelligence operations. As public concern about the chilling of the Cold War grew in the early 1980s, Congress did indeed begin to take a more active role in decisions on the development of new weapons and in urging adherence to the second Strategic Arms Limitation Talks treaty and a resumption of negotiations

toward a comprehensive test ban treaty. Congress also took an uncommonly activist stance in restricting U.S. military involvement in Central America. But these actions were never linked to a formal mechanism for Senate oversight of the President's international diplomacy. As a result, congressional activism lasted only as long as the freeze movement was able to maintain public visibility and pressure on the issue.

Ultimately, the freeze movement strategy of attempting to alter policy by passing a specific congressional resolution was a failure. The 1984 elections returned President Reagan to office in a landslide, despite the efforts of freeze activists on behalf of his opponent. Without any clear strategy to achieve change, the freeze movement rapidly collapsed. Within three years, the much reduced national staff of the Nuclear Weapons Freeze Campaign had merged with the long-established antinuclear organization SANE. Despite the massive support gained during the Cold War chill of the early 1980s, the freeze movement soon melted without a trace.

PROTEST AGAINST
HAZARDOUS WASTES

Second only to the freeze movement in size and scope during the 1980s was the widespread outpouring of protest against the reckless management of hazardous wastes and toxic materials by American business and government. In addition to the environmental activists mobilized a decade earlier over issues of air and water pollution, the problems of toxics and hazardous waste brought pre-

16. The Constitution says in part that "[the President] shall have Power, by and with the Advice and Consent of the Senate, to make Treaties, provided two-thirds of the Senators present concur; and he shall nominate, and by and with the Advice and Consent of the Senate, shall appoint Ambassadors, other public Ministers and Consuls . . . and all other Officers of the United States." U.S., *Constitution*, art. 2, sec. 2, para. 2.

17. Louis Fisher, *American Constitutional Law* (New York: McGraw-Hill, 1990), p. 308.

viously uninvolved citizens into the political arena in numbers rarely experienced.[18] Traditional organizations such as the Sierra Club saw a doubling of membership in the early 1980s, while hundreds of newly formed local groups monitored the implementation of Superfund hazardous waste site cleanup efforts by the government. The resulting mobilization of thousands of citizens in hundreds of protest groups caused hazardous waste policy to be shifted from the closed circle of government agencies and private industry to the politics of public outcry and protest.

The toxics movement differs from the freeze movement in several notable respects. Rather than addressing Congress, protest against hazardous waste treatment has focused on the thousands of past and present waste treatment and storage facilities across the nation. Although most activists were initially mobilized to change a specific policy or decision, such as a local Superfund site cleanup or waste treatment facility, they soon came to feel that it was just as important to secure an opening of the policy process to greater public participation. This would enable continuing intervention by movement activists in the myriad local siting, health, safety, and land-use issues that constantly arise in the toxics arena.

The shift in attention from policy to the ongoing governing process reflects a reorientation under way in the broader environmental movement, for which toxics happened to be the most salient topic during the

1980s. As successful as the efforts of the 1970s were to win passage of new federal legislation to protect the environment,[19] most activists believed that the changes in environmental practices called for by new legislation were too little, too late, and too often simply ignored. The conviction grew that movement activists would have to take an active role in the implementation of this legislation, that this could not be entrusted to public officials and business leaders alone.

Within this context, groups sprang up across the nation demanding to participate in negotiations on hazardous waste regulation and in the implementation of specific agreements on facility siting and operation. In effect, environmental groups insinuated themselves into the established working relations between government and business. As the focus of these groups moved from battles over particular policies and statutes to involvement in regulation and implementation, the political process evolved from one of representative democracy through organized interest groups in distant federal and state capitals to a far more decentralized democracy with the active participation of citizens mobilized through movement organizations. The pace of change has not been even across all levels of government or in all regions of the country. Nevertheless, the participatory experiments of the 1980s have evolved into commonly adopted procedures in the

18. Dick Russell, "The Rise of the Grass-Roots Toxics Movement," *Amicus Journal*, 12:17-21 (Winter 1990).

19. This legislation includes toxics and hazardous waste legislation such as the Resources Conservation and Recovery Act, as well as the Comprehensive Environmental Response, Compensation, and Liability Act, popularly known as Superfund.

1990s. The involvement of environmental organizations in the policy process is here to stay.[20]

Businesses and movement organizations alike have come to realize that there are advantages to direct involvement by movement activists in the design and implementation of hazardous waste programs and projects. By accepting this involvement in the policy process, environmental groups do weaken their ability to bring a proposed project to a halt through litigation and public confrontation—a point that continues to trouble some environmental organizations. Increasing numbers of environmental organizations have found, though, that simply saying no is insufficient. For one thing, the strategy does not always work. Even more serious is the problem of maintaining credibility with the broad public when one does not have a positive agenda for environmentally sensitive growth and development.

This strategic decision by environmental organizations to focus on the policy process was also affected by the narrowing of opportunities during the Reagan administration for movement activists to get involved through internal and often informal channels of the U.S. Environmental Protection Agency. Faced with the decidedly anti-environmental Reagan presidency, environmental leaders realized they would have to find alternative channels of influence.

At the same time, the environmentalists' strategy of mobilizing the public in order to block projects was sufficiently successful that the business and governmental architects of various projects were eager to move beyond the threatened stalemate with environmental groups. As a result, both sides began to search for new kinds of policy forums beyond the legislature, courts, administrative hearings, and public protests. This search converged on alternative dispute resolution (ADR), which, as regards the environmentalism field, may be described broadly as "any effort to use informal, face-to-face negotiations and consensus building to resolve disputes over environmental issues."[21]

Initial experiments in ADR proved sufficiently successful that by the mid-1980s the approach had a growing record of success in resolving site-specific environmental disputes.[22] Many states and several federal agencies began to incorporate ADR mechanisms into their formal administrative procedures. The Environmental Protection Agency adopted a form of ADR as a new method of obtaining public input on the regulation of business and industry called for under the Clean Air Act, in order to avoid lengthy court challenges to its rule making.

20. The involvement of the environmental movement in regulation and implementation is analyzed further in two excellent anthologies: James P. Lester, ed., *Environmental Politics and Policy: Theories and Evidence* (Durham, NC: Duke University Press, 1989); Norman J. Vig and Michael K. Kraft, eds., *Environmental Policy in the 1990s* (Washington, DC: C. Q. Press, 1990).

21. Douglas J. Amy, "Environmental Dispute Resolution: The Promise and the Pitfalls," in *Environmental Policy*, ed. Vig and Kraft, p. 212.

22. Gail Bingham, *Resolving Environmental Disputes: A Decade of Experience* (Washington, DC: Conservation Foundation, 1986).

Examples of successful collaboration between business and environmentalists include their jointly negotiated proposal for the 1986 Federal Insecticide, Fungicide, and Rodenticide Act, a process that brought together long-time foes from environmental organizations and the chemical industry.[23] It has even led to agreement on the siting of a new hazardous waste facility.[24]

At the state and regional level, ADR mechanisms have been extended into full-scale collaborative processes to address regional urban water allocation in Colorado and to agree on the decision process for local and regional hazardous waste management throughout California.[25] The collaborative agreement developed in California requires that the planning process include the active consultation of citizen groups and movement organizations with environmental, health care, occupational safety, and fire protection interests. Most recently, a collaborative mechanism has been used in helping devise energy conservation policy in California. Collaboration in this area was initiated by environmental organizations as a strategy for ensuring that

energy conservation and environmental protection become cornerstones of energy development by the major utilities in the state.[26]

ADR and collaboratives are not a substitute for the formal processes of making and implementing laws. Nevertheless, when such discussions are conducted with the encouragement of political leaders, the resulting agreements between environmentalists and businesses are adopted as laws and regulation. In effect, these new forms of dialogue and conflict resolution have created a new channel for movement influence over policy. The outcome is not only the incorporation of movement organizations into the governmental process but a level of influence over policy that far exceeds the achievements of the all-or-nothing gamble of mobilizing to block a project.

CONCLUSION

The relative success of the environmental movement in helping to shape laws, regulations, and the implementation of hazardous waste policies is due only in part to the focus of many environmental organizations on involvement in the policy process. In fairness to the freeze movement, it must be noted that presidential prerogatives are deeply entrenched in the areas of foreign policy and military security and that efforts to open up arms control negotiations to de-

23. Christopher J. Bosso, "Transforming Adversaries into Collaborators: Interest Groups and the Regulation of Chemical Pesticides," *Policy Sciences*, 21(1):3-22 (1988).

24. Barry Rabe, "Beyond the NIMBY Syndrome in Hazardous Waste Facility Siting," *Governance*, 4(2):184-206 (Apr. 1991).

25. Daniel Mazmanian and Michael Stanley-Jones, "Reconceiving LULUs: Changing the Nature and Scope of Locally Unwanted Land Uses," in *Confronting Regional Challenges: Approaches to LULUs, Growth, and Other Vexing Governance Problems*, ed. Joseph DiMento and LeRoy Graymer (Cambridge, MA: Lincoln Institute of Land, 1991), pp. 55-75.

26. Daniel Mazmanian, "Toward a New Energy Paradigm for California," in *California Policy Choices*, vol. 8, ed. John Kirlin and Donald Winkler (Sacramento: University of Southern California, School of Public Administration, Sacramento Center, 1992).

tailed oversight by the Senate would represent a major departure from recent practice. But it should also be remembered that until the last decade there were no precedents for the role that many environmental movement organizations now take in negotiating toxic waste regulations and implementation. Indeed, a good definition of the task of any social movement may be that it takes an unlikely idea, makes it seem feasible, and then puts it into practice.

Despite its ability to generate widespread support at the polls and to organize the largest demonstration in American history, the freeze movement failed to translate its goals into public policy. The movement sought to affect policy directly by lobbying Congress to pass a resolution advocating the freeze. The resolution that passed in 1983 had no practical significance because it did not affect the actual conduct of superpower diplomacy.[27] By becoming a lobbying organization, the freeze movement gave control over its issue to Congress and ultimately failed to affect policy.

The environmental movement has had a greater policy impact due to its direct involvement in the policy process. Widespread concern about the handling of hazardous wastes was translated into citizen involvement in regulation and oversight of implementation, not simply pressure on Congress to act. That the increased use of consultation is largely a re-

sponse to movement politics is suggested by both the timing of the initiation of consultation mechanisms—often just after a movement has derailed some project—and the fact that procedures for consultation are most rigorous in issue areas where popular mobilizations have been the most widespread—for example, in the siting and construction of toxic waste storage facilities and nuclear power plants.

The success of environmental movement organizations in affecting policy by gaining access to the policy process is a strategy that should be examined by other movements. The fear of co-optation makes many movement leaders, including those in the environmental movement, wary of becoming institutionally involved in decision making. Indeed, one problem faced by environmental organizations that do take part in the policy process is criticism from environmental organizations that do not. The problem of being outflanked by more militant organizations is a source of instability in the development of negotiated arrangements for policy implementation. Nonetheless, ADR mechanisms have become institutionalized as a major avenue through which environmental movement organizations can be directly engaged in the decision-making processes of government. The involvement of movement activists in the policy process has greatly expanded the range of interests and perspectives that are expressed in the making of environmental policy, with important implications for the quality of the democratic process.

27. Other than indirectly, by pressuring the Reagan administration to create at least the appearance of arms control progress.

ANNALS, *AAPSS*, **528**, July 1993

Greenpeace U.S.A.:
Something Old, New, Borrowed

By RONALD G. SHAIKO

ABSTRACT: Greenpeace U.S.A. is unique among environmental organizations in the United States. While it is one of the wealthiest and largest membership groups in the environmental movement, its organization and political strategies are quite different from those employed by the more mainstream groups such as the Sierra Club or the National Wildlife Federation. Its status as a new social movement is evaluated on four dimensions: ideology, motivations to participate, organizational structure, and political structure. Greenpeace U.S.A. exhibits characteristics of both new and old social movements and is thus classified as an organizational hybrid. Today, the organization struggles with several challenges. In two decades, it has grown to become part of the largest worldwide environmental network. Greenpeace U.S.A. must decide on the proper mix of old and new methods to continue its mission into the next century.

Ronald G. Shaiko is an assistant professor of government at The American University in Washington, D.C. His research is focused on public interest organizations. The analysis presented here is based on a larger study of environmental groups presented in his forthcoming book, Voices and Echoes for the Environment: Public Interest Representation in the 1990s.

GREENPEACE U.S.A., the largest of the thirty national organizations worldwide that compose the Greenpeace International network, is an organizational anomaly. With a 1992 net operating budget of more than $25 million and a membership of 1.8 million in the United States, Greenpeace U.S.A. ranks as one of the largest and wealthiest American environmental groups. Greenpeace does not easily fit the American interest group model, however. At the same time, it is not exactly a new social movement either. Journalists and activists alike have wrestled with the mission and activities of this organizational hybrid. Peter Dykstra of Greenpeace acknowledges the controversial position held by the organization: "Depending on whom one asks in the U.S. conservation community, Greenpeace is either one of the most effective environmental groups or one of the most irresponsible. Perhaps the easiest way to dodge the issue is to describe Greenpeace as unique."[1]

Environmental writer Tom Horton expands upon the unique character of the organization: "There simply is no guidebook for running Greenpeace. There has never been anything like it. After twenty years of existence, the group's motto (if it could agree on one) might well be a sentiment often expressed by Greenpeace's managers: We're Running a Big Experiment Here."[2] It is this characterization that draws criticism as well as praise from those attentive to the environmental agenda. Greenpeace will often attempt to employ strategies deemed unacceptable by mainstream environmental organizations, thereby drawing fire not only from big business but from those supposedly fighting on the same side of the battle. Timber industry representative Adam Zimmermann has little time for Greenpeace antics: " 'They are zealots. Society is being forced to defend practices which shouldn't require defense and to spend time fixing non-problems.' "[3]

From within the environmental movement, the methods utilized by Greenpeace are also closely scrutinized. Jay Hair, executive director of the National Wildlife Federation, reflects a view held by many environmentalists attempting to reform the political system by working within it: " 'I don't agree with [Greenpeace's] tactics. Some people feel that environmentalists will do anything, including deceiving the public, to make their point.' "[4] Yet there are some within the movement who feel that Greenpeace provides a service to the cause that other organizations are either unwilling or unable to offer. John Adams, executive director of the Natural Resources Defense Council, argues that Greenpeace " 'fills a need. It provides an outlet for frustrations that develop because the system doesn't take care of problems. Anybody who is really trying to do

1. Peter Dykstra, "Institution: Greenpeace," *Environment*, 28(6):5 (July-Aug. 1986). Used by permission of Heldref Publications.

2. Tom Horton, "The Green Giant," *Rolling Stone*, 5 Sept. 1991, p. 44. © By Tom Horton From Rolling Stone, September 5, 1991. By Straight Arrow Publishers, Inc. 1991. All Rights Reserved. Reprinted by Permission.

3. John DeMont, "Frontline Fighters," *Maclean's*, 16 Dec. 1991, p. 47. Reprinted by permission.

4. Dykstra, "Institutions: Greenpeace," p. 5. Used by permission of Heldref Publications.

anything gets a lot of heat, a lot of criticism.' "[5]

While most of the within-movement criticism emanates from the more mainstream organizations, Greenpeace is not without its critics from the more radical wing of the movement. Paul Watson, one of the cofounders of Greenpeace in 1971, left the organization in 1977 to create a more radical direct-action group, the Sea Shepherd Society. Dissatisfied with what he perceived to be a betrayal by Greenpeace organizers of the group's original direct-action mission, Watson criticizes Greenpeace for shifting the focus toward fund-raising and media baiting: " 'It doesn't matter what is true, it only matters what people believe is true. You are what the media defines you to be. [Greenpeace] became a myth and a myth-generating machine.' "[6]

In addition to the criticisms leveled at the activities of Greenpeace, those who have looked closely at the organizational aspects of the group also have found weaknesses in internal management and leadership when measured against the American standards of organizational professionalization in the public interest movement. Financially, Greenpeace U.S.A. is well ahead of most American environmental groups, yet organizationally it looks much like the environmental groups of the 1960s. Bob Ostertag succinctly summarizes this somewhat contradictory predicament: "To exercise its power effec-

tively will require skills that have not so far had top billing in the Greenpeace circus: constituency mobilization, coalition building—in a word, politics. But here Greenpeace is rather limited. For all its growth and expansion, Greenpeace remains an eminently 'European' organization."[7]

Despite the wide-ranging critiques, Greenpeace U.S.A. has managed to capitalize on its unique character and to mobilize and maintain an exceptionally large membership base. How, then, should one judge or evaluate the effectiveness of Greenpeace U.S.A.? From an academic perspective, this question is particularly intriguing given the various approaches to the study of organized interests in society. The recent dialogue that sheds the most light on this topic incorporates and delineates standards drawn from disparate literatures revolving around the distinction between old social movements and new social movements. Elsewhere in this issue, various authors pursue this debate from various theoretical perspectives. In this article, the defining set of characteristics that separate old movements from new ones will be applied to Greenpeace U.S.A.

Russell Dalton, the special editor of this volume, along with several colleagues, has provided a frame of reference through which one may evaluate the degree to which an organization adheres to new social movement principles. The dimensions upon which Greenpeace U.S.A. will be evaluated are ideology, motiva-

5. Michael Brown, "The Zeal of Disapproval," *Oceans*, 20:41 (May-June 1987).

6. Leslie Spencer, "The Not So Peaceful World of Greenpeace," *Forbes*, 11 Nov. 1991, p. 174. Reprinted by permission.

7. Bob Ostertag, "Greenpeace Takes Over the World," *Mother Jones*, 16:84 (Mar.-Apr. 1991).

tions to participate, organizational structure, and political style.[8]

IDEOLOGY: CORE LEADERSHIP VERSUS CORE MEMBERSHIP

Of the four dimensions, most researchers have argued that the ideological dimension provides the clearest point of delineation between old and new movement organizations. The vast majority of analytical assessments of actual groups are carried out on European organizations, however. It is quite difficult to impose a model derived from one set of cultural or political experiences on another, distinct culture, namely, that of the United States. Interestingly, Bob Ostertag's comments, quoted earlier, reflect the feeling that there is something different about Greenpeace U.S.A., yet his only conclusion was that it is "eminently 'European.'" Similarly, Peter Bahouth, executive director of Greenpeace U.S.A., was not familiar with the concept of new social movement.[9] It is within this American context that the following analysis is pursued.

It is important when analyzing American environmental organizations to distinguish between the ideology, values, and attitudes of the leadership and those held by membership. One should not assume that there is congruence of opinion within groups between leaders and members. Perhaps the best example of this problem is found in the only other environmental or conservation organization that rivals Greenpeace U.S.A. in size and budget, the National Wildlife Federation. During the first term of the Reagan presidency, James Watt was appointed and confirmed as Secretary of the Interior. Quickly and forcibly, most of the major environmental groups called for his removal. The National Wildlife Federation did not respond in similar fashion. It was not until they commissioned a membership poll to find out where their members stood on the issue that the federation took a position against Watt. They took this position only after learning that the majority of their rank-and-file members were not familiar with James Watt. On another substantive issue, nuclear power, the federation's membership is evenly split. The leadership has a position on nuclear power, but it does not make that position clear to its membership for fear of losing half of it.

This is not to say that the Greenpeace U.S.A. membership is at all like the membership of the National Wildlife Federation. However, whenever 1.8 million citizens are drawn to any cause, one should assume there is some substantial degree of diversity within that membership base.

Core leadership ideology:
True believers

Within the leadership ranks of Greenpeace U.S.A., there is an ideological clarity consistent with new social movement theory. It is their

8. Russell J. Dalton, Manfred Kuechler, and Wilhelm Bucklin, "The Challenge of New Movements," in *Challenging the Political Order*, ed. Russell J. Dalton and Manfred Kuechler (New York: Oxford University Press, 1990), pp. 6-16.

9. Personal interview, Peter Bahouth, Executive Director, Greenpeace U.S.A., Washington, DC, 21 July 1992.

adherence to a decentralized, almost libertarian pursuit of issues and agendas that leads its critics to question the anarchistic nature of the organization. Bahouth views the entire environmental realm in ideological terms: "Environmental issues are moral and ethical, not just scientific and political."[10] Even their mission statement reflects the condemnation of the existing social order and their quasi-religious fervor to overcome the attendant barriers—"Greenpeace will both personally bear witness to atrocities against life and take direct action to prevent them."[11]

Organizationally, the leadership ideology is manifest in the management of personnel as well as issues. Bahouth would much rather have a support staff of true believers than one composed of neutrally competent policy wonks. " 'We've got to the point where we could pay for professional people across the board and we don't do it, because we make a commitment to keep people who come in to help out for awhile, get interested, and want to stay.' "[12] Similarly, the structure of the issue agenda, divided into "campaigns," reflects the pragmatism as well as the idealism of the staff. There is no blueprint for implementing each campaign. The toxics campaign might employ a strategy totally separate and distinct from the oceans campaign, for example. According to former Greenpeace executive director Stephen Sawyer, " 'All

campaigning must be individual acts of conscience.' "[13] This intermixing of ideology and free will, combined with the relative youth of more than 175 staffers, each earning a quite modest salary, has obvious consequences. Internecine battles are common within the organization. Nonetheless, the basic adherence to an ideological anchor allows Greenpeace U.S.A. to continue its mission.

Core membership ideology:
  Direct mail and the
  politics of emotion

Given the ideological clarity found among the leaders and staffers of Greenpeace U.S.A., how does one attract similarly oriented citizens from a diverse population? In the United States in the 1990s, the method of choice remains direct mail. While this technology is viewed by some as having run its course, virtually all environmental groups remain addicted to direct mail as a mobilization and retention tool; Greenpeace U.S.A. is no exception. While Greenpeace utilizes canvassing, for fundraising purposes, in 27 cities across the United States, it remains dependent upon direct mail for the bulk of its funding. According to figures cited in the rather harsh appraisal of Greenpeace in *Forbes* magazine in late 1991, Greenpeace U.S.A. raised $64 million in 1990, with 60 percent coming from more than 40 million solicitations sent out by the direct-mail firm Craver, Matthews, Smith, and Co.[14] According to Roger Craver,

10. Ibid.

11. Personal interview, Blair Palese, Media Director, Greenpeace U.S.A., Washington, DC, 22 July 1992.

12. Michael Harwood, "Daredevils for the Environment," *New York Times Magazine*, 2 Oct. 1988, p. 76. Reprinted by permission.

13. Ibid.

14. Spencer, "Not So Peaceful World of Greenpeace," p. 179.

" 'Direct mail is a medium of passion when used politically. . . . Causes which can easily arouse that passion are naturals. But, whatever the issue, a direct mail letter must evoke a strong emotional response to be successful.' "[15]

Mobilizing the
Rainbow Warriors

Perhaps better than any other environmental cause in the United States, Greenpeace U.S.A. is consistently successful in marketing itself in starkly emotional terms. One issue-event in particular epitomizes Greenpeace's ability to mobilize a constituency: the blowing up of the Greenpeace flagship, *Rainbow Warrior*, on 10 July 1985 by French government agents. Ironically, this event resulted in a doubling of the group's membership, from 400,000 to 800,000, and a tripling of its revenues in less than two years following the *Rainbow Warrior* incident.[16] In a single mailing shortly after the bombing, Greenpeace gained 43,000 new members with a response rate of almost 10 percent, a rate unheard of in the direct-mail industry. The mailing, which included a blueprint, suitable for framing, of the new *Rainbow Warrior II* under construction, received the Echo Award from the direct-marketing industry as the best piece of nonprofit direct mail in 1986.[17]

It is probable that a substantial number of readers of this journal have received direct mail solicitations from Greenpeace as well as a host of environmental, consumer, peace, animal rights, civil rights, and political organizations. Greenpeace mailings are distinctive in several respects. First, the packaging is usually colorful and eye-catching. Second, the message involves enjoyment of what Bahouth calls "the vicarious thrill of living through the group's activists who do things that members themselves would not do."[18]

In an excellent book on the direct-mail phenomenon, Ken Godwin equates the messages of Greenpeace with those of the Reverend Jerry Falwell's Moral Majority:

Their direct mail informs recipients that the leaders of the Moral Majority and Greenpeace place themselves in personally dangerous situations. Reverend Falwell describes threats on his life and the verbal abuses he and his family receive from enemies of the Christian Right. Greenpeace chronicles the arrests that the group's activists have undergone and the dangers to them that their radical actions in behalf of wildlife and environment create. Then both groups tell the readers that they will not be asked to subject themselves to these dangers. All they need do is send money, the leaders will take the risks. This "participation through contribution" is the ersatz participation that alarms many of the critics of direct marketing.[19]

The messages delivered by door-to-door canvassers across the country are similar to those transmitted

15. Susan Rouder, "Mobilization by Mail," *Citizen Participation*, (Sept.-Oct. 1980), p. 4.

16. Spencer, "Not So Peaceful World of Greenpeace," p. 179.

17. Personal interview, Vicky Monrean, Membership Development, Greenpeace U.S.A., Washington, DC, 29 June 1988.

18. Personal interview, Bahouth.

19. R. Kenneth Godwin, *One Billion Dollars of Influence: The Direct Marketing of Politics* (Chatham, NJ: Chatham House, 1988), p. 48.

through direct mail. While not all of the messages are as emotionally gripping as the *Rainbow Warrior* incident, mailings based on the various campaigns, whether toxics, Antarctica, whaling, energy, nuclear proliferation, or rainforest preservation, tend to stress an eminent threat to potential members' very existence. Whether or not this direct-mail strategy constitutes the dissemination of a new environmental ideology is open for debate. One might argue that it is antithetical to the tenets of the new environmental paradigm or postmaterialistic values as it is a method of economic manipulation perfected on Madison Avenue and permanently borrowed by the public interest sector in America.

Without the aid of membership data relating to individual attitudes and opinions, it is difficult to speak to the ideological predispositions of members of Greenpeace U.S.A. Information at the aggregate level, however, does shed some light on the composition of the membership. It is known that multiple membership is the norm among individuals who join environmental organizations. A member of the Sierra Club, for example, is likely to belong to at least three other organizations; for a member of the Environmental Defense Fund, the number of affiliations is likely to approach six or seven. Given that the Greenpeace U.S.A. membership is twice as large as the Sierra Club's, the likelihood of multiple membership among its followers is great. This being the case and given that the average donor to Greenpeace is contributing a comparatively small amount vis-à-vis the costs of belonging to other environmental organizations—the average contribution is less than $20 annually—it is not clear that Greenpeace donors understand or acknowledge the significant ideological differences between the leaders of Greenpeace and those of other organizations to which they belong, if they are aware of the differences at all.

Americans are indeed joiners, as Alexis de Tocqueville once observed. There exists, however, a consistent historical pattern in this country of climbing aboard political bandwagons or supporting political causes for reasons having little or nothing to do with ideology. One need look no further into our past than the Ross Perot phenomenon of last year. Perot managed to activate almost 20 million citizens with the most simplistic, nonideological message imaginable: "Can Do!"

American youths are also distinctly nonideological. Yet Greenpeace does better than most groups in attracting younger members. The Greenpeace concerts, albums, and compact discs featuring groups such as U2, REM, and other major acts make the environmental message quite palatable to American youths. Still, it remains to be seen whether this soft connection made at a younger age results in full-fledged environmental awareness in future years. Nonetheless, Greenpeace should be applauded for reaching out to American youths when other organizations find younger members too difficult to maintain because they rarely give beyond the minimum—student—rate and they want services that older members are not interested in receiving.

After an examination of the motivations of individuals for belonging to various environmental or conservation organizations across the political spectrum of environmentalism, one general pattern has emerged that is applicable to Greenpeace members. What one tends to find among these citizen activists is that while they feel strongly about the environmental cause, generally defined, they are not particularly committed to any one or set of organizations. In essence, they are constantly looking for change or at least different agents of change. In this manner, these citizen activists tend to choose organizations much as they would order a meal in a Chinese restaurant—one from column A, one from column B. It is difficult to attribute to this method of selection any significant degree of ideological connection between leaders and members.

MOTIVATIONS TO PARTICIPATE:
GREENPEACE U.S.A.
AS PART OF A FULL PLATE

Continuing with the Chinese-restaurant analogy, members of Greenpeace U.S.A. are also likely to be members of a number of related organizations (column A) as well as participants in unrelated causes (column B). Their reasons for selecting group A over group B are as numerous as the organizational incentives provided by group leaders. The Sierra Club, for example, is a multiple-incentive organization, that is, it attracts members on a variety of dimensions. However, given that an individual citizen is presented with a choice of seventy or eighty groups in a year's worth of mail and given that

an average response rate for each solicitation is 1-2 percent, groups offering a unique package of incentives tend to fair better than those offering incentives replicated throughout the industry. Here Greenpeace U.S.A. has clearly developed its niche: direct nonviolent action.

By offering this tactic as an incentive, Greenpeace U.S.A. is able to position itself within the broad range of activities attractive to potential members. Therefore, it is probable that Greenpeace is attracting membership on the direct-action dimension. But this is not the only incentive provided by the leadership. *Greenpeace* magazine is an attractive, informative, selective material incentive provided to all members. This incentive has become less selective as Greenpeace leaders have recently followed the lead of *Sierra* editors as well as other magazine publishers who have attempted to capitalize on this upscale constituency hungry for environmental news and information—publishers of, for example, *E Magazine*, *Buzzworm*, and *Garbage*—by selling *Greenpeace* magazine on newsstands to the general public.

In terms of satisfying individual motivations, a typical environmentalist is likely to belong to the Sierra Club for its outings and grass-roots organizational structure, to the Natural Resources Defense Council for its ability to litigate environmental cases, to the National Wildlife Federation in order to receive *Ranger Rick* magazine for his or her children, to the Wilderness Society for its ability to lobby on wilderness-preservation issues, to the National Audubon Society for its attractive magazine for the coffee table, and, finally, to Greenpeace for the "vicarious thrill." At base, though, lies the purposive motivation that places adherents in the ranks of new social movement membership.

ORGANIZATIONAL STRUCTURE: FLUIDITY OR MONEY PIT?

Organizationally, Greenpeace U.S.A. falls squarely within the new social movement parameters. As an integral part of the large Greenpeace International, Greenpeace U.S.A. is organizationally and financially linked to the parent headquarters in Amsterdam. With at least one office in 30 countries, an international headquarters, a U.S. headquarters in Washington, D.C., a half dozen regional offices, and canvassing operations in 27 cities, Greenpeace U.S.A. is in the middle of a hyperdecentralized organization, yet with little linkage to the grass roots in this country. Overlaid upon this organizational shell are the issue campaigns, conducted and administered in isolation vis-à-vis other campaigns.

Given the issue-driven nature of organizational activity, planning and strategy are based on demands and needs as they arise; therefore, there is little task-based division of labor. At times, Greenpeace has become an environmental free-for-all. Battles rage between national headquarters and the international office. Campaigns compete for attention and funding from disparate sources. Clearly, if one were to impose a standard of organizational effectiveness, utilized when evaluating mainstream environmental organizations in the United States, Greenpeace

U.S.A. would fail miserably; it would be looked upon as a $25 million money pit. However, the organizational complexity masks part of the organizational uncertainty.

From a membership perspective, the relationship between Greenpeace U.S.A. and the International is less than clear. Just under one-quarter of every dollar raised by Greenpeace U.S.A. goes directly to Greenpeace International in Amsterdam; in essence, leaders in Washington are paying for the use of the Greenpeace trademark in their fund-raising. An additional $0.23 is spent conducting direct-mail fund-raising and canvassing. In a study of 12 environmental or conservation organizations conducted in 1990, it was found that Greenpeace U.S.A. spent the largest portion of its budget on fund-raising: 23.1 percent, more than double the 10.6 percent average of the remaining 11 groups.[20] Combined, almost half of every dollar given to Greenpeace U.S.A. by members either leaves the country or is spent on organizational maintenance.

Structurally, operating in the United States presents some unique organizational choices. Recently, Greenpeace U.S.A. moved the bulk of its operation into its 501(c)(4) action arm, Greenpeace Action. Greenpeace U.S.A. remains a 501(c)(3) tax-exempt entity, thereby allowing big donors to give generously with the benefit of deducting their contributions from their tax bills. This action is consistent with an emerging pattern identified elsewhere in a study of more than 200 public interest organi-

20. Ronaleen R. Roha, "Giving Back," *Changing Times*, 44:107 (Nov. 1990).

zations. With this action, Greenpeace U.S.A. is behaving much like its mainstream counterparts.[21]

POLITICAL STYLE: GUERRILLA THEATER FOR THE 1990S

New social movements are characterized by their extrasystemic political behavior. Such organizations are more likely to attempt to influence the governmental process through distinctly indirect means by utilizing the mass media to influence public opinion. While earlier movements utilized social protest as a political resource, many of the actions tended to be spontaneous and haphazardly organized. Today, new social movements are much more adept at orchestrating their guerrilla theater efforts. Greenpeace U.S.A. has become the model for new social movements in this regard.

Tactics such as blocking entrances to power plants, clogging waste valves that deposit carcinogens into waterways, hanging banners from smokestacks and skyscrapers, intercepting whaling vessels, dying seal skins to render them worthless to hunters, disrupting nuclear testing, and organizing marches are all part of the ecodrama orchestrated by Greenpeace activists and campaigners. The impact of such staged events is dependent upon the degree of media coverage and the political salience of the issue within the general population. Greenpeace U.S.A. has

an interesting relationship with the media. To a point, each is reliant on the other. The media need the picture as well as the story, whereas Greenpeace needs the coverage to demonstrate its impact. One might ask, philosophically, If Greenpeace activists hold a protest rally in the woods and the media are not there to cover it, do they really make a sound?

Greenpeace has sought to become less reliant on direct media coverage by producing its own pictures through films and videos. Nevertheless, the basic strategy of guerrilla theater, not exactly a novel approach in American politics, remains a significant weapon in the Greenpeace arsenal. Thirty years ago Abbie Hoffman, Jerry Rubin, and their fellow yippies made guerrilla theater into an art form.[22] Similarly, groups such as the Jesus Movement of the late 1960s found their own unique way of expressing their faith.[23] Whether or not these groups constitute the genesis of new social movements remains a topic for further study. The point is that the tactics of Greenpeace are not particularly new on the American scene. Perhaps it is the application of these tactics to the environmental arena that sets it apart.

Greenpeace U.S.A. has found some difficulty in defining the boundaries of acceptable protest. As mentioned earlier, the Sea Shepherd Society was formed by disgruntled Greenpeace activists who felt that the organization was not going far enough to

21. Ronald G. Shaiko, "More Bang for the Buck: The New Era of Full-Service Public Interest Organizations," in *Interest Group Politics*, 3d ed., ed. Allan J. Cigler and Burdett A. Loomis (Washington, DC: Congressional Quarterly Press, 1991), pp. 117-23.

22. Bernard Ohanian, "Fighting That Bushed Feeling," *Mother Jones*, 14:49 (Jan. 1989).

23. Steve Rabey, "Remembering the Jesus Movement," *Christianity Today*, 22 Nov. 1985, p. 53.

make its presence known. Likewise, dissatisfied activists affiliated with Friends of the Earth, including Dave Foreman, created an ecoterrorist organization, Earth First! Both organizations have employed a strategy of "monkey-wrenching" and "ecotage" that includes destruction of property through means ranging from vandalism of construction equipment to spiking of trees ready to be harvested.[24] Greenpeace U.S.A. draws the line short of ecoterrorism. In fact, some of the recent activities of the leadership indicate a greater willingness to begin acting in concert with the mainstream reform organizations.

"Only a dream in Rio": [25]
  *Juggling the
  insider-outsider role*

Greenpeace U.S.A. leaders as well as those in Amsterdam are struggling with the proposition of dealing directly with public policymakers as well as other environmental groups. The 1992 Earth Summit in Rio de Janeiro provides an illuminating example of this internal struggle. Greenpeace campaigners played an active role in all of the preparatory meetings around the world prior to the summit. At each meeting, they sat down with other environmental leaders, scientists, and government representatives and argued for their positions. At this stage, they were less than successful; however, they did participate in the process and had some degree of influence.

Their strategy at the Rio summit was entirely different. Greenpeace sent twenty representatives to the summit, many of whom had actively participated in the earlier meetings. Upon their arrival, their immediate ecodrama involved a blanket condemnation of the summit, before a single word was uttered by conference delegates. This was the message the media received and what it relayed to attentive environmentalists in the United States. In the eyes of many environmental participants, Greenpeace had legitimized itself by being part of the process and subsequently delegitimized itself by condemning the effort publicly when it did not get its way in the negotiation process.

This same insider-outsider approach takes place in Washington as well, but to a lesser extent. It occurs in the relationship between Greenpeace and the U.S. Congress. For instance, Dean Tousley, a senior staffer on the House Interior and Insular Affairs Subcommittee on Energy and the Environment, acknowledged his interaction with the Greenpeace nuclear coordinator on the recent energy bill, but he also noted the coordinator was laid off midway through the process.[26]

While some Greenpeace staffers do attempt to influence the process through traditional lobbying efforts,

24. Jamie Malanowski, "Monkey-Wrenching Around," *Nation*, 2 May 1987, pp. 568-70; Tim Vanderpool, "Monkey-Wrenching for Planet Earth," *Progressive*, 53:15 (Sept. 1989); Christopher Manes, *Green Rage: Radical Environmentalism and the Unmaking of Civilization* (Boston: Little, Brown, 1990), pp. 175-90.

25. James Taylor, "Only a Dream in Rio" (Country Road Music, Inc., 1985).

26. Personal interview, Dean Tousley, Staff Member, U.S., Congress, House, Committee on Interior and Insular Affairs, Subcommittee on Energy and the Environment, Washington, DC, 19 July 1992.

other campaign activists employ more public tactics. Another senior staffer on the House Energy and Commerce Subcommittee on Energy and Power noted two incidents in which Greenpeace activists "marginalized themselves." In both subcommittee and full committee markups on the 1992 Resource Conservation and Recovery Act bill, Greenpeace activists staged a protest by wearing T-shirts that read "Ban, Don't Burn." They were quickly escorted out of the subcommittee markup session. At the full committee hearing, they were ejected from the committee room prior to the appearance of any congressman.[27]

With its current budget volatility, Greenpeace U.S.A. has only two full-time lobbyists. A survey of senior staffers on the House and Senate committees with primary jurisdiction over environmental issues found that Greenpeace often adds its name to efforts conducted by various environmental coalitions. The general consensus among congressional staff, however, is that Greenpeace is not itself a major actor in the policymaking process.

CONCLUSION

Greenpeace U.S.A. is at a crossroads in its existence. Bob Ostertag argues that "to survive in this environment, Greenpeace will have to remake itself. Greenpeace always leaped before it looked."[28] Such impulsive behavior has brought the organization to its present point of development. Even Executive Director Peter Bahouth recognizes the difficulty inherent in growing at such a rapid pace and now attempting to move on to the next level: "We must move from a place between the harpoon and the whale to dealing with transnational corporations. Our agenda is changing; we are beginning to offer positive alternatives at a concrete level."[29] Media Director Blair Palese feels that the next two years are critical. "We must prioritize, choose our fights more carefully, and work together as an organization to have the most effect."[30]

These comments are similar to those voiced in the late 1970s by social movement leaders attempting to create professionalized political interest groups. These earlier activists recognized what environmental lawyer David Roe noted in his book, Dynamos and Virgins: "Public interest work is nonprofit, inevitably and proudly, but it is hardly immune from economics."[31] William Turnage, former executive director of The Wilderness Society, put it more bluntly: "There is no need to be sloppy and inefficient just because we're a liberal cause."[32]

Today, Greenpeace U.S.A. is a marriage of old and new social movement ideas and activities. Its leadership and organizational structure clearly reflect new social movement

27. Personal interview, Shelley Fidler, Senior Staff Member, U.S., Congress, House, Committee on Energy and Commerce, Subcommittee on Energy and Power, Washington, DC, 18 July 1992.

28. Ostertag, "Greenpeace Takes Over the World," p. 85.

29. Personal interview, Bahouth.

30. Personal interview, Palese.

31. David Roe, Dynamos and Virgins (New York: Random House, 1984), p. 186.

32. Personal interview, William Turnage, former executive director, Wilderness Society, Washington, DC, 25 Oct. 1986.

ideals. Its method of membership recruitment and maintenance is derived from the old school. The membership base, while motivated by purposive incentives, is less ideological than its European counterparts. The current methods of influence are unique in the movement, even if borrowed from the 1960s social activists.

How stable is this marriage? If Greenpeace U.S.A. is more American than it is European, then the organization will adapt to the American process to become more like its mainstream potential allies, rather than gravitate toward the Sea Shepherds and Earth First! If the reverse is true, its future in the United States is more tenuous.

ANNALS, *AAPSS*, **528**, July 1993

Protesters, Counterprotesters, and the Authorities

By DIARMUID MAGUIRE

ABSTRACT: This article focuses on a comparison of direct action and its political effects in Italy and Northern Ireland in the period from 1967 to 1992. It traces how these two unstable one-party democracies were profoundly affected by waves of protest with similar origins that began in the late 1960s. The analysis leads to a consideration of some of the positive and negative consequences of protest and direct action. Central to these political outcomes are the structures and processes of interactions between protesters, counterprotesters, and the authorities.

Diarmuid Maguire has published a number of articles on protest movements and is preparing a book on the British Campaign for Nuclear Disarmament. He is a lecturer in European and international politics in the Department of Government and Public Administration at the University of Sydney.

DOES greater citizen protest lead inevitably to the introduction of reforms and the expansion of democracy? Or are there circumstances whereby direct action can provoke the opposite responses?

Students of social movements tend to answer the first question in the affirmative, albeit with some disagreement about the inevitability or permanence of progress. At the same time, they give little consideration to those cases where protest itself can result in the withdrawal of rights and the contraction of participation.

This gap in the literature may reflect some sort of ideological bias in this epistemic community toward the objects of its study. After all, most of us think that citizen movements are a good thing for democracy. More likely, though, it is due to the fact that most of the movements that we study operate within stable Western democracies. In these societies, the triangular relationship between popular protest, legislative reform, and expanded participation has been shown to be largely positive and reinforcing.[1]

The complexities of this relationship continue to fascinate those who analyze the old labor movement, which emerged in the nineteenth century, and the new social movements—greens, women, and pacifists—born in the late 1960s. Indeed, there has been a tendency to see some sort of evolutionary logic in the shift from old to new, with the manifesta-

tion of the latter taken as a sign that advanced societies are becoming more concerned with quality of life or postmaterial issues. As Ronald Inglehart has put it, such societies may be "reaching a nobility a little lower than the angels."[2]

But how are we to understand those countries that are not stable democracies and where popular struggle elicits neither reform nor greater opportunities for political access? What sense can we make of societies that have not shifted from the old politics to the new politics but seem to be enmeshed, often violently, in their traditions and their history? In other words, how can we theorize about citizen protest in nations that are a little less heavenly than those described by Inglehart?

Here I shall compare two unstable Western democracies that were affected profoundly by the "international cycle of protest" that characterized the late 1960s.[3] The events set in motion by the protests of that period propelled these two countries along very different paths. One path led to significant reforms, greater democracy, and acceptance of popular participation. The other led to the removal of rights, the denial of democracy, and the repression of citizen protest. Put simply, a cycle of protest that began in the late 1960s resulted in one society's becoming better and the other's becoming even worse. Exploring the comparative questions of how and why this occurred should

---

1. See, for example, Sidney Tarrow, *Struggle, Politics, and Reform: Collective Action, Social Movements, and Cycles of Protest*, Occasional Paper no. 21 (Ithaca, NY: Cornell University, Center for International Studies, Western Societies Program, 1989).

2. Ronald Inglehart, *Culture Shift in Advanced Industrial Society* (Princeton, NJ: Princeton University Press, 1990), p. 433.

3. Sidney Tarrow, *Democracy and Disorder: Protest and Politics in Italy, 1965-1975* (New York: Oxford University Press, 1989), p. 37.

allow an assessment of some of the positive and negative consequences of direct action.

COMPARING PROTEST IN ITALY AND NORTHERN IRELAND, 1967-92

In 1967, Italy and Northern Ireland were unstable one-party democracies. Their instability stemmed from the polarized nature of domestic political cleavages—Christian Democrat versus Communist, Protestant Unionist versus Catholic Nationalist, respectively. They were one-party states because Christian Democratic and Protestant Unionist control depended on the political exclusion of significant minorities: Italian Catholics excluded Communists; Ulster Protestants excluded Catholics. Yet these societies were democracies despite the distortions of patronage, discrimination, and periodic bouts of repression. Elections were held regularly and citizens enjoyed a modicum of civil liberties.

Before the mass challenges of the 1960s, the structures of exclusion in both societies were broadly similar. Italian Communists and Northern Irish Nationalists sat in parliament but had little hope of sharing executive power. State patronage was denied to these groups, and this meant limited access to public service positions. The power of the Christian Democrats and the Unionist Party was based on religious populism, business, and interclass unity.[4] Hold-

ing these coalitions together meant demonizing their political others, using the threats of the Red Menace and the Green Menace as ideological strategies for continual reelection.

But it is one thing to base the politics of inclusion and exclusion on class and party choice, and another to use religious affiliation. Cleavages in Italy formed around the axes of religious versus secular cultures and class conflict. In Northern Ireland, all conflicts were subsumed within a political division based on different religious denominations—in general, Catholics favored a united Ireland while Protestants fought to remain part of the United Kingdom. In Italy, religious culture was linked to class power. In Northern Ireland, the equation was similar except that control over territory was also at stake.

This crucial difference over cleavage structures meant that the pattern of conflict in these two unstable one-party democracies ran along different trajectories. "Challengers to the polity" in Italy used the ballot box, the strike, and the mass demonstration as their means of seeking access.[5] The Italian Communist Party (PCI) had participated in the founding of the Republic and, following Togliatti's postwar strategy, had abandoned the tactics of mass insurrection. The PCI developed strong cultural networks based on the party branch, the factory, and front organization. The PCI's main competitor on the Left, the Socialists, was more

---

4. See the characterizations of Christian Democratic and Unionist rule in ibid., p. 46; Paul Bew, Peter Gibbon, and Henry Patterson, *The State in Northern Ireland, 1921-72: Polit-*

ical Forces and Social Classes (Manchester: Manchester University Press, 1979).

5. Term used in Charles Tilly, *From Mobilization to Revolution* (Englewood Cliffs, NJ: Prentice-Hall, 1978).

moderate but adopted the same political tactics. Until the 1960s, both lived in a cultural ghetto isolated from centers of power.

Challengers to the polity in Northern Ireland zig-zagged between the ballot and the bullet. The constitutional Nationalist Party represented Catholic grievances in the Unionist-dominated Stormont Parliament. Pleas for reform and an end to discrimination fell on deaf ears, and the Nationalists would exit Parliament altogether following a policy of abstention. Their main political competitor, the Irish Republican Army (IRA), launched successive military campaigns that were designed not to reform but rather destroy the Northern Irish statelet. These campaigns always ended in failure, with IRA members being rounded up for incarceration or execution. Neither constitutional attempts at reform nor military struggles for revolution were successful in changing the political situation for the Catholic minority.[6]

Despite the differences in the patterns of conflict in these two societies, the political outcomes were similar. Opponents of one-party rule were weak and divided and unable to win greater political access or representation. Their tactical repertoire was forged during the foundation of these two regimes and had changed little over the following decades. The members of the polities, that is, their elites, had to put up with considerable conflict and disruption in the

postwar period but nothing that seriously challenged their rule.

Changing cleavages and political opportunities in the 1960s

The 1960s changed all that. The largely global processes of social, economic, and political transformation that came with that decade turned Italy and Northern Ireland upside down. The dominant elites were divided over how to respond to widespread social and economic change. Their opponents united, temporarily and sporadically, as new social actors entered the political arena. New protest tactics were deployed and old ones revamped as opportunities for radical change presented themselves. Novel demands were made on systems whose defenders thought that the entire world had come to an end.

To the extent that such a complex process can have a clear beginning, it can be said that economic change initiated these interactions. In the 1960s, Italy became a predominantly industrial nation whose continued development seemed to rest on the successful mix of state intervention, cheap southern labor, and a strong export performance. Yet Italy's first economic miracle opened up a series of social contradictions, which the Christian Democrats tried to control through an alliance with the Socialist Party beginning in the mid-1960s. This opening to the Left—excluding the PCI—only increased expectations of radical reform, which state and industrial elites were either unable or unwilling to deliver. Furthermore, one important element of the

6. For a detailed account of these shifting protest tactics and the response of the Northern Ireland state, see Michael Farrell, *Northern Ireland: The Orange State*, 2d ed. (London: Pluto, 1980).

economic miracle's formula—cheap labor—which had helped keep the Left weak and the economy strong, was coming to an end.[7]

The economic transformation of Northern Ireland had begun in the late 1950s. By contrast with Italy, Northern Ireland's political elite did not have to deal with the problems of full-scale industrialization and labor shortages. Rather, its dilemma was how to cope politically with the consequences of deindustrialization and unemployment. Industrial unemployment in Northern Ireland had a disproportionate impact on the Protestant working class, whose predominance in the manufacturing work force was largely a function of discrimination. The interclass alliance that held the Unionist Party together was sorely tested, and Protestant working-class dissent was manifested at the ballot box in votes for the Northern Ireland Labour Party at the expense of the Unionists.[8]

Northern Ireland's economic transition weakened the system's defenders, in contrast to the Italian experience. A new leader emerged in the Unionist Party, Terence O'Neill, who developed a new economic strategy for resolving the crisis. It centered around making Northern Ireland attractive for foreign investment. Politically, he matched his economic modernism with a progressive outlook toward the Catholic minority. In this way, jobs and growth were to keep the Unionist power bloc intact and an opening to the Catholics, through reforms, would provide further political stability.

Of course, there was much more to the crises of the 1960s in Italy and Northern Ireland than elite strategies and mass responses to changing economies. Events in Rome affected both countries, with the papacy of Pope John XXIII and Vatican II opening the way for greater liberalism and ecumenicalism. The Catholic Church opened a dialogue with the secular world and with other denominations. This represented a cultural challenge to the political cleavages that divided the peoples of Northern Ireland and Italy.

More mundane threats to the existing order came in various forms: the miniskirt and the birth-control pill, the pop record and long hair—a set of evil twins for conservatives—represented the cultural expression and freedoms of a new postwar generation. The political vanguard of this generation emerged from the universities of Italy and Northern Ireland, which had both seen a massive increase in student numbers in the 1950s and 1960s. The fact that the Northern Irish university system was controlled by London rather than Belfast meant that Catholics were able to gain access without discrimination.

The student movements that gelled in these societies "were central to disorderly politics from the mid-1960s."[9] They challenged the dominant political divisions of Christian

---

7. Tarrow, *Democracy and Disorder*, p. 48.

8. For accounts of this period, see Farrell, *Northern Ireland*; Bew, Gibbon, and Patterson, *State in Northern Ireland*.

9. Tarrow, *Democracy and Disorder*, p. 87. For the role of students in the Northern Ireland Civil Rights Association and People's Democracy, see Liam De Paor, *Divided Ulster* (London: Penguin, 1970), chap. 7.

Democrat versus Communist, Unionist versus Nationalist. They imported but also created new protest tactics that became part of an international repertoire of direct action. At the beginning of their respective campaigns, they shared a broadly similar ideology despite different domestic contexts. It was an ideology derived from Marxism with a new theoretical twist: a student-worker alliance was essential for successful popular struggle.

These new social actors used their protest tactics and ideological packages to pressure political systems that were already in crisis economically, culturally, and politically. The student movements were joined by other citizen groups anxious to settle grievances and win social and political reforms. But these mobilizations provoked countermobilizations and a variety of state responses. The interactions between protesters, counterprotesters, and state authorities that emerged in this period had deep and lasting effects.

PROTESTERS,
COUNTERPROTESTERS, AND
THE AUTHORITIES IN ITALY

In Italy, the new forms and demands of citizen protest were spread from student to worker and then to other categories similarly bound by interest and identity. University students, whose numbers had increased by 117 percent between 1961 and 1968, initiated the process.[10] The students' disruption was based on various forms of occupation and ob-

struction. Their demands ranged from the end of written exams to the end of the Vietnam war. Their protests led to some reforms of the university system and to their recognition as a social collectivity by leading political actors and state institutions.

The vanguard of protest was soon taken up by the workers. The Hot Autumn of 1969 saw an explosion of strikes by workers in northern factories that spread to other sectors of employment. Italy's wage bill shot up and workers saw their pay approach, and in some cases exceed, that of their northern European counterparts. The *Statuto dei lavoratori* (Workers' Charter) of 1970 gave the workers important rights. Shop-floor operations were increasingly regulated and subject to negotiations with trade unions. Manufacturing workers enjoyed a shorter work week; they were guaranteed time off for study and meetings; and they exercised greater control over their daily working lives. Unionization consequently increased from 29 percent in 1968 to 49 percent in 1977.[11] The social wage also increased dramatically as the state met societal demands and sought to offset some of the increasing costs for capitalists.[12]

Then came the middle-class radicals. The women's movement became a pillar of general agitation for social

10. A. De Grand, *The Italian Left in the Twentieth Century* (Bloomington: Indiana University Press, 1989), p. 148.

11. M. Kreile, "The Crisis of Italian Trade Unionism in the 1980s," *West European Politics*, 11:54-67 (Jan. 1988).

12. Lange notes that, by 1972, Italy's social expenditure was only 1 percent behind that of West Germany. Peter Lange, "Semiperiphery and Core in the European Context," in *Semiperipheral Development*, ed. G. Arrighi (Beverly Hills, CA: Sage, 1985), p. 187.

change.[13] The high point of this mobilization was the success of the referendum that legalized divorce in 1974. Although the content of this policy change was important, its symbolism was more important still. Catholic Italy was becoming secular Italy and the church and the Christian Democrats were increasingly on the defensive. The legalization of abortion in 1978 and the failure of the pope's anti-abortion referendum in 1981 further highlighted this important transformation.

By the 1980s, the new social movements—greens, pacifists, and feminists—were launching significant challenges to the old politics of the Christian Democrats and the Communists. The PCI, in particular, was sensitive to this phenomenon. The party's continued exclusion from executive power meant that it relied on its dominance of left-wing mobilization to maintain its base. Competition with the new movements led to significant changes in the PCI's structures and policies. The party's youth federation was rebellious on the issues of nuclear energy, disarmament, and feminism. It was the first organization to abandon democratic centralism—a move that the PCI itself later followed—and it was instrumental in getting the party to oppose nuclear energy in 1987.

By the 1990s, we might characterize Italy as having followed a certain logic of societal evolution that has affected other advanced democracies.

Citizen protest led to the expansion of democratic participation and the introduction of significant reforms. As Tarrow puts it, "Disorder contributed to the broadening of democracy where it was strong and to its consolidation where it was weak."[14] Over the years, old cleavages based on class and religion were eroded through structural change and the action of collective agents. After the events of 1989, Italy no longer has a Communist party, and the Christian Democrats have been robbed of the Red Scare. This is the democratic Italy that has somehow muddled through an epochal transformation and has earned the congratulations of a former critic, Joseph La Palombara.[15]

The costs of transition

This process of democratic transition in Italy has not been without its costs, and we should be wary of falling into deterministic explanations founded on the notion of structural inevitability. The protests of the students, the workers, and the new social movements brought on their heads the often unfriendly attentions of counterprotesters and the authorities. Street fights, assassinations, and bombings were particularly prevalent in the 1970s as Italy went through its "years of lead." The fact that Italy survived the terrorisms of the Left and Right and the plots of undemocratic forces within the state should not erase our memory of their existence.

13. For a very interesting study of the Italian women's movement, see Judith Hellman, *Journeys among Women: Feminism in Five Italian Cities* (New York: Oxford University Press, 1987).

14. Tarrow, *Democracy and Disorder*, p. 1.

15. Joseph La Palombara, *Democracy Italian Style* (New Haven, CT: Yale University Press, 1987).

Italian politics in the 1960s and 1970s saw the revival of the most important countermovement of the interwar years, namely, the Fascists. The far-right Italian Social Movement enjoyed an electoral upsurge as it capitalized on some of the citizen backlash against leftist and student protest. Street Fascists clashed with left-wing demonstrators using fists and clubs. Military Fascists planted their bombs in banks, on trains, and in railway stations. The neo-Fascists' "strategy of tension" was aimed at eroding popular respect for democracy and ushering in the strong state.

Yet, despite the disturbing tendency of the secret services and elements of the military and police to collude in these actions, the Christian Democratic state remained democratic. It enjoyed a high degree of autonomy from a countermovement constituency that was associated with a defunct and stigmatized regime.

In the same period, left-wing terrorism emerged with the foundation of the Red Brigades. The Red Brigades declared war on capitalism and the state by kidnapping leading industrialists and state functionaries in the early 1970s. Assassination followed kidnapping as the key tactic of this group's activities. The seizure and murder of Christian Democrat leader Aldo Moro in 1978 was its most spectacular operation. Yet by the 1980s, the Red Brigades, for all intents and purposes, no longer existed. The state cleverly exploited the tactic of light sentencing in exchange for information from *pentiti* (turncoats) and, in this way, broke the organization. The state also refused to use the heavy instruments of coercion and repression, which would have played into the hands of leftist and rightist terrorists.

It should also be noted that the political base of the Red Brigades was isolated by mass mobilizations against terrorism led by the PCI and the democratic Left. Indeed, throughout the entire protest wave of the 1960s and 1970s, the PCI worked to temper militancy in order not to provoke a strong backlash by countermovements or undemocratic forces within the state.

PROTESTERS,
COUNTERPROTESTERS,
AND THE AUTHORITIES IN
NORTHERN IRELAND

Terence O'Neill's premiership of Northern Ireland from 1963 to 1969 brought a rapid shift in political opportunities in favor of the Catholic minority. His reformist policies toward the area's social and economic crisis encouraged the Nationalists and angered many of his fellow Unionists.

Indeed, some of the first protests that were launched in this period were by militant Unionists rather than by Nationalists. The Reverend Ian Paisley led a radical Protestant movement that was determined to resist religious ecumenicalism and any reforms in the political system. The Ulster Volunteer Force—a Unionist paramilitary group that had resisted home rule at the turn of the century—was revived and engaged in a campaign of sectarian assassinations. In short, Northern Ireland's new countermovement emerged before the movement itself! Reform from above rather than revolution from below inspired the hard-liners to take to the streets.

But it was not long before the traditional challengers to the regime sought to exploit the opportunities provided by a reformist premier and a divided political elite. In 1967, the Northern Ireland Civil Rights Association (NICRA) was founded by a collection of groups and individuals some of whom came from the Nationalist Party, the Northern Ireland Labour Party, the Communist Party, civil libertarian organizations, and a leftist faction of the IRA that was disillusioned with military-style campaigns. NICRA attempted to avoid the territorial issue and reproduction of communal conflict by demanding "British rights for British citizens." The anthem of this organization, "We Shall Overcome," evoked the comparison with the U.S. civil rights movement. The demand of civil rights rather than Irish unity was also designed to win sympathy in London from the media and the Labour government.

The tactics of nonviolent direct action were used by NICRA with great effect. The occupation of public houses that had been unfairly distributed to Protestants and the mass marches through city streets had the authorities confused. The regime was used to dealing either with IRA campaigns or Nationalist Party representations. It proved to be tactically inept when handling new forms of protest. Policemen clubbed peaceful protesters and camera crews alike during mass demonstrations. This led London and the international community to focus on this insular province, and the protesters enjoyed a high degree of external support.

Student participation in the civil rights struggle radicalized the move-

ment. They used the tactics of the sit-down, obstruction, and occupation to challenge the authorities. They founded their own organization, People's Democracy, in October 1968 and rejected the moderate leadership of NICRA. Some of the students' left-wing political leaders believed that articulating the demands of civil rights with socialism would win over a "misguided" Protestant working class. Inspired by class ideologies, they acted as if Northern Ireland's deep communal and religious divisions did not exist.

Like NICRA, though, the students found that practically every protest they organized attracted Paisleyite counterprotesters and a hostile Royal Ulster Constabulary (RUC). Meanwhile, the opponents of civil rights believed that the movement was for revolution rather than for reform. The conflicts that ensued radicalized the movement and the reaction to it.

In January 1969, the students organized a "Long March" from Belfast to Derry which was "consciously modelled on Martin Luther King's march from Selma to Montgomery, Alabama."[16] Outside Derry they were attacked by Paisleyites with the collusion of the RUC. Later on, the arrival of wounded protesters in the city's Catholic ghetto of the Bogside sparked widespread rioting.

The failure of transition

Through these conflictual interactions, a movement that was based on the association of all those who advo-

16. Paul Arthur and Keith Jeffrey, *Northern Ireland since 1968* (London: Basil Blackwell, 1988), p. 6.

cated civil rights—which included some prominent Protestant liberals —was forced inexorably into the logic of communal conflict around the ties of residence and religion. Terence O'Neill was politically paralyzed by competing claims from protesters, counterprotesters, and hard-line elements in the state. He was unable to deliver reform or prevent state repression. His moderate Unionists lacked any real autonomy from a countermovement constituency that provided the institutional and popular framework for the existence of the regime. Faced with electoral challenges from Paisley's anti-O'Neill Unionists, a bombing campaign by the Ulster Volunteer Force, and the mobilization of a radical civil rights movement, O'Neill resigned in April 1969.

The tactics of nonviolent direct action, which had been imported from the United States, and the ideology of the student-worker alliance, which came largely from continental Europe, were replaced very quickly with more traditional forms of protest and belief. Ghettos became "no-go" areas as barricades and riots were used to keep out violent adversaries. Residential defense associations sprang up in both communities as intercommunal conflict worsened. These organizations became the bases for future paramilitary organizations such as the Provisional IRA and the Protestant Ulster Defence Association.

Yet, when the British Army entered Northern Ireland in 1969, many believed that there was now a possibility for concrete reforms. The British government enjoyed a high degree of political autonomy from the Unionists and was sympathetic to the demands of the Nationalists. Certainly, the first manifestations of British political intervention were promising. The RUC was disarmed and its hated auxiliary force, the B-Specials, was abolished. Civil rights reforms were introduced in local elections by introducing the one man, one vote principle and by ending gerrymandering.

But not long after, the RUC was rearmed and the B-Specials were reconstituted in the shape of the Ulster Defence Regiment. In addition, while the reform of the electoral system endured, the evidence shows that discrimination in the work force and housing continued.[17] Meanwhile, a security state grew which has used the tactics of curfews, internment without trial, special no-jury courts, torture, and the practice—if not the policy—of shooting to kill when dealing with terrorist suspects.[18]

Civil liberties and democratic rights, therefore, have contracted significantly in the past two decades. All attempts at political reform, such as the power-sharing experiment of 1973-74, have been abandoned in the face of Unionist counterprotest. Fear of majority disorder—such as the Protestant Backlash—has been one of the guiding features of British policymaking in the province.

17. See Liam O'Dowd, Bill Rolston, and Mike Tomilson, Northern Ireland: Between Civil Rights and Civil War (London: CSE Books, 1980).

18. For some examples of these practices, see John McGuffin, The Guinea Pigs (London: Penguin, 1974), and, more recently, Mark Urban, Big Boys' Rules: The Secret Struggle against the IRA (London: Faber & Faber, 1992).

Furthermore, the violent struggles that ensued among Nationalist and Unionist paramilitaries and the state effectively ended mass protest in the 1970s. Any tactical innovations in protest repertoires were really the renewal of old forms of contention. The hunger strike, the political funeral, and the paramilitary display were revived within the context of the modern conflict. The diffusion of protest tactics went in strange directions, with Protestant groups sometimes adopting those of NICRA and with Unionist paramilitaries copying the IRA.[19]

To date, this conflict has crowded out the issues of other movements. Northern Ireland, with the worst unemployment and highest infant mortality in Western Europe, has seen its workers strike over the right to display flags and to prevent their religious protagonists from entering government. New social movements are smothered by the violence and the overriding issue of nationalism. In this way, the issues of nuclear waste in the Irish Sea, reform of homosexual and abortion laws, and international peace rarely get a political mention.

In Northern Ireland, the four Rs of revolution, reform, reaction, and repression are all tactics in continuous use rather than outcomes of particular conflicts. Cycles of protest are not followed by cycles of reform or, indeed, by all-out revolution. Instead, Nationalist protest has led to occasional attempts at reform, but the re-

19. For an example of the latter, see David Boulton, *The UVF 1966-73: An Anatomy of Loyalist Rebellion* (Dublin: Torc Books, 1973), pp. 173-74.

sult is usually a massive wave of Unionist counterprotest. The subsequent abandonment of reforms—which is the typical result of this process—has radicalized the minority community and provoked further rounds of violence and state repression.

A COMPARISON OF CASES

Italian protesters from myriad social groups have been successful in mobilizing support and gaining significant reforms since the late 1960s. The experience of fascism and concern about its resurgence tempered the demands and the militancy of the democratic Left, led by the PCI. This helped weaken the rightist backlash and keep the state democratic. The terrorism of the Red Brigades was as much a reaction to the success of reformism as the desire for revolution. The terrorism of the Right stemmed from similar concerns with a different kind of revolution in mind. The Christian Democratic state resisted using heavily repressive tactics and sought to incorporate rather than exclude its democratic challengers. All of this is not to say that this transition was not without significant problems and tragedies; rather, it is to argue that these were insufficient to prevent the expansion of democratic reform and participation.

By contrast, Northern Irish protesters have achieved few successes and a number of significant reversals. Many of those who led the protests in the late 1960s believed that Unionism was a paper tiger that would not bite. In part, this was due to wishful thinking, but it was also the result of a class-based ideology that did not take the sectarianism of Protestant workers seriously. For example, the Long March from Belfast to Derry through Protestant areas in January 1969 was based on a false comparison with the U.S. case. Territorial sovereignty over Alabama was finally settled in the American Civil War of the 1860s. Political control of Northern Irish soil was still a live issue at the beginning of its civil war in the 1960s. This is why the American and Northern Irish long marches had very different consequences.

Unionist counterprotesters derailed Premier O'Neill's reforms. He lacked the political autonomy from sections of his own constituency to grant civil rights to Catholics. After the entry of British troops into the area in 1969 and the assumption of direct rule in 1972, a similar pattern of conflict emerged. Successive British governments have refused to stand up to Unionist counterpressures and introduce significant reforms. It is partly this lack of reform that keeps the Provisional IRA from losing its strength like the Italian Red Brigades. The British would rather fight a war on one front and deal with minority disruption than have to cope with conflict on two fronts and widespread majority disorder. Northern Ireland's rulers from across the water pay few direct costs for maintaining the current impasse, and they would like to keep it that way.

CONCLUSION

Citizens can use protest to redress grievances, gain political access, and expand democratic participation. Alternatively, they can use the same techniques to deny those rights to others. Direct-action tactics forged by one citizen group can later be adopted by its enemies. Even protest songs and slogans can be rearticulated by opponents to convey a different message entirely. The originators of tactics of disruption enjoy the benefits of neither monopoly nor copyright.

Protesters who take advantage of a favorable political situation make judgments about the way they should structure their claims and the likely reaction of other social actors and the authorities. Eventually, they may achieve the right mix of demands and tactics to bring about reforms. On the other hand, they may miscalculate politically and invite reaction and repression.

These concerns about the functional aspects of protest make it difficult to formulate general theoretical statements. The contingent factors of political context shape the emergence, evolution, and institutional impact of citizens' direct action. A new protest tactic or demand, in a particular setting, can inspire followers, mobilize mass support, and lead to the introduction of progressive reforms. In a different context, the same innovation can enrage opponents, lead to violence, and result in state repression.

Protesters who are inspired by actions and ideas developed elsewhere need to consider whether they are appropriate to local conditions. They must also calculate the possible countermoves of adversaries and weigh the possible outcomes. Counterprotesters need to ensure that they do not confuse mass movements for reform with preparations for total revolution. In addition, these defenders of the existing order should be concerned that their actions do not lead to its demise. Finally, state authorities who want political stability should not fall into the temptation of following a self-defeating strategy of repression and the denial of reform.

These lessons are pressing and urgent, for it seems that more than a handful of Northern Irelands are emerging out of the new democratic transitions in Central and Eastern Europe. It might be helpful if the actors involved in these conflicts tried to be a little more Italian in their politics.

ANNALS, *AAPSS*, **528**, July 1993

Movements and Media
as Interacting Systems

By WILLIAM A. GAMSON and GADI WOLFSFELD

ABSTRACT: In this article, some organizing principles and hypotheses are offered concerning the ways in which social movements interact with the news media and the outcomes for both parties. The structural part of the analysis focuses attention on the power and dependency aspects of the relationship and the consequences of the asymmetries. The cultural part focuses attention on the more subtle contest over meaning. Hypotheses on how social movement characteristics affect media coverage focus on movement standing, preferred framing, and sympathy. The authors argue for the importance of organization, professionalism, and strategic planning and for the benefits of a division of labor among movement actors. Hypotheses on how media characteristics affect movement outcomes focus on leadership, action strategy, and framing strategy. The authors argue for audience size, emphasis on the visual, and emphasis on entertainment values as influencing movements.

William A. Gamson is professor of sociology at Boston College and codirector of the Media Research and Action Project. His books include Talking Politics *(1992) and* The Strategy of Social Protest *(second edition, 1990). He is currently president-elect of the American Sociological Association.*

Gadi Wolfsfeld is director of the Smart Family Institute of Communication at the Hebrew University of Jerusalem and has a joint appointment as senior lecturer in political science and communication at that institution. His most recent publication is an edited volume (with Akiba Cohen): Framing the Intifada: People and Media *(1993).*

MOST conversations between social movement activists and journalists take a drearily predictable form: "Send my message," say the activists; "Make me news," say the journalists. In this dialogue of the deaf, neither activists nor journalists make an effort to understand how the other views their relationship or, better yet, the complex nature of these transactions.

We offer here some organizing principles and hypotheses about the ways in which social movements interact with the news media and the outcomes for both parties.[1] This is really a transaction between two complicated systems of actors with complex internal relationships. The media world has its internal transactions between journalists and camera crews

in the field and editors and producers in the home office; they operate in systems with quite different political economies in different countries, and the norms and practices vary, both nationally and internationally. Journalists have their own distinctive culture, and individual media organizations often have distinctive subcultures.

Similarly, social movements vary in many ways.[2] Many involve alliances between groups with quite different strategies of change and ways of approaching the media. They do not represent a unified actor but an array of actors who are affected by each other's media transactions, sometimes in contrasting ways. Movements often have a distinctive and evolving culture that may, in various ways, conflict with media and mainstream political culture.

Useful explanations will need to reflect the internal complexities of both parties in this transaction as well as the social and political context of their interaction. There are both structural and cultural dimensions. The structural part of our analysis focuses attention on the power and dependency aspects of the relationship and the consequences of the asymmetries. The cultural part of our analysis focuses attention on the more subtle contest over meaning.

POWER AND DEPENDENCY

Each side in the media-movement transaction is dependent on the other

---

1. We draw here on a growing literature about this relationship, including especially Harvey Molotch, "Media and Movements," in *The Dynamics of Social Movements*, ed. Mayer N. Zald and John McCarthy (Cambridge, MA: Winthrop, 1979); Todd Gitlin, *The Whole World Is Watching* (Berkeley: University of California Press, 1980); David L. Paletz and Robert M. Entman, *Media, Power, Politics* (New York: Free Press, 1981); Richard B. Kielbowicz and Clifford Scherer, "The Role of the Press in the Dynamics of Social Movements," in *Social Movements, Conflict, and Change* (Greenwich, CT: JAI Press, 1986), 9:71-96; Clarice N. Olien, Phillip J. Tichenor, and George E. Donahue, "Media Coverage and Social Movements," in *Information Campaigns: Balancing Social Values and Social Change*, ed. C. T. Salmon (Newbury Park, CA: Sage, 1992); William A. Gamson, "Challenging Groups since 1945," in *The Strategy of Social Protest*, 2d ed. (Belmont, CA: Wadsworth, 1990); Charlotte Ryan, *Prime Time Activism* (Boston: South End Press, 1991); Gadi Wolfsfeld, "The Symbiosis of Press and Protest: An Exchange Analysis," *Journalism Quarterly*, 61:550-56 (1984); idem, "Media, Protest, and Political Violence: A Transactional Analysis," *Journalism Monographs*, no. 127 (1991).

2. By "social movement," we mean a sustained and self-conscious challenge to authorities or cultural codes by a field of actors—organizations and advocacy networks—some of whom employ extra-institutional means of influence.

but not equally so. Movements are generally much more dependent on media than the reverse, and this fundamental asymmetry implies the greater power of the media system in the transaction. We begin by examining the needs of each in what Wolfsfeld calls the "competitive symbiosis" between them.[3]

Movements need the news media for three major purposes: mobilization, validation, and scope enlargement. Regarding mobilization, most movements must reach their constituency in part through some form of public discourse.[4] Public discourse is carried out in various forums, including the movement's own publications and meetings. But media discourse remains indispensable for most movements because most of the people they wish to reach are part of the mass media gallery, while many are missed by movement-oriented outlets.

Beyond needing the media to convey a message to their constituency, movements need media for validation. When demonstrators chant, "The whole world is watching," it means that they matter, that they are making history. The media spotlight validates the fact that the movement is an important player. Receiving standing in the media is often a necessary condition before targets of influence will grant a movement recog-

nition and deal with its claims and demands. Conversely, a demonstration with no media coverage at all is a nonevent, unlikely to have any positive influence either on mobilizing followers or influencing the target. No news is bad news.

Finally, movements need the media to broaden the scope of conflict. "If a fight starts, watch the crowd," Schattschneider advised us more than thirty years ago.[5] The scope of a conflict, he observed, frequently changes during its course, and the introduction and subtraction of players alters the power relations between the contestants. Where the scope is narrow, the weaker party has much to gain and little to lose by broadening the scope, drawing third parties into the conflict as mediators or partisans.

Making a conflict more public offers an opportunity for the movement to improve its relative power compared to that of its antagonist, and mass media coverage is a vehicle for this. Here it is not merely attention but the content of the media coverage that affects whether and in what ways third parties will enter the conflict. Third-party sympathy can be an important constraint on the social control measures used by authorities against movements and can also lead to new alliances. Movements, then, depend on the media to generate public sympathy for their challenge.

If we flip the question of need around, social movements often make good copy for the media. They provide drama, conflict, and action;

3. Wolfsfeld, "Media, Protest, and Political Violence," p. 2.

4. There are significant exceptions, especially if one focuses on the Third World. The Faribundo Martí National Liberation Front's movement against the regime in El Salvador, for example, was not dependent on the mass media for reaching its constituency. Arguments made here require appropriate modifications to fit such cases.

5. E. E. Schattschneider, The Semi-Sovereign People (New York: Holt, Rinehart, & Winston, 1960), p. 3.

colorful copy; and photo opportunities. But they operate in a competitive environment with many rival service providers; they are only one source of news among many. When reporters are given continuing assignments or beats, it is rare for them to be assigned to cover a social movement, and they are less likely to develop routine relationships with movement sources. Hence movements must not only compete with other potential newsmakers but are forced to start the race much further back on the track.

The fact that movements need the media far more than the media need them translates into greater power for the media in the transaction. Power dependency theory distinguishes two components of power: value and need.[6] "Value" refers to how much the other party needs one's own services; "need" refers to how much one needs the other party's services. The relative power of actors is determined by the ratio of their value to their need.

6. Power dependency theory—essentially a subcategory of exchange theory in social psychology—has its roots in the work of Richard Emerson, "Power-Dependence Relations," *American Sociological Review*, 27:31-41; idem, "Exchange Theory, Part II," in *Sociological Theories in Progress*, vol. 2, ed. Joseph Berger et al. (New York: Houghton Mifflin, 1972), pp. 58-87; Peter Blau, *Exchange and Power in Social Life* (New York: John Wiley, 1964). Its application to the media has been led by Sandra Ball-Rokeach and her colleagues under the rubric of media system dependency theory. See Sandra Ball-Rokeach and Melvin DeFleur, "A Dependency Model of Mass Media Effects," *Communication Research*, 3:3-21 (1976); Sandra Ball-Rokeach, "The Origins of Individual Media System Dependency: A Sociological Framework," *Communication Research*, 12: 485-510 (1985).

For social movements, the ratio is rarely favorable. Unlike public officials and heads of large established organizations, movement actors do not receive automatic standing in the media. They must struggle to establish it, often at what they regard as serious costs for the message that they wish to convey. Their dependency forces them to pay a price of entry that affects the subsequent transaction in various ways, which will be discussed later in this article.

Not only are institutional actors given standing automatically, but, having access to institutional channels of influence, they do not have the mobilization and validation needs of movements. The powerful usually prefer and are able to lobby in private; media coverage is often the last thing they need or want. Hence those who are most needy have least access to the media services they desire and pay a higher price for them—an example of the principle of cumulative inequality.

FRAMING

We have focused so far on the exchange of services in an unequal power relationship, but there is another aspect of the transaction between movements and media: a negotiation over meaning. Movements and media are both in the business of interpreting events, along with other nonmovement actors who have a stake in them. Events do not speak for themselves but must be woven into some larger story line or frame; they take on their meaning from the frame in which they are embedded.[7]

7. For development of the concept of frame in work on media and social movements, see

The movement-media transaction is characterized by a struggle over framing. A frame is a central organizing idea, suggesting what is at issue. It deals with the gestalt or pattern-organizing aspect of meaning. W. Lance Bennett attempts to capture this idea with the concept of political scenario, suggesting that scenarios provide a "lay theoretical framework in which to organize the sense data of politics."[8] He points to the use of paradigmatic or compelling examples to provide a highly abstract symbolic container to deal with an unfolding reality. Frames are expressed over time as a story line.

Charlotte Ryan provides some excellent examples of movements contesting the dominant media framing of issues, sometimes with at least modest success. The movement opposing the U.S. war against Nicaragua faced a prominent, officially supported media frame that depicted the war as a struggle against Communist expansion. She shows how a local group in New Bedford, Massachusetts, was able to counter this frame by making

the issue one of whether the United States should continue a war whose human costs were so high that it violated basic American values.[9]

The group organized a delegation that visited Nicaragua. The story in the *New Bedford Standard Times* on their return was headlined, "Nicaragua Trip Sears Delegates," and the article began, "With their arms clutching each other and tears rolling down their faces, members of the New Bedford delegation to Nicaragua came home Monday, emotionally wrought with the images of war." The movement frame was provided in comments and quotations:

Nicaragua is nothing resembling a repressive, military state, that is, for example, El Salvador. Mr. Pina said the message he heard over and over again from the Nicaraguans was: "We're hungry, we have no arms. We're poor, but we're not asking anything but to let us go about our business of maintaining peace in our land for our children . . . because our children are our future.[10]

Note the complicated double role that the media system plays in this framing transaction. On the one hand, journalists play a central role in the construction of meaning; they choose a story line in reporting events, and media commentators develop arguments and images that support particular frames. News stories are put together out of raw happenings, and this necessarily means framing these happenings and giving them meaning.

On the other hand, media output is an arena in which symbolic contests are carried out. Journalists

especially Gaye Tuchman, *Making News* (New York: Free Press, 1978); Gitlin, *Whole World Is Watching*; Gladys E. Lang and Kurt Lang, *The Battle for Public Opinion: The President, the Press, and the Polls during Watergate* (New York: Columbia University Press, 1983); William A. Gamson and Andre Modigliani, "Media Discourse and Public Opinion on Nuclear Power," *American Journal of Sociology*, 95:1-37 (1989); David A. Snow et al., "Frame Alignment and Mobilization," *American Sociological Review*, 51:464-81 (1986); Ryan, *Prime Time Activism*; Gadi Wolfsfeld, "Framing Political Conflict," in *Framing the Intifada: Media and People*, ed. Gadi Wolfsfeld and Akiba Cohen (Norwood, NJ: Ablex, 1993).

8. W. Lance Bennett, *The Political Mind and the Political Environment* (Lexington, MA: D. C. Heath, 1975), p. 65.

9. Ryan, *Prime Time Activism*, pp. 34-37, 63-66.

10. Ibid., p. 65.

serve as gatekeepers here, deciding which frame sponsors will be granted standing and selecting what to quote or emphasize. Journalists, however, do not invent the rules of access; these are structural, reflecting power differences between actors in the larger society. In some cases, the media output may simply reflect the frames of the most powerful actors with little independent contribution from journalists.

Participants in symbolic contests read their success or failure by how well their preferred meanings and interpretations are doing in various media arenas. Prominence in these arenas is an outcome measure by which one judges the success of one's efforts.

Media norms and practices and the broader political culture in which they operate have major effects on this framing transaction. Not only are certain actors given standing more readily than others, but certain ideas and language are given a more generous welcome. It is not simply that certain ideas are unpopular—some are rendered invisible.

One realm of media discourse is uncontested. It is the realm where the social constructions rarely appear as such to the reader and may be largely unconscious on the part of the writer as well. They appear as transparent descriptions of reality, not as interpretations, and are apparently devoid of political content. Journalists feel no need to get different points of view for balance when they deal with images in this realm.

There is also a contested realm of media discourse in which struggles over meaning and interpretation are central. It is a major achievement of some movements that they succeed in moving issues from the uncontested to the contested realm. Even if the subsequent contest is played on a tilted playing field, it is still a contest, and many movements have scored media successes in spite of the odds.

Movement disadvantages in the struggle over meaning reflect cultural obstacles as well as handicaps in access and resources. Movement-media communication is like a conversation between a monolingual and a bilingual speaker. The media speak mainstreamese, and movements are pushed to adopt this language to be heard since journalists are prone to misunderstand or never hear the alternate language and its underlying ideas. But it is a common experience of movement activists to complain that something has been lost in translation. Movements that accept the dominant cultural codes and do not challenge what is normally taken for granted will have less of a problem, but for many movements, this would involve surrendering fundamental aspects of their raison d'être.

There is, then, a fundamental ambivalence and, for some, estrangement between movements and media. Movement activists tend to view mainstream media not as autonomous and neutral actors but as agents and handmaidens of dominant groups whom they are challenging. The media carry the cultural codes being challenged, maintaining and reproducing them. In this sense, they are a target as much as a medium of communication. But they are also the latter and, in this sense, one tries to speak through the media rather than to them. This dual media role is the central problematic of the transaction from the movement standpoint.

Given the power-dependency relations, journalists can afford to be more detached in their attitudes toward movements, but there are definite points of friction when their own more pragmatic and cynical subculture encounters the more idealistic and righteous culture of the movements. Movements seem to demand unreasonable and unrealistic things and often have a righteousness that is unappealing to those who are living with the inevitable compromises of daily life. Movements hector people and call them to account. This means that internal movement conflicts and peccadillos will have a special fascination for journalists, giving them an opportunity to even the score from their standpoint. The fall of the righteous is a favored media story wherever it can be found, and movements offer a happy hunting ground.

Finally, the subcultures of specific media organizations may clash more with some movements than with others. A religious newspaper in Israel, covering a demonstration of ultra-orthodox Jews (*Haredim*) against driving cars on the Sabbath, will have less cultural distance than a secular newspaper covering the same event. Cultural distance between movements and media, whatever the source, is more likely to mean that movement frames will get lost in translation.

HYPOTHESES

Movement and media systems vary on many important dimensions that affect their transaction. Movements differ in the breadth and depth of their challenge and in the centrality of the media to the success of their collective action. Within the movement system, some actors focus heavily on media strategies, while, for others, these are secondary to face-to-face interactions.

Media systems vary both organizationally and ideologically. Media organizations vary in prestige and in the size of their audience. Some are multimedia giants with worldwide reach; others are specialized and local. In some media organizations, the production of news is permeated by entertainment values, while in others, journalistic values are more dominant. Some target political and cultural elites, while others aim at a broader, popular audience. Some produce news as a commodity that can attract an audience to sell to advertisers, while others produce news to promote a worldview, to further the interests of a political party, or as a public service for the citizenry. Some emphasize the visual, while, for others, visual aspects are secondary.

An explanation of the movement-media transaction needs to relate these variable elements of the two systems to both media and movement outcomes. The hypotheses that we will suggest run in both directions: some of them suggest how movement characteristics and actions will affect media products, while others suggest how media characteristics and actions will affect movements.

Effects of movements on media coverage

There are three elements of media coverage of particular interest to movement actors: (1) standing, that is, the extent to which the group is taken seriously by being given extensive media coverage, regardless of content; (2) preferred framing, that is, the prominence of the group's frame in media discourse on the issues of concern; and (3) movement sympathy, that is, the extent to which the content of the coverage presents the group in a way that is likely to gain sympathy from relevant publics.

Hypothesis 1. The greater the resources, organization, professionalism, coordination, and strategic planning of a movement, the greater its media standing and the more prominent its preferred frame will be in media coverage of relevant events and issues.

Some movements are either unable or unwilling to dedicate resources to media strategies, to coordinate their stance in transactions with the media, or to gain an understanding of the world of journalists and media systems. Those movements that are able and willing to allocate resources to working with the media frequently have more experience and sophistication in this area as well as ongoing relationships with working journalists. These movements are in a much better position to provide and package information in ways that meet the needs of the media. Organization, resources, and media sophistication are all markers journalists use to identify who the serious players are.

A movement that does not have its act together in this regard is less likely to be granted standing. From the perspective of journalists, the burden of proof is on the movement to show that it is a potential force. Here journalists act as self-appointed surrogates for political elites, assuming, perhaps unconsciously, that if a movement seems sloppy and disorganized in dealing with them, the authorities it is challenging will be unlikely to take it seriously.

Once granted standing, movements will be most successful in getting their message across when they are both clear and consistent in what issue framing they prefer and devote time and resources to conveying their wishes in a way that makes that frame most likely to be used. This means dedicating effort to meeting the news needs of journalists, by providing sound bites, backgrounders, photo opportunities, and ready-to-use video footage. To compete with sophisticated rivals, movements must be ready to make it as easy as possible for journalists to send their message with a minimum of alteration.

Hypothesis 2. The greater the complementary division of labor among movement actors, the greater the ability of the movement to gain both standing and preferred frames.

As has been discussed, movements have a dilemma that many other news sources do not experience. Officials are granted automatic standing and can concentrate simply on the message they wish to convey. Movements, in contrast, must deal with a potential contradiction between gaining standing and getting their message across.

Members of the club enter the media forum through the front door when they choose, they are treated with respect, and they are given the benefit of the doubt. Challengers must contend with other would-be claimants for attention at the back door, finding some gimmick or act of disorder to force their way in. But when they do so, they enter defined as upstarts and the framing of the group may obscure any message it carries. Those who dress up in costume to be admitted to the media's party will not be allowed to change before being photographed.

Movements can solve this dilemma in part through an intentional or unintentional division of labor among actors. When this occurs, those who engage in actions designed to gain standing do not themselves attempt to be the main carriers of the issue frame; for this, they defer to partners who do not carry the baggage of deviance but can articulate a shared frame. In the antinuclear movement, for example, standing was greatly enhanced by the site occupation of the Seabrook, New Hampshire, reactor by the Clamshell Alliance. This action helped to define nuclear power as controversial, and once it was designated as such, the media's balance norm was invoked. This norm requires seeking spokespersons for both sides in what journalists typically reduce to a dyadic conflict.

In the case of nuclear power, the more respectable movement actor was most frequently represented in the United States by the Union of Concerned Scientists (UCS). The actions of the Clam plus other antinuclear demonstrations and site occupations across the country helped to create the conditions for media-initiated contacts with movement actors. As Gamson puts it, "when demonstrators are arrested at Seabrook, phones ring at UCS."[11]

The Palestinian *intifada* provides another good example. The most intensive violence came from bloody clashes between young Israeli soldiers and sometimes even younger Palestinians. The *intifada* provided additional media standing for the Palestinian movement, especially with the international press. But it was not the youth groups (*shabiba*) who became media spokespersons for the Palestinian cause. The international press turned to the Palestinian intellectual community living in East Jerusalem, to people with whom they already had some relationship. Schiff and Ya'ari describe this group "as men of the middle class and middle ground [whose] natural inclination was to set the *intifada* on a more familiar, 'respectable' footing by calling a press conference in Jerusalem, inviting the international news media, announcing a plan of action for the uprising, and establishing themselves as its leadership."[12] Some members of this group of intellectuals later became the Palestinian representatives in the Madrid and subsequent peace talks. Media standing translated into broader political standing.

11. William A. Gamson, "Political Discourse and Collective Action," in *From Structure to Action*, ed. Bert Klandermans, Hanspeter Kriesi, and Sidney Tarrow (Greenwich, CT: JAI Press, 1988), p. 235. For an account of changes in media discourse on nuclear power in the United States, see Gamson and Modigliani, "Media Discourse and Public Opinion on Nuclear Power."

12. Ze'ev Schiff and Ehud Ya'ari, *Intifada: The Palestinian Uprising—Israel's Third Front* (New York: Simon & Schuster, 1990), p. 204.

Internal rivalries between movement actors can undermine such convenient divisions of labor. Movements frequently offer multiple frames, each identified with particular groups. Those whose action creates a broader movement standing may find that their preferred frame is poorly represented by those who become the media-designated spokespersons. They may attack and attempt to undercut their rivals. This internal movement contest can easily become the media's story, thereby distracting attention or blurring the preferred issue frame. A division of labor is likely to work only if there is a common frame and a willingness to subordinate concerns about who gets credit for being the messenger.

Hypothesis 3. The narrower the movement's demands, the more likely it is to receive coverage that presents it sympathetically to a broader public.

This points to another fundamental dilemma that movements face in their transaction with the media. Do they challenge powerful groups and institutions and cultural codes in fundamental ways, thus risking being denied standing altogether or being branded as dangerous threats? Or do they challenge as little as possible and risk being forced to settle for a few symbolic gestures that change little or nothing? Successful movements must walk a tightrope between these two perils.

The environmental movement provides examples of the risks involved in seeking broad public support. Some groups avoid targeting corporate or governmental actors, focusing their attention on consumer behavior instead. Recycling or anti-littering campaigns, for example, make few enemies and put the movement on the side of the angels. But the favorable image is purchased at the cost of leaving broader structural and cultural sources of environmental problems unchallenged and implicitly reinforced.

Effects of the media on movements

The hypotheses here treat media characteristics as independent variables and examine their effects on three different movement outcomes: (1) leadership, that is, the role of the media in influencing who has standing in the movement; (2) action strategy, that is, the role of the media in influencing which collective-action strategies and tactics are pursued; and (3) framing strategy, that is, the role of the media in influencing how the movement represents its message in the contest over meaning.

Hypothesis 4. The larger and more elite the audience of the media outlet, the greater the impact on movement framing strategies.

Movements challenging political authorities or fundamental cultural codes are reluctant to water down their message to make it palatable to a mass audience. It is frequently not merely a matter of sending one's frame in diluted form but of reframing one's message in the dominant language. But this is a matter of degree, not all or nothing.

If a media outlet offers a prime-time forum with national or global reach, it is valuable enough for the movement to make some compromises in the purity of the message.

The problem here for the movement is how to condense its message effectively without losing it. The right catchphrase or the telling concrete example can convey an underlying frame in shorthand in a compelling way. The message is not reduced to this simplification; rather, the shorthand provides a handle for holding on to the underlying idea. As Ryan puts it, "A bite is merely an extremely abbreviated form of story-telling foisted upon us by high-tech media in a hurry."[13]

Hypothesis 5. The more the media actor emphasizes entertainment values relative to journalistic values, the more likely it is to influence the leadership choices and action strategies of the movement.

Media oriented toward a mass audience, particularly those media that are profit driven, are especially likely to favor entertainment values over journalistic values in news production. The media influence internal movement leadership by certifying some people or groups and ignoring others. They follow their own principles of selection, and some media-designated leaders may have had few followers before their anointment. With their media-created celebrity, they soon find followers where none may have existed before. Gitlin describes this effect for the American New Left movement of the 1960s: "The all-permeating spectacular culture insisted that the movement be identified through its celebrities; naturally, it attracted personalities who

enjoyed performance, who knew how to flaunt some symbolic attribute, who spoke quotably."[14]

Gitlin also points out how the structure of movements enables the celebrity process to operate. In contrast to countries where political parties and other institutions provided adult roles for former student leaders, the American political scene lacked such opportunities. "Celebrity became a substitute for a continuing radical role," he writes.[15] The result was the creation of leaders who rose to glory as spokespersons without accountability to a movement base.

The media's awarding of celebrity status sometimes leads movements to reject the idea of having any movement spokespersons. Sale describes how Paul Booth, as national secretary of Students for a Democratic Society, was attacked for making statements to the media on behalf of the organization. One member suggested he should have referred reporters to local chapters, which would tell them what was going on in their particular area.[16] Such a strategy simply compounds the celebrity system since by failing to provide its own spokesperson, a movement invites the media to designate who will speak for the movement.

Hypothesis 6. The more the media actor emphasizes visual material in its news production, the more likely it is to produce action strategies that emphasize spectacle, drama, and confrontation.

13. Ryan, *Prime Time Activism*, p. 104. Ryan's book provides the most thorough and compelling analysis of the possibilities and pitfalls involved in attempts by challengers to speak through the media without losing the essence of their message.

14. Gitlin, *Whole World Is Watching*, p. 153.
15. Ibid., p. 156.
16. Kirkpatrick Sale, *SDS: Students for a Democratic Society* (New York: Random House, 1973), p. 235.

Because visual material puts a higher premium on spectacle, television is more likely than print media to emphasize it. Spectacle means drama and confrontation, emotional events involving people who have fire in the belly, who are extravagant and unpredictable. This puts a high premium on novelty, on costume, and on confrontation.

Violent action has most of these media-valued elements. Fire in the belly is fine, but fire on the ground photographs better. Burning buildings and burning tires make better television than peaceful vigils and orderly marches. Furthermore, as Gitlin argues,[17] it is precisely those leaders who are attached to followers only through their media image and are unaccountable to the rank and file who are likely to advocate the extravagant and dramatic actions that generate good media copy.

Visual spectacle is high in entertainment value. When news is a vehicle for procuring an audience to sell to advertisers, then one needs to worry a lot about people's tuning out. The fear is that these people will turn to alternative providers who have higher flames and more action on their news. Movements that want to keep the spotlight of such media organizations will adopt action strategies that provide strong visual material.

CONCLUSION

Many of the hypotheses stated in this article concerning movements are based on principles that apply to other political actors as well. Important parameters change, but power-

17. Gitlin, *Whole World Is Watching.*

dependency relations can be applied to the transaction between any actor and the media. In the transaction between government and the media, for example, the relative power of the media is also asymmetrical—but in this case, it is the media with the unfavorable ratio of value to need.

It is not only movements that gain standing through resources, organization, and professionalism or do better when they have a planned media strategy. But other actors do not need the kind of division of labor that movements employ to prevent their efforts to gain standing from obliterating their message.

All actors must deal with the media's interest in spectacle. Presidents have as much occasion to provide photo opportunities as any movement does. Framing strategies of powerful actors are often dictated by what is likely to play in the media. The selection of leadership, however, is determined by institutional roles, not celebrity. In sum, the movement-media transaction is a special case of media transactions more generally, one with some unusual and unique features.

We have sketched a model of the transaction between movements and media that is long on general arguments but short on specific applications. Every transaction takes place under a particular set of conditions and the hypotheses are intended to suggest what is relevant for understanding the outcome. Only the detailed application to specific cases will enable us to see how helpful these are in generating insights and in understanding the limiting conditions under which they hold.

Coordinating Demands for Social Change

By DENNIS CHONG

ABSTRACT: Mass protest movements resemble assurance games, in which individual decisions to contribute are contingent on the aggregate level of participation. While participation in ineffective movements carries high costs and returns few collective and selective benefits, participation in successful social movements can be more advantageous than abstention. Supporters of a movement therefore try to coordinate their decisions with those of other activists, participating when it appears that the movement has sufficient popular support to be politically effective, but not otherwise. Such decisions, however, typically have to be made with considerable uncertainty about both the intentions of other individuals and the prospects of the movement as it develops. Given this individual calculus, a number of deductions can be drawn about the resources, strategies, goals, and political conditions that will be required to coordinate and organize mass social protest.

Dennis Chong is an assistant professor of political science at Northwestern University. He has written papers on political attitudes and beliefs, collective action, and cooperative behavior, as well as a book, Collective Action and the Civil Rights Movement. *Currently he is studying how ideas and values are used strategically in politics and society.*

THE public goods sought by mass protest movements can be enjoyed equally by those who contribute to their achievement and those who do not. It is generally accepted that to discourage people from getting a free ride on the efforts of others, a movement that depends on popular support for its influence has to provide additional selective incentives to participants beyond its collective goals. In social movements, these selective incentives for cooperation are more likely to be social and psychological in nature than material. People might do their fair share, for example, to receive praise or avoid criticism from others, to preserve their social standing, or to experience expressive benefits from the process of participation itself.[1]

It would seem that adding selective incentives to the cost-benefit calculus of individuals would be enough to produce cooperation except that these benefits are usually contingent upon the prospects of collective action. Members of a group tend to be enthusiastic about participating in protests and demonstrations, or feel pressured by others to do so, only to the extent that they believe they can achieve their goals through collective action. When collective action is widely regarded to be futile, these

social and psychological incentives are significantly diminished. Moral prescriptions and social obligations hold more sway when there is a reason to do one's duty or contribute one's fair share, and psychological incentives to participate increase when one has an opportunity to be a member of a winning cause.

In this article, I will show that the conditional nature of these selective benefits turns mass collective action into an assurance game, in which contributions depend on the perceived strength of the social movement. Political activists face various problems trying to organize collective action when support for the movement is linked to its prospects for success. Their biggest obstacle is that everyone may insist on following the lead of others. Until the movement becomes viable, social pressures and psychological incentives to contribute are not strongly felt by the ordinary participant. Therefore, barring leaders or entrepreneurs who are willing to absorb the high start-up costs of collective action, the movement may never reach its potential. I will also show that by thinking about a popular movement as an assurance game, we can deduce a number of strategies that organizers will use to gain mass support and the political conditions in which these tactics are likely to be effective. In addition, analysis of the model will reveal why popular movements are so difficult to sustain over an extended period and why the types of goals they can pursue and achieve tend to be limited to relatively uncomplicated, singular—albeit sometimes grand—pursuits.

---

1. The theoretical status of these kinds of selective incentives is a separate topic in itself, which I will not pursue here. See the discussion in Dennis Chong, *Collective Action and the Civil Rights Movement* (Chicago: University of Chicago Press, 1991); Jon Elster, *The Cement of Society* (New York: Cambridge University Press, 1989); Russell Hardin, *Collective Action* (Baltimore, MD: Johns Hopkins University Press, 1982).

CONDITIONAL BENEFITS

Brian Barry speculated that "whatever the reason why a person may attach himself to a cause, more enthusiasm for its pursuit is likely to be elicited if it looks as if it has a chance of succeeding than if it appears to be a forlorn hope. Nobody likes to feel that he is wasting his time, and that feeling may be induced by contributing to a campaign which never looks as if it has a chance."[2] I would add that this sense of futility predominates whether one participates for socially instrumental or expressive reasons. Much of the expressive pleasure of political activism comes from the feeling that others are paying attention to one's protests. While a famous person might be able to get a message across single-handedly, ordinary individuals need the company of others if they are to have any chance of attracting public attention to their cause. There may be some visceral relief, but little expressive value to shouting in the wilderness.

Likewise, the socially instrumental value of participation often hinges on the viability of collective action. A successful movement receives widespread recognition and publicity, and its activists receive credit for having done their part in a worthy cause. Because unsuccessful movements are generally denied such publicity, people are less likely to have heard of the exploits of those who participated in them. For example, veterans of the civil rights movement look back fondly on their experiences and continue to receive the plaudits and es-

teem of each new generation for having been leaders in their time. In contrast, participants in, say, the nuclear freeze movement may well be accused of having wasted their time. Indeed, whereas winners are praised, losers are sometimes scorned. Mancur Olson made a passing comment on this point in *The Logic of Collective Action* when he wrote, "Selfless behavior that has no perceptible effect is sometimes not even considered praiseworthy. A man who tries to hold back a flood with a pail would probably be considered more of a crank than a saint, even by those he was trying to help."[3]

Fruitless activity, therefore, even when it is selflessly devoted to the interests of the group, often goes unrewarded. This claim runs against the grain—correctly so, I believe—of various equity theories that stipulate that people believe there should be a relationship between an individual's effort to achieve a goal and the rewards that he or she receives.[4] By this account, people who work diligently to achieve something deserve to be repaid for their efforts even if the product of their labor in itself merits little esteem. On the contrary, I suspect that bad acting, bad piano playing, bad cooking, and bad political activism are judged no better, and the performers no better rewarded,

---

2. Brian Barry, *Sociologists, Economists and Democracy* (Chicago: University of Chicago Press, 1978), p. 30.

3. Mancur Olson, Jr., *The Logic of Collective Action* (1965; reprint ed., Cambridge: Harvard University Press, 1971), p. 64.

4. J. Stacy Adams, "Inequality in Social Exchange," in *Advances in Experimental Social Psychology*, vol. 3, ed. Leonard Berkowitz (New York: Academic Press, 1965), pp. 267-99; George C. Homans, *Social Behavior: Its Elementary Forms* (New York: Harcourt, Brace, Jovanovich, 1974).

simply because we discover that they have trained long hours or dedicated themselves to the task. As much as we may wish to praise the industrious worker, we are probably even more likely to question his or her character in the wake of a poor performance. For this reason, a movement's failure may cast suspicion on the wisdom, tactics, and efforts of the participants and make them the targets of disrespect as opposed to admiration. This might explain the cold shoulder accorded veterans of the Vietnam war in comparison to our treatment of those who served successfully in World War II.

Lastly, group members will feel more obligated to participate in collective action when it is clear that collective action is useful. There is little if any obligation to participate in a hopeless cause. If the social pressure to participate in any cause originates from the obligation not to take advantage of the efforts of others, then that obligation is lightened in lost causes. Since collective benefits are not forthcoming, there is no advantage to be taken. If it appears that the venture will fail, each individual can decide for prudential reasons—while maintaining a clear conscience—to withhold any contribution on the grounds that it would be good money (or labor or time) thrown after a bad cause. Nor would this decision likely harm one's reputation for being a decent person who lives up to other, mutually profitable agreements. Under better conditions, one might argue, one would do one's duty, but mitigating circumstances make it conscionable to refrain from, in essence, sacrificing oneself. "Acts, including speech acts, are to be evaluated by their probable consequences; no one is morally required to take risks unless the probable consequences are beneficial; what is commendable is regard for the best results, not futile gestures."[5]

When social and psychological incentives enjoy a conditional status, individuals make prospective calculations to ascertain the short- and long-run benefits they can expect to receive for their own participation. The issue for them is whether the movement can attract enough support to stand a reasonable chance of succeeding. If the level of participation is high enough, individual participants are in line to receive not only a share of the public goods produced by the movement but also the collateral benefits associated with playing a role in an important cause. By their actions, cooperators enhance their reputations, gain the esteem of others, experience the excitement of a successful cause, and ensure that they will continue to enjoy good relations with other members of their community. As long as the collective and selective benefits that would accompany a successful movement exceed any individual's share of their cost, the movement profits everyone.

The reason why collective action might not materialize is that it appears that few people actively support it. Should this be true, no public goods will be produced and any individual contribution of time and energy will go largely unrewarded, as

5. Thomas E. Hill, Jr., "Symbolic Protest and Calculated Silence," *Philosophy and Public Affairs*, 9:83 (1979).

there are few if any compensatory social and expressive benefits for isolated efforts. Given these contingencies, each individual's choice will be conditional on the aggregate level of involvement. He or she will participate if the size of the movement exceeds a particular threshold but abstain if it does not. This is therefore an assurance game, in which a person will contribute only when assured that a sufficient number of others intend to do likewise.[6]

COORDINATION OF DEMAND

Whereas coordination can be a relatively simple matter in everyday interactions, it presents a serious obstacle to the initiation of mass political activism. Even if members of an aggrieved group harbor strong desires to engage in collective action, they must still reassure each other of their willingness to contribute. This prerequisite is more difficult to satisfy than it may appear at first glance, largely because of the size and concomitant vagaries of a social movement.

Individual decisions in the assurance game are based on assessments of the likelihood that the aggregate level of involvement needed to achieve success will be realized, but these estimates are muddled by two sources of uncertainty. Potential supporters of the movement are un-

6. Amartya K. Sen, "Isolation, Assurance and the Social Rate of Discount," *Quarterly Journal of Economics*, 80:112-24 (1967); idem, "Choice, Orderings and Morality," in *Practical Reason*, ed. Stephan Korner (Oxford: Basil Blackwell, 1974), pp. 54-67.

aware of the sort of collective effort that is required to give the movement enough leverage to accomplish its agenda, and they are uncertain about the perceptions and intentions of other people who may contribute to the movement.

Consider how these sources of uncertainty alter the calculations of activists. Each individual has to determine how the costs and benefits of participation vary according to the aggregate level of participation. Let us assume that the benefits of participation increase, while the costs decrease, with the size, N, of the movement. The cost-benefit functions can take various functional forms. For purposes of discussion, assume an S-shaped benefits curve; that is, collective and selective benefits are nonexistent at low levels of participation, rise sharply if the movement gathers widespread popular support, and then level off. Costs, on the other hand, vary inversely; they are steep when few people participate, but then decline as the movement gains momentum before eventually leveling off. Therefore, at low levels of N, the movement generates few if any collective or selective benefits and is extremely costly for individual contributors, making defection the preferred alternative. If the movement is able to attract more widespread support, several favorable developments occur: its prospects for success improve, selective incentives become more salient, and the costs of participation decline with the growing safety of numbers. In accordance with the assurance game, I assume that there is some threshold level of participation, $N = n'$, above which cooperation provides more net benefits than defection does.[7]

A person participates if the expected value of cooperation exceeds the expected value of defection. Let $EV(C)$ be the expected value of cooperation and $EV(D)$ be the expected value of defection or abstention; then $EV(C) = \Sigma_N$ [collective benefits (n) + selective benefits (n) − costs (n)] × probability (n), and $EV(D) = \Sigma_N$ collective benefits (n) × probability (n). The threshold level, n', is the point at which the selective benefits of participation equal the cost of participation; beyond n', the total benefit for participation exceeds that for nonparticipation. Therefore, although there are high start-up costs to collective action, the benefit of individual cooperation increases with the total level of contributions, until cooperation is the preferred course of action.

The difference between the expected values of C and D clearly increases inversely with costs and directly with the magnitude of selective incentives and the likelihood that total participation will exceed the threshold level. Therefore, everything else being equal, developments that lower the cost of participation, increase the selective benefits accompanying contributions, or raise the probability that total participation will reach the critical threshold— which might be accomplished by reducing the perceived threshold level itself—will abet the cause.

SOURCES OF UNCERTAINTY

Estimates of the threshold value for participation will vary among group members depending on their assessment of the prospects and selective benefits of collective action, and estimates of the probability that there will be at least n' cooperators will also be unsettled. Someone who thinks that collective action has little chance of succeeding will set very high levels for n'; in the most pessimistic case, n' will exceed the size of the group seeking benefits—in other words, even total cooperation will be assumed to be futile. Obviously, much depends on the responsiveness of the government or other petitioned party to these demands. To further complicate matters, not only will an individual be uncertain in his or her own mind about these parameters, but he or she will also know that others are uncertain about them, too, and that everyone is aware of each other's uncertainty. These combined sources of doubt are prone to undermine anyone's confidence in the likelihood of coordinated action.

Knowledge of the calculations and intentions of fellow group members is, of course, alleviated when collective action is built out of existing organizations and community relationships. The sociological literature is rich with examples of social movements capitalizing on existing social

7. For other discussions of threshold models, see Mark Granovetter, "Threshold Models of Collective Behavior," *American Journal of Sociology*, 83:1420-43 (1978); Mark Granovetter and Roland Soong, "Threshold Models of Diffusion and Collective Behavior," *Journal of Mathematical Sociology*, 9:165-79 (1983); Thomas C. Schelling, "Hockey Helmets, Concealed Weapons, and Daylight Savings," *Journal of Conflict Resolution*, 17:381-428 (1973); idem, *Micromotives and Macrobehavior* (New York: W. W. Norton, 1978).

networks of individuals with common interests and goals.[8] Community ties facilitate communication between people with common grievances, and discussion reduces uncertainty about the preferences and intentions of group members. Nevertheless, social movements are mass phenomena that depend not only on the steadfastness of small groups of dedicated activists but also on the more chronic participation of those in the public who are intermittently drawn to the movement based on its changing fortunes. As a result, even those movements that are favored by organizational resources will face difficult coordination problems.

We can think of this collective action problem more generally as an iterated assurance game or supergame in which prospective activists must continually make decisions about whether to participate based on the information they receive about the outcome of the game in preceding trials, that is, in previous campaigns of the movement. The early trials of this supergame allow participants and spectators to evaluate the nature of the game they are playing and, in particular, to estimate the costs, collective benefits, selective incentives, contribution levels, and prospects of the movement. The parameters of

8. See, for example, Michael Hechter, *Principles of Group Solidarity* (Berkeley: University of California Press, 1987); Gerald Marwell, Pamela E. Oliver, and Ralph Prahl, "Social Networks and Collective Action: A Theory of the Critical Mass. III," *American Journal of Sociology*, 94:502-34 (1988); Aldon Morris, "Black Southern Student Sit-In Movement: An Analysis of Internal Organization," *American Sociological Review*, 46:744-67 (1981).

the game therefore are established by the successes and failures of the movement. Forays by the movement in its nascent stages provide information about the relative difficulty or ease of attaining the group's objectives, the number of people who support the cause, the force of social pressures and other selective incentives, and so on. The initial plays of the game reveal both the strategies of the players in the community and the payoffs for those strategies. This trial-and-error process clarifies the values of the payoff functions for cooperation and defection at different levels of participation. These functions are initially ambiguous to the participants and become defined gradually by their experiences in the political process. Moreover, these functions are constantly being reevaluated as old campaigns wind down and new ones are begun.

DYNAMICS OF
COLLECTIVE ACTION

A number of implications about the resources, tactics, goals, and political circumstances that are required for a successful movement can be deduced from this model. The first two key elements that I will discuss have already been alluded to—leadership and community resources.

Drafting leaders

The cost of participation is greatest, while the benefits are most uncertain, when collective action has the least support. Prior to organizing, people suffer diffuse grievances and contemplate various means by which to address them. Leadership is therefore necessary to develop a common understanding of the problems that people face and to provide convincing arguments in favor of collective action. All analysts of social movements point to the importance of having an ideology that interprets people's circumstances and offers prescriptions for action. The task of leadership is to use such ideological appeals to create a group identity among those who are discontented and to train the energies of group members on a set of targets and solutions to their problems. Leaders therefore help to define the assurance game for others by persuading them of the promise entailed in collective action. In addition to defining the game for others, leaders help mightily to solve it by constituting, in effect, the critical mass that instigates the growth of collective action.[9]

The rationality or irrationality of leaders of causes is open to debate. Such individuals may simply be the most morally committed individuals within the entire social movement. Alternatively, rationally calculating political entrepreneurs are conventionally described as people who will pay the costs of soliciting and coordinating contributions in exchange for individual benefits such as power, prestige, or a disproportionate share of the profits derived from collective action.[10] One might get the impression from this that any number of individuals can step into the breach if the cost-benefit calculus is favorable. In practice, however, it is likely that only a few members of a community will have the credentials and social standing necessary for effective and successful leadership. Consequently, there may be substantial community pressure on such individuals to lend the prestige and leadership skills associated with their current roles to the new political enterprise, especially if it is perceived that coordination is impossible without their active involvement. Such pressures, which are not imposed on ordinary citizens, will likely lower the rate at which these individuals can discount the future repercussions of their actions.[11]

In this fashion, community leaders occupying nonpolitical positions may be drafted into the political arena because of the unique resources they possess. The combination of entrepreneurial opportunity and conformity to social pressure therefore helps explain why the leaders of public-spirited collective action tend to be respected community members with considerable resources already at their disposal. Existing leaders command respect, followers, and monitoring capabilities that increase their chances of favor-

9. Cf. Anthony Oberschall, "Loosely Structured Collective Conflict: A Theory and an Application," Research in Social Movements, Conflicts and Change, 3:45-68 (1980); Pamela Oliver, Gerald Marwell, and Ruy Teixeira, "A Theory of the Critical Mass. I. Interdependence, Group Heterogeneity, and the Production of Collective Action," American Journal of Sociology, 91:522-56 (1985).

10. Jean Hampton, "Free-Rider Problems in the Production of Collective Goods," Economics and Philosophy, 3:256 (1987).

11. Norman Frohlich, Joe A. Oppenheimer, and Oran R. Young, Political Leadership and Collective Goods (Princeton, NJ: Princeton University Press, 1971).

ably resolving coordination problems. At the same time, these capabilities carry responsibilities and obligations that the community may demand that they fulfill as a price for its allegiance to them.

Building on
social networks

Solving the assurance game requires creating confidence among political activists that they share a common understanding of their situation. Preexisting social networks therefore play a central role in the emergence of collective action as uncertainty is removed and coordination facilitated when people belong to the same social and political organizations. Groups in general are more readily mobilized than individuals. Individuals in groups bonded by a distinct ethnicity, race, or social status; ties of friendship and kinship; and common membership in religious, fraternal, social, and political clubs, associations, and organizations have greater solidarity and are in closer communication than groups that are not constrained by similar functional and social linkages. Solidarity and affection, in turn, go hand in hand with the establishment of personal obligations and exchange relationships. Members of these preexisting networks have reputations to protect, respect and affection for each other, and reliable information about the preferences and probable behavior of others. If we closely examine various forms of collective action, from the mob or crowd to the social reform movement to the full-scale revolutionary movement, we find

that, at all levels, collective action invariably involves the confederation of smaller organized units rather than the aggregation of previously isolated, atomized individuals.[12]

Informing through
mass media

Modern communication technology can compensate for weak grassroots organizations and expand the popular base of a social movement by facilitating the rapid transmission of information. Whereas small groups can be coordinated through meetings and face-to-face interaction, the coordination of large masses of people in disparate locations depends on central sources of information transmission. Through the electronic media, people can learn about the plans of the movement to initiate new campaigns, the size and impact of demonstrations in distant cities, how authorities are responding to collective action, whether third parties are sympathetic or hostile to the struggle, and other relevant information that updates their evaluation of the movement's prospects. Not only do the media inform interested parties, but they convey information that the recipient will interpret as common knowledge based on his or her as-

12. On the general importance of community, see Michael Taylor, *Anarchy and Cooperation* (New York: John Wiley, 1976); idem, *Community, Anarchy and Liberty* (New York: Cambridge University Press, 1982); idem, *The Possibility of Cooperation* (New York: Cambridge University Press, 1987); idem, "Rationality and Revolutionary Collective Action," in *Rationality and Revolution*, ed. Michael Taylor (New York: Cambridge University Press, 1988), pp. 63-97.

sumption that access to this information is widely shared.

A key factor behind the massive size of the recent upheaval in Eastern Europe is that people were extremely well-informed and aware of political developments in their own country and abroad. With the aid of modern telecommunications, the opposition movements were able to coordinate strikes, demonstrations, and other activities. For example, one of the most effective ways that Solidarity leaders in Poland transmitted information was to provide foreign radio networks with details about their strike activities, which would then be broadcast in news reports throughout the country. When the Czechoslovak opposition gained access to the radio and television waves, it was able to provide updates on the progress of the movement to parts of the country beyond Prague. Moreover, through print, radio, and television, people throughout Eastern Europe were able to stay apprised of developments in the West and in the Soviet Union. It was easy to learn from the media about Gorbachev's support for the upheaval in Eastern Europe, his plans for reform in the Soviet Union, and the consequences of those reforms, namely, competitive elections and the development of an independent national legislature.[13]

Using cultural resources and traditions

Mass political activism can also be coordinated by common knowledge of historical precedents and traditions that synchronize people's actions. As Schelling explained,

Overt leadership solves the [coordination] problem; but leadership can often be identified and eliminated by the authority trying to prevent mob action. In this case the mob's problem is to act in unison without overt leadership, to find some common signal that makes everyone confident that, if he acts on it, he will not be acting alone.[14]

To reduce the need for explicit communication, activists can capitalize on famous locations, significant anniversary dates, focal events such as deaths and funerals, and other cultural signposts when staging mass demonstrations and protests. A striking feature of the revolutions in Eastern Europe was the manner in which the opposition movements took advantage of salient historical precedents to coordinate their activities. Much of the protest activity in Hungary, Poland, and Czechoslovakia in 1989 occurred at the same sites where earlier protests had been held. There were obvious parallels between the processions organized by the opposition in Budapest in 1989 and similar processions staged during the 1848 and 1956 Hungarian Revolutions. In Czechoslovakia, the demonstrators conducted their rallies at the symbolic Wenceslas

13. Examples in this article drawn from recent events in Eastern Europe are developed further in Valerie Bunce and Dennis Chong, "The Party's Over: Mass Protest and the End of Communist Rule in Eastern Europe" (Paper delivered at the annual meeting of the American Political Science Association, Washington, DC, 30 Aug.-2 Sept. 1990).

14. Thomas C. Schelling, *The Strategy of Conflict* (New York: Oxford University Press, 1960), p. 90.

Square, the historic setting for most of the nation's greatest political events. Similarly, Leipzig's famous tradition for opposing authority, dating from the Protestant Revolution and extending through the Peasants Rebellion, the 1848 revolution, the workers' uprising in 1923, and the sympathy protests for the Prague Spring, may help to explain why the mass demonstrations that brought down the regime in East Germany were initiated in that city before diffusing to the rest of the country.[15] All of these examples illustrate how history and tradition can supplement overt leadership and formal organizations in coordinating mass political activism.

*Raising hope and
    winning concessions*

Since political mobilization is easier when people have hope of achieving their goals, the leaders of collective action will try to convince their followers that the demands of the group will not fall on deaf ears. Leaders will emphasize to the rank and file that they will prevail in the conflict if they persevere and work together. An abiding faith among the activists that they will succeed keeps frustration down while increasing the contagiousness of the movement. In the course of the Russian Revolution, for instance, "when the terminal point was distant the revolutionary movement was small; it was a secret society. When the chances of revolution increased—the secret society ex-

panded into a real revolutionary party and mass movement."[16]

Participation in the assurance game depends on the belief that enough pressure can be applied to win concessions from the opposition. Sooner or later, however, collective action will have to produce real dividends because the activists will not be able to suspend their disappointment indefinitely. Therefore, in addition to trumpeting the potency of collective action, the leaders of a movement will try to get some concrete victories under their belts as quickly as possible. Doing so establishes a level of proficiency and success that reinforces their followers and makes the movement attractive to others. Notable successes spur a bandwagon of new participants to join based on their revised estimates of the prospects of the movement. In addition, concessions establish the responsiveness of the authorities to political pressure.

The establishment of Solidarity in Poland in 1980, for example, signified the willingness of the state to make concessions, thereby emboldening Polish citizens to express their grievances against the Communist regime. Although the protests that occurred in 1980-81 were not revolutionary in scope, they nevertheless kindled an important psychological revolution in mass attitudes and political consciousness. Before Solidarity, anger toward the regime had no viable outlet, and people felt helpless to change their society. After Solidarity stepped into this void, the Polish

15. David Binder, "Leipzig: Where Indignation Has Transformed Politics," *New York Times*, 6 Dec. 1989.

16. F. Gross, *The Seizure of Political Power in a Century of Revolutions* (New York: Philosophical Library, 1958), p. 356.

masses believed they had a vehicle for engaging in public action.

Projecting strength

Leaders may also try to increase the credibility of the movement by providing inflated estimates of the size of their organization and the anticipated or actual attendance at rallies, marches, and demonstrations. Membership and attendance figures convey information to the authorities about whether the movement enjoys considerable popular support. Therefore, misrepresentation of the size of the movement can prompt greater concessions than would have been provided if support for the movement had been assessed correctly. Crowd estimates, for example, were inflated for this purpose by organizers of a 1989 Washington, D.C., rally in support of the right to an abortion. "The United States Park Police estimated that 300,000 people marched from the Washington Monument to the Capitol . . . some organizers contended that the crowd was twice as large."[17]

Oftentimes, the media will inadvertently assist a cause—as it did, for example, in the case of the Moral Majority in the 1980s—by accepting at face value and publicizing inflated figures that an organization provides about the size of its own membership. The media may also lend a hand by overreporting the number of participants at marches and rallies. Typically, reporters will confuse spectators and even opponents at these events with the actual sympathizers. Organizers of civil rights demonstrations capitalized on the journalists' errors by scheduling their rallies at times of the day when it was assured that a larger number of onlookers would be present. For example, there were occasions during the Birmingham protests, according to Southern Christian Leadership Conference leader Wyatt Walker, when "we weren't marching but 12, 14, 16, 18. But the papers were reporting 1,400."[18]

Actual demonstrations of numerical strength will encourage participation by those who are skeptical that the inchoate movement is too ineffectual to have an impact on society. The level of mobilization in any period is in this fashion partly determined by the level of mobilization in the preceding period. During the recent uprising in Czechoslovakia, confidence in the size of the opposition had so risen by the eighteenth day of protests that people joined demonstrations reassured in their knowledge that participation would be widespread. The assurance game had become child's play. "Wenceslas Square. Despite the freezing cold, the demonstration will be huge, and a success. Everyone knows it. They file into the square slowly and matter-of-factly, as if they had been doing this for years."[19] This example shows how widespread expectations that an upcoming rally will attract a large number of supporters can amount to a

17. Robin Toner, "Right to Abortion Draws Thousands to Capital Rally," *New York Times*, 10 Apr. 1989.

18. Adam Fairclough, *To Redeem the Soul of America* (Athens: University of Georgia Press, 1987), p. 121.

19. Timothy Garton Ash, "The Revolution of the Magic Lantern," *New York Review of Books*, 37:50 (1990).

self-fulfilling prophecy. An individual will attend because he or she wants to be part of a memorable and successful historical event; in turn, his or her contribution and the contribution of hundreds or thousands of like-minded individuals ensure that the rally is both successful and memorable.

Devising new strategies

The premium that is placed on continual success gives rise to an evolution of tactical strategies over the course of the movement based on what succeeds. Tactics that work in forcing the opposition to supply concessions will become popular while those that prove ineffective will be abandoned. Each innovative tactic will lose its appeal within a movement once its effectiveness is reduced by the tactical countermaneuvers of the opposition. Leaders of collective action must therefore devise a continuing series of novel tactics in order to retain their followers and maintain the leverage of the movement.

During the civil rights movement, for example, several innovative tactics, such as the bus boycott, sit-in, and freedom ride, grabbed the spotlight at different times. After a new tactic was introduced, the following months of activity in the civil rights movement tended to be dominated by copycat campaigns in other locales around the country.[20] The popularity of various tactics used over the course of the civil rights movement rose and fell according to their suc-

cess in gaining media attention, provoking southern authorities, and extracting meaningful concessions. Each tactic enjoyed its greatest success immediately after it was introduced, when both the opposition and the public were caught by surprise; as the opposition developed an effective response to the new tactic, civil rights activists gradually abandoned it in favor of a newer one.

Adjusting to the law of supply and demand

The incentive structure of the assurance game also shows how fluctuations in demands for social change will be linked to the disposition of the agencies capable of supplying such change. A sympathetic government or a government that is expected to be responsive to popular demands will obviously encourage collective action. In premodern Japan, for example, protest was believed to enjoy greater prospects of success because there existed a

culturally recognized obligation of the government to rule with *jinsei* ("benevolently"). The notion of *jinsei* did not obligate the government to be kind but only to maintain conditions under which the populace could endure, in exchange for which the people were obligated to offer up taxes.[21]

This relationship between supply and demand has also been confirmed in studies of the farm workers' movement in the 1960s, the popular movement in West Germany against

20. Doug McAdam, "Tactical Innovation and the Pace of Insurgency," *American Sociological Review*, 48:735-54 (1983).

21. James W. White, "Rational Rioters: Leaders, Followers, and Popular Protest in Early Modern Japan," *Politics and Society*, 16:41 (1988).

nuclear power, the contemporary environmental movement, the civil rights movement, and the women's movement.[22]

By the same token, if those in power are antagonistic, they will attempt to dampen the movement by refusing to capitulate to its demands. To show they mean business, the authorities will try to remove the movement's leaders, step up their arrests of protesters, pass laws that restrict the tactics available to them, and use other maneuvers that increase the cost of political activism. The employment of these strategies will often result in a battle of wills in which each side attempts to outlast the other.

It seems reasonable, for example, to suppose that extremely repressive countermeasures in the early stages of the demonstrations in Eastern Europe in the late 1980s could have halted the popular movements there. Once compliance with government ideology dissolved at both the private and public levels, the only restraints

on mass dissent were the twin threats of internal repression and Soviet intervention. The two methods of repression were not independent, however. State resistance and countermeasures were evident in Poland, East Germany, and Czechoslovakia in the early stages of these movements; but once it became apparent that the Soviet Union would not interfere—except to send encouraging signals about its nonintentions—the option of internal repression also became limited. By the summer of 1989, fears that either form of repression would occur had diminished greatly even in the more hard-line states of Czechoslovakia and East Germany.

What is remarkable nevertheless is the speed with which the publics in Eastern Europe sized up current events and seized the moment when it became apparent that the Communist system was ready to collapse. When the popular revolts succeeded in Poland and Hungary, the model for success was established. For the Czechoslovaks and East Germans, not to mention the Yugoslavs and Bulgarians, there was a sense of security gained from the dress rehearsals in Poland and Hungary. The Party had proved to be weaker than many had assumed, considerable liberalization was shown to be achievable, and the Soviets appeared unwilling to block, and might very well aid and abet, the transformation of the political system. By the time the revolutions had spread to East Germany and Czechoslovakia, the assurance problem was solved in a fraction of the time that it had taken in Poland and Hungary. Hence Garton Ash's now famous quip to Václav

22. J. Craig Jenkins and Charles Perrow, "Insurgency of the Powerless: Farm Workers' Movements, 1946-1972," *American Sociological Review*, 42:249-68 (1977); Dorothy Nelkin and Michael Pollak, *The Atom Besieged* (Cambridge: MIT Press, 1981); Richard P. Gale, "Social Movements and the State: The Environmental Movement, Counter-Movement, and Governmental Agencies," *Sociological Perspectives*, 29:202-40 (1986); Doug McAdam, *Political Process and the Development of Black Insurgency 1930-1970* (Chicago: University of Chicago Press, 1982); Anne Costain, "Social Movements as Interest Groups: The Case of the Women's Movement," in *The Politics of Interests*, ed. Mark P. Petracca (Boulder, CO: Westview Press, 1992), pp. 285-307. For a general discussion of these issues, see Doug McAdam, "Social Movements," in *Handbook of Sociology*, ed. Neil J. Smelser (Beverly Hills, CA: Sage, 1988), pp. 695-737.

Havel: "In Poland it took ten years, in Hungary ten months, in East Germany ten weeks; perhaps in Czechoslovakia it will take ten days!"[23]

Setting precedents

While antagonistic authorities hamper efforts to organize collective action, activists who manage nonetheless to initiate protests and extract concessions thereby weaken the opposition and make subsequent campaigns easier to conduct. The outcomes of past confrontations therefore serve to preview the costs and benefits of future engagements. By winning a showdown, the activists may convince the authorities that resistance will only use up valuable resources while forestalling the inevitable.

Protest groups therefore benefit by acquiring a reputation for toughness and endurance. In discussing the art of commitment among nations, Schelling notes the importance of persuading the other side in a conflict that one actually possesses the intentions one claims to have:

To fight abroad is a military act, but to *persuade* enemies or allies that one would fight abroad, under circumstances of great cost and risk, requires more than a military capability. It requires projecting intentions. It requires *having* those intentions, even deliberately acquiring them, and communicating them persuasively to make other countries behave.[24]

Obviously, the ability to make credible threats is very important for any

group trying to exert pressure on the government or some other party. The group has to convey that it is resilient and capable of persevering until the other side is ready to concede. Therefore, if the activists provide evidence from past confrontations that the movement can enlist mass support for any of its campaigns, then the authorities may recognize the latent potential for collective action and be more inclined to respond favorably early in the contest. Success breeds success.

A special characteristic of the upheaval in Eastern Europe is that learning on both sides of the conflict took place not only within countries but across them as well. Because political, economic, and social conditions were parallel from one country to the next within the bloc, the outcome of protests in one country provided a lesson to the regime and opposition in the others. There is some irony here in that the Soviet Union itself was responsible for the creation of a regional system that, by its very structure, was susceptible to contagion effects. Indeed, the Soviets were always conscious that disorder in one country could easily spread to other countries, including their own. There was considerable empirical support for these fears given, for instance, the impact of Hungarian unrest on Poland in 1956, the effects of the Czechoslovak reform movement on the Ukraine—which is a major reason why the Soviets invaded in 1968— and the reverberations of the 1980-81 Polish crisis in the Baltic states, the consequences of which we are witnessing today.

    23. Ash, "Revolution of the Magic Lantern," p. 42.
    24. Thomas C. Schelling, *Arms and Influence* (New Haven, CT: Yale University Press, 1966), p. 36.

Whither social movements?

In closing, I would contend that the incentive structure of popular movements typically makes them both hard to maintain and ill-suited to accomplishing complex social and political agendas. Social movements depend on rallying and holding the support of masses of people. In order to do this, they must have simple, clear, and usually grand objectives to stimulate and unify large numbers of people. Competing ideologies and elaborate schemes and programs serve only to dilute energies, create conflicts of interest, and hinder coordination.

When collective action succeeds, it pays a stream of material, social, and psychological benefits to participants, but it also tends to sap the movement of its vitality. As the goals of the movement are achieved, new and equally attractive—and equally feasible—goals have to be devised to ensure the continued contribution of current members. Unless the new generation of goals displays the same luster as the earlier goals, participation in the movement will not carry the same participatory benefits that accrue to those who take part in historic or memorable causes. Furthermore, if the new set of goals is not as practicable, or if they cannot be reached through application of mass protests, then supporters of the original cause will feel less obligated to lend their time and energy to fighting for them through direct action. Most people are reluctant to participate in lost causes. Unfortunately, to tired radicals who are satisfied with their efforts or disappointed over the impact of their achievements, no new agenda may be sufficiently attractive for them to want to sustain their level of commitment and participation.[25] Consequently, in the latter stages of the movement, the benefits of cooperation may become almost as obscure as they were prior to the development of group identities and strategies, when it appeared that little of consequence could be gained through collaboration.

SUMMARY

I have argued that selective social and psychological benefits of participation in collective action often turn popular movements into assurance games, in which contributions are contingent on the actions of others. Individuals attracted by these selective incentives prefer cooperation over defection if there is sufficient participation for the movement to stand a reasonable chance of succeeding, but they prefer to abstain if the movement fails to secure enough popular support. Uncertainty about the requirements of a successful movement and about the intentions of other potential activists, however, creates difficult coordination problems. The successful resolution of these coordination problems requires effective leadership, community and organizational resources, favorable political conditions, focused objectives, and the careful implementation of tactics and strategies that establish and maintain the viability of the movement.

25. On the dissipation of public spirit, see Albert O. Hirschman, *Shifting Involvements* (Princeton, NJ: Princeton University Press, 1982).

ANNALS, *AAPSS*, **528**, July 1993

Citizens' Groups and Political Parties in the United States

By MARJORIE RANDON HERSHEY

ABSTRACT: The relationship between political parties and citizens' groups in the United States contains elements of both competition and cooperation. Citizens' groups have the potential to compete with parties for individuals' loyalty, time, and money; for influence on the media's agenda; and for candidates' attention. In fact, voter attachment to the major parties began to decline just at the time that the number of citizens' groups was increasing, during the 1960s and 1970s. But other aspects of the parties either held their own or strengthened during this time. During the Reagan era, the increasingly ideological tone of national politics polarized both groups and parties and stimulated greater efforts at collaboration between them. Substantial conflict between groups and party leaders remains in the presidential nominating process, however, as can be seen in a case study of the 1992 Republican platform.

Marjorie Hershey is a professor of political science at Indiana University. Her primary fields of study are political parties and elections, about which she has published two books and two dozen articles.

EXERCISING popular control over government is not among most people's favorite daily activities. Instead, we rely on intermediary institutions such as political parties, interest groups, and the media of mass communication to gather and spread information about candidates, track the progress of public issues, monitor the ethics of leaders, and simplify the choices that the public is asked to make. Without these intermediaries, it is difficult to imagine how a democracy could function in a nation of 250 million people.

Political scientists' research on the workings of intermediaries has heavily emphasized parties and interest groups, with a strong normative presumption in favor of the former. As Jack Walker put it, when most political scientists are asked to judge whether parties or interest groups are preferable as a means of mobilizing citizens, "the parties win, hands down."[1] Parties are typically regarded as the only intermediaries capable of aggregating broad sets of interests and providing coherent leadership in the American setting. Citizens' and other interest groups, in contrast, are thought to polarize legislators and citizens, speak primarily for narrow interests, and prevent the parties from performing their vital organizing role.[2]

These two types of intermediaries, then, are usually described as competitors: when one gains strength, it causes the other to weaken. And when it is the parties that weaken, democ-racy suffers. But is that necessarily so? Are citizens' groups an antiparty development, or can they be integrated into existing patterns of partisan politics? This article will examine the links between citizens' groups and the political parties: the ways in which these groups compete with parties, work with or use the parties, or circumvent party organizations. It will include a brief case study of how some citizens' groups attempted to change or defend the controversial abortion plank in the 1992 Republican platform. Finally, it will consider this evolving relationship in light of the needs of a democracy.

CITIZENS' GROUPS AND
THE POLITICAL PARTIES

There is a complex relationship between parties and citizens' groups, described by Sorauf as one of "mixed competition and cooperation."[3] Both parties and groups recruit leaders and mediate interests. Both want power; they help elect their allies to office by giving money and training campaigners. Both also want to affect public policy, through developing programs and influencing policymakers and the public. They differ, in part, in terms of their emphasis. The traditional view is that citizens' and other interest groups focus on issues and policies, whereas parties are primarily concerned with winning power.

According to the common wisdom, "party and organized interest strength are proportional: where parties are

1. Jack L. Walker, Jr., *Mobilizing Interest Groups in America* (Ann Arbor: University of Michigan Press, 1991), p. 20.

2. Ibid., pp. 21-23.

3. Frank J. Sorauf, "PACs and Parties in American Politics," in *Interest Group Politics*, 3d ed., ed. A. Cigler and B. Loomis (Washington, DC: Congressional Quarterly Press, 1991), p. 220.

strong, organized interests are weak and vice versa. Our own era is one of interest group strength and party weakness."[4] But researchers disagree as to which way the causal arrow runs. Some feel, for instance, that the weakening of party organizations in the 1920s prompted an increase in interest group politics.[5] Others feel the reverse is true: that it was the Progressive movement, a citizens' movement, that passed legislation weakening the parties by changing the incentives that had forced elements of the parties to work together.[6]

Still other writers see one or more third factors as the cause of both party decline and interest group expansion. To Jeffrey Berry, for example, it was a sense of alienation from an unresponsive government that produced a weakening of the parties *and* an increase in citizens' groups during the 1960s.[7] The parties had failed to resolve the problems of civil rights and Vietnam; protest groups had much greater success. For people who wanted major change, the lesson was to abandon the parties and support group advocacy.

These causal questions are difficult to answer; scholars are limited by a lack of some relevant data and by differences in interpreting the data we have. But it is clear that the rise of citizens' groups in the 1960s and 1970s coincided to some degree with a concern about party decline.

Are the American parties in decline?

Political parties in the United States have always faced an ambivalent climate of opinion. The early leaders of the republic, including George Washington, expressed intense hostility toward parties and other "factions"—even though many of these same leaders were instrumental in the development of a party system within the next decade. This ambivalence has affected the strength and coherence of the parties they created and those that followed, which have tended to be less unified, disciplined, and ideological than their counterparts in other nations.

Party organizations reached their pinnacle in the patronage-rich era of the late 1800s. But they soon fell under successful attack by the Progressive movement of the early 1900s. As the Progressive-sponsored direct primary was adopted by states, for instance, parties lost much of their power over nominations. The party machines were also weakened by pressures for professionalization in the delivery of services and by the post-World War II expansion of the middle class and the movement into the suburbs, where people were out of the reach of, and had less need of, the urban party's services.[8]

4. Kay Lehman Schlozman and John T. Tierney, *Organized Interests and American Democracy* (New York: HarperCollins, 1986), p. 201.

5. Mark P. Petracca, "The Rediscovery of Interest Group Politics," in *The Politics of Interests*, ed. M. Petracca (Boulder, CO: Westview, 1992), pp. 26-27.

6. Joseph A. Schlesinger, "The New American Political Party," *American Political Science Review*, 79:1156 (Dec. 1985).

7. Jeffrey M. Berry, "Public Interest vs. Party System," *Society*, 17:44 (May-June 1980).

8. Walker, *Mobilizing Interest Groups*, pp. 23-26.

So the recent increase in citizens' groups could not have caused the phenomenon of party decline in general, because several aspects of party functioning had been weak or in decline long before these groups appeared;[9] indeed, the climate had been hostile to parties well before the Progressive movement. Further, other aspects of party functioning either held their own or gained strength while citizens' groups have been on the rise. Party cohesion in Congress, normally limited, reached an all-time low in the late 1960s but then increased through the 1980s.[10] Party organizations showed no evidence of weakening in the 1960s and 1970s.[11] In fact, the parties' national organizations—especially that of the Republicans—are now better funded and more active in the provision of services than ever before.[12]

But there was substantial further erosion of one important party function during the 1960s and 1970s: citizens' attachment to parties. It could be seen in declines in the proportion of strong partisans, positive evaluations of the parties, and straight-ticket voting. The erosion halted later; with the first Reagan administration came an increase in the proportion of party-identified in-

dividuals. But the parties' current relationships with voters have not yet recovered to pre-1960 levels.

One reason was the increasing educational level of voters. The party label can be an important cue to citizens who must make large numbers of choices in an election without much information. As educational levels and literacy increased, however, voters could process more complex cues than "Democrat" and "Republican." Indeed, in the large number of cities with nonpartisan elections—also a Progressive reform—party cues were of little help.

Alternative sources of political information were also proliferating at this time. In addition to radio and newspapers, television was becoming a more important source of information about candidates and issues, and after the mid-1960s, direct mail provided still more cues. The mass media were coming to rival the parties as intermediaries between government and citizens—and access to the media did not depend on party loyalty. Parties became less important to voters, cognitively and emotionally, than they had been in the 1950s.

Another cause of this erosion was the change in issues that catalyzed public attention beginning in the 1960s. Questions arose concerning women's rights, environmental issues, abortion, nuclear energy, constituting what Russell J. Dalton has called "the agenda of advanced industrial societies." According to Dalton, this agenda "often appears unsuited for mass political parties. . . . [The parties] are reluctant to take clear positions on these issues because of

9. Sorauf, "PACs and Parties."

10. Paul Allen Beck and Frank J. Sorauf, *Party Politics in America*, 7th ed. (New York: HarperCollins, 1992), pp. 389-91.

11. Cornelius P. Cotter et al., *Party Organizations in American Politics* (New York: Praeger, 1984).

12. James W. Ceaser, "Political Parties—Declining, Stabilizing, or Resurging?" in *The New American Political System*, 2d version, ed. A. King (Washington, DC: American Enterprise Institute, 1990).

the uncertain electoral benefits."[13] The issues are too narrow to bring in major new party support, and in many cases they have the potential to split the established parties. While increasingly sophisticated citizens paid more attention to these new and complex issues, the major parties remained wedded to the old New Deal issues, "the Old Politics cleavages of class and religion."[14] Their group ties showed the same pattern, with the Democrats remaining close to organized labor and the Republicans to business. But by clinging to the old alignments, the parties have not been able to escape the pull of the new issues; New Left activists have rent the Democratic Party, as have New Right elements in the Republican Party.

These declines in voter attachment to the major parties during the 1960s and 1970s occurred just at the time that the number of citizens' groups, and citizens' attachment to them, were increasing (see Figure 1). As is discussed elsewhere in this volume, large proportions of citizens' groups were founded in these two decades, resulting in "an explosion in the number of groups representing the interests of broad publics and the disadvantaged."[15]

These new groups were motivated by the very issues that proved so damaging to citizens' relationships with the major parties. Thus they were quickly expected to challenge the parties' role as primary political intermediaries. In addition, as citizens' groups worked to promote their views, they came increasingly to see partisan politics as a relevant terrain and thus to place new demands on the parties. The threat to party cohesion soon became apparent. For example, pro-life groups' efforts to get the Republican Party to work for a ban on all abortions were successful beginning in 1980, but at the cost of ongoing conflicts not only with pro-choice Republicans but with party activists who feel that hot-button issues distract from the traditional Republican agenda.

This conflict between parties and citizens' groups has been more muted in the United States than in many other nations. U.S. citizens' groups have tended to be less broadly ideological and less interconnected than is the case in most European nations; Mothers Against Drunk Driving is quite a different phenomenon from the French antinuclear movement. But the timing of the trends shown in Figure 1 indicates the possibility that the rise of citizens' groups is directly related to the decline of voters' party attachments in the period 1960-80, if not to changes in other aspects of party activity.

13. Russell J. Dalton, *Citizen Politics in Western Democracies* (Chatham, NJ: Chatham House, 1988), p. 191.

14. Ibid., p. 148.

15. Schlozman and Tierney, *Organized Interests*, p. 75. See also Jeffrey M. Berry, "Citizen Groups and the Changing Nature of Interest Group Politics in America," in this issue of *The Annals* of the American Academy of Political and Social Science.

IN WHAT WAYS DO CITIZENS' GROUPS WEAKEN THE PARTIES?

How might citizens' groups cause or encourage party decline? One possibility is that groups and parties compete for the same resources— citizens' emotional attachments and

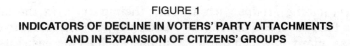

FIGURE 1
INDICATORS OF DECLINE IN VOTERS' PARTY ATTACHMENTS
AND IN EXPANSION OF CITIZENS' GROUPS

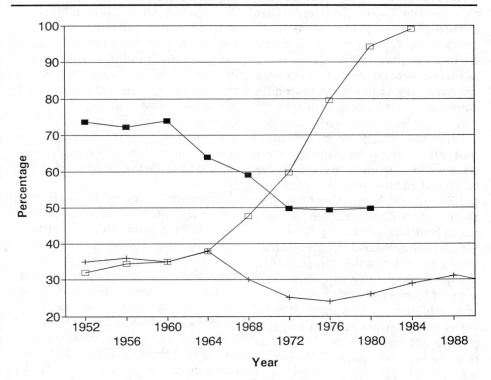

—■— Percentage expressing a positive evaluation of at least one of the two major parties.

—+— Percentage claiming to be strong Democrats or strong Republicans.

—□— Cumulative proportion of citizens' groups by the year of their founding. Note that this data line starts at 32 percent because 32 percent of all citizens' groups existing in 1983 had been founded prior to 1952.

SOURCES: For the positive evaluation of the political parties, Martin P. Wattenberg, *The Decline of American Political Parties 1952-1988* (Cambridge, MA: Harvard University Press, 1990), tab. 4.4, p. 61. For strength of party identification, Paul Allen Beck and Frank J. Sorauf, *Party Politics in America*, 7th ed. (New York: HarperCollins, 1992), tab. 6.2, p. 153. For the founding of citizens' groups, Jack L. Walker, Jr., "Activities and Maintenance Strategies of Interest Groups in the United States, 1985" (Codebook made available by the Inter-University Consortium for Political and Social Research, Ann Arbor, MI, n.d.).

their time and money—so that when citizens' groups get more, the parties get less. In the 1950s, someone fascinated by the arms race might have felt that the best way to make a dif-

ference in that area was to become a party activist; there were not many alternative means. With the decline in partisan loyalties, he or she might seek another organizational avenue of influence, joining groups such as Americans for Peace, SANE, or Nuclear Freeze, many of which did not exist in the 1950s. To Berry, these groups channel people away from party work. "The essence of the public interest philosophy is that party politics cannot be trusted. Parties are impure; they stand for compromise rather than hard-fought principles."[16]

The antiparty message may not take, of course. The vivid, dramatic, and often negative appeals that citizens' groups must make in order to attract media coverage, and thus public support, have a short half-life; their impact decays rapidly, according to Salisbury, on both public opinion and policymakers.[17] There is little evidence that people who join such groups consequently withdraw their support from a political party; in fact, research shows that most politically active people who take part in party politics are also associated with one or more interest groups.[18] Nevertheless, the simple existence of larger numbers of citizens' groups offers individuals an avenue outside the parties through which to become involved in campaigns and issues—an avenue that has greatly expanded in the last two decades.

Citizens' groups expand the options for candidates as well. The more group money that comes into campaigns, the less candidates need to rely on other sources of funds, includ-

ing their party's. In the late 1960s and early 1970s, new campaign techniques such as increased use of television and polling left candidates in critical need of cash. The parties of that time were not well designed to fill the need.[19] Political action committees (PACs), some formed by citizens' groups, moved into the void. These new PACs also put interest groups in more direct competition with parties, by giving groups a more secure role in the campaigning process, which is the parties' primary focus.

The parties might have tried to ally with citizens' groups at that time, to help guide the competition. But that proved difficult to do. Structural differences worked against cooperation; because many citizens' groups were not highly structured, cohesive organizations with a stable membership that could reliably deliver votes, the parties had less incentive to seek them as allies.[20] Nor were many groups eager to choose sides in partisan politics; that would limit their access to legislators of the other party.

The protest and unconventional political tactics used by citizens' groups can also compete with the parties' ability to gain media attention and set the public agenda. The outside strategy that citizens' groups follow, seeking media coverage in order to gain members and do grassroots lobbying, may, especially during campaigns, compete with the parties' grass-roots activities.

16. Berry, "Public Interest," p. 43.
17. Robert H. Salisbury, "The Paradox of Interest Groups in Washington—More Groups, Less Clout," in New American Political System, ed. King, p. 216.
18. Walker, Mobilizing Interest Groups, p. 22.

19. Sorauf, "PACs and Parties," p. 219.
20. Russell J. Dalton et al., "The Challenge of New Movements," in Challenging the Political Order, ed. R. Dalton and M. Kuechler (New York: Oxford University Press, 1990), pp. 14-15.

CAN CITIZENS' GROUPS AND PARTIES COMPLEMENT ONE ANOTHER?

In more recent years, however, the increasing involvement of citizens' groups in elections has probably brought about a closer relationship with the parties. As Walker argues, the Reagan administration's ideological and partisan tone, expressed particularly in its effort to "defund the [interest group] left," was the cause. During the Reagan years, ideological compatibility with the administration's goals seemed to be a prerequisite for groups seeking cooperation from the administration, to a greater extent than before. Because Reagan was attempting to make basic changes in the nature of public policy, large numbers of liberal groups found their favorite programs in jeopardy. It became clear that the results of presidential elections would affect their ability to achieve their policy goals. As the ideological polarization continued, in Walker's view, citizens' groups and other interest groups were pushed into contending conservative and liberal camps. Political parties, becoming more ideologically distinct themselves, were in a good position to lead these coalitions. These groups therefore found themselves "being drawn into alliances with one of the two major political parties in order to protect their futures, whether they like[d] it or not."[21]

This is not unprecedented, of course; consider the lengthy, close relationship between the Democratic Party and the American Federation of Labor and Congress of Industrial Organizations. This relationship has taken on a new dimension, however, with the increase in PACs, including those of citizens' groups. In recent years, the fastest-growing category of PACs has been the "non-connected" category, most of which are ideological organizations.[22] Both parties—and especially the Republicans—have begun working with PACs to fund campaigns. PAC liaisons have been appointed to share information about candidates and legislation of mutual interest. The parties select close races where interest group money could make a difference and then guide groups to targeted candidates with compatible stands. This clearly benefits the parties, whose contributions to targeted candidates are augmented by citizens' groups' money. It also helps the more partisan and ideological PACs, because it provides information—about the election chances and policy stands of candidates—that would otherwise be more costly.

Since the early 1980s, a few citizens' groups' PACs have begun to follow the lead of labor PACs in taking on partylike functions, such as registering voters. Most citizens' groups, however, have not taken these further steps into the electoral arena. Their PACs' efforts consist mainly of soliciting and making campaign contributions, rather than offering expertise and services to candidates. The parent groups' efforts are centered around the articulation of new issues, many of which the major parties are not prepared to champion.

21. Walker, *Mobilizing Interest Groups*, pp. 10, 150.

22. Clyde Wilcox, "Political Action Committees and Abortion: A Longitudinal Analysis," *Women & Politics*, 9(1):3 (1988).

"Seen in this light, the two forms of political organization are complementary and together constitute a much more responsive and adaptive system than either would be if they somehow operated on their own."[23]

In short, although the relationship between citizens' groups and parties is potentially conflict filled, there has been recent movement in the direction of greater complementarity. Earlier, Jeffrey Berry, in his highly regarded book *Lobbying for the People*, could report an extensive 1972-73 survey of public interest groups and hardly mention political parties. But after the late 1970s,

many elements of the interest-group system expanded and became more active at the same time the party system's role as a coordinating and mobilizing force, especially within the government, also began to strengthen.

The American public is much more thoroughly mobilized for political action in the 1990s than it was 35 years ago, and both political parties and interest groups have contributed to this development.[24]

When citizens' groups work from within

The picture changes, however, when we examine the activities of citizens' groups within the parties, with respect to presidential nominations. Citizens' groups may become involved in the internal dynamics of the major parties for several reasons. For one, the American party system is not nearly as hospitable to the workings of third parties as are many European party systems. If citizens' groups are to be involved in partisan politics, then, they must expect to deal with the two existing parties.

Second, groups were virtually invited to become involved by the Democratic Party reforms of the 1970s. The reforms encouraged a shift from a party-based to a candidate-based system of presidential nominations.[25] Reformers had assumed that once the party bosses were out of the way, their place in the process would be taken by a more representative set of grass-roots activists. Candidates, however, still needed an organizational base for winning delegates. A variety of citizens' and other interest groups provided a ready alternative, in the form of an organized base of supporters, funds, and endorsements.

The groups that gained the most from this change were those capable of affecting the results of the reform-produced primaries and caucuses: groups that could turn out small armies of members in a large number of states, especially those with early or otherwise important delegate-selection events. Groups most able to turn out large numbers were those whose members were highly dedicated to a cause—in short, citizens' groups. The groups benefited as well. Prior to the reforms, citizens' and other groups had to work through the party organizations in order to affect presidential campaigns, but that diluted their influence. After the reforms, they could gain more direct access.[26]

The change left a giant imprint on the national party conventions. The

23. Walker, *Mobilizing Interest Groups*, p. 14.
24. Ibid., p. 22.

25. Byron E. Shafer, *Bifurcated Politics* (Cambridge, MA: Harvard University Press, 1988), p. 108.
26. Ibid., p. 115.

organized interests that had long held sway—labor unions in the Democratic Party and business associations in the Republican—now had to fight to be heard. The ideological motivation of citizens' groups meant that rhetoric and demands within the convention became less moderate, and, to some, more radicalized, than when party leaders were clearly in control of the process and could serve as effective brokers.[27] Presidential nominations and campaigns became less predictable. A reaction quickly set in, led by an effort to bring back the "peer review" that party leaders serving as convention delegates could provide. But that only highlighted the irony, as Shafer notes, that the official party had been transformed into yet another organized interest.[28]

The increasing role of citizens' groups has been felt more in Democratic Party functions than in Republican. It was the Democratic Party in which the participatory reforms began and where they reached full flower. Further, the grass-roots character—or perhaps the ideological slant—of many citizens' groups may be tolerated better by the Democratic nominating process, given its greater emphasis on participation. To Jo Freeman, the bigger role of citizens' groups within the Democratic Party is explained by its coalitional nature.[29] Because power in the party flows upward from its various constituency groups, the Democrats are more permeable to organized pressure, whereas in the Republican Party, which is more unitary, the greater deference to the leadership tends to discourage competing group loyalties.

The prominence of feminist groups in the Democratic nominating process shows the extent to which citizens' groups have penetrated the post-reform party. Feminist groups were virtual outsiders when they first made demands on the party at the 1972 Democratic convention.[30] But by the 1980s, once the party had come to perceive them as a prospective source of group support at a time when other such sources were diminishing, feminist organizations had become an important force within the nominating process. At the 1980 Democratic convention, more than one in five delegates were members of the National Women's Political Caucus or the National Organization for Women (NOW). Organized groups of feminist delegates successfully lobbied the convention to adopt a platform plank calling for government funding of abortions for poor women.[31] Feminist strength was even more evident in 1984, when a vice president of NOW served on the platform committee, where she was "given the leading role on matters of concern to NOW."[32] Women's groups' preferences were also heard in the choice of the vice presidential nominee, Representative Geraldine Ferraro. The visible influence of feminist groups in

27. Salisbury, "Paradox of Interest Groups," pp. 222-23.

28. Shafer, *Bifurcated Politics*, p. 136.

29. Jo Freeman, "The Political Culture of the Democratic and Republican Parties," *Political Science Quarterly*, 101(3):328-32 (1985-86).

30. Jo Freeman, "Women at the 1988 Democratic Convention," *PS*, 21(3):875 (Fall 1988).

31. Joyce Gelb, "Feminism and Political Action," in *Challenging the Political Order*, ed. Dalton and Kuechler, p. 145.

32. Ibid.

that convention led to concern by some Democrats that the party was perceived as the captive of special interests. Yet in 1988, feminist groups' issues were again negotiated into the platform, over the initial objections of Democratic National Chair Paul Kirk.[33] Several sets of citizens' groups, including women and gays, won formal recognition as "official caucuses" of the Democratic National Committee in the early 1980s. Other citizens' groups have also played an active role in party conventions:

In 1980, abortion opponents focused on the Republican platform, antinuclear and gay activists on the Democratic platform. These groups launched carefully coordinated campaigns: attending candidate forums, participating in the delegate selection process, placing them on appropriate platform subcommittees, attending regional platform committee meetings, and lobbying other platform committee members.[34]

A case in point: The 1992 Republican platform faces the abortion issue

These campaigns clearly had an impact. By 1980, the two parties' platforms had become almost mirror images on the subject of abortion, and the differences were maintained through the decade. The 1988 Democratic platform stated "that the fundamental right of reproductive choice should be guaranteed regardless of ability to pay." The 1984 and 1988 Republican platforms read,

The unborn child has a fundamental individual right to life which cannot be infringed. . . . We oppose the use of public revenues for abortion and will eliminate funding for organizations which advocate or support abortion . . . and we reaffirm our support for judges at all levels of the judiciary who respect traditional family values and the sanctity of innocent human life.

These striking differences between the two platforms were not caused by issue voting among the parties' constituencies; before 1984, there was no significant correlation between voters' abortion attitudes and their choice of candidates. A slight correlation began to appear after 1984, but even then, the two parties' stands on abortion were considerably more extreme than the stands of a majority of citizens. Nor do the parties' stands reflect the views of the majority of the parties' campaign contributors or convention delegates, at least in the case of the Bush campaign.[35]

Why should the parties take positions so clearly out of the mainstream of public opinion and so different from one another? It seems likely that the change was driven by the activities of pro-life and pro-choice citizen groups within the two parties' organizations and conventions. Feminist groups, as shown earlier, were the primary lobbyists on abortion at Democratic conventions and succeeded in getting their pro-choice views written into the platform. Among Republicans, the New Right movement that had spearheaded the

    33. Freeman, "Women at the 1988 Democratic Convention," pp. 875-77.
    34. Schlozman and Tierney, *Organized Interests*, p. 209.

    35. Elizabeth Adell Cook et al., "The Electoral Politics of Abortion" (Paper delivered at the annual meeting of the American Political Science Association, Washington, DC, 1991), pp. 7-9.

nomination of Ronald Reagan included a number of pro-life groups and others sympathetic to banning abortion. In 1980, these groups were responsible for the party's first explicit platform language opposing abortion. One New Right leader described the power of the National Right to Life Committee, a pro-life citizens' group with a substantial budget and grass-roots organization, as deriving from "an intimate relationship with the administration and an intimate relationship with the Republican party. . . . They are the arbiter of who gets into a meeting or not."[36]

Other Republicans might have accepted this change to a pro-life plank either because the abortion issue was not important to them or in the sure knowledge that abortion rights had been secured by the Supreme Court's 1973 *Roe* v. *Wade* decision. In 1989, that security crumbled. The Court's *Webster* decision narrowed a woman's right to abortion and signaled that the Court might be ready to reverse its earlier ruling. By 1990, several groups of pro-choice Republican activists were preparing to argue strongly for a new platform plank on abortion.

The 1992 Republican platform committee scheduled a hearing on the issue in Salt Lake City, where pro-life sentiment runs strong. Prior to the hearing, a citizens' group called Republicans for Choice mounted a billboard campaign in the city to remind readers that most Republicans favor abortion rights. Leaders of Republicans for Choice and other groups appealed to the platform committee to drop the pro-life plank, arguing that it would harm the election chances of Republican candidates and that it was inconsistent with the party's traditional stand against government intrusion. The groups warned of a floor fight at the convention if the platform were not revised. Pro-life groups responded, threatening to target Republican lawmakers who failed to take pro-life stands. Both sides staged pickets, rallies, and press conferences.

Compromise was impossible, but party leaders tried anyway. The party could not abandon the pro-life plank; its nominee, George Bush, had switched to a pro-life position in 1980 and certainly could not switch back, especially after having disappointed Republican conservatives by abandoning his "no new taxes" pledge. Party leaders worked to keep the controversy away from the convention. Top Republican leaders reminded anti-abortion activists that the Republican Party is a "big tent," "large and diverse" on abortion and other issues, suggesting that pro-choice as well as pro-life Republicans are welcome in the party.[37] But it was apparent that such language in the platform would enrage pro-life groups, while not going far enough to satisfy pro-choice groups. In the end, the conflict was muzzled and the strong pro-life plank stayed.

This pattern of conflict appeared in state politics as well. In Oregon, for example, the conservative, pro-life Oregon Citizens Alliance ran suc-

36. Joan Biskupic, "The Pressure's On," *Congressional Quarterly Weekly Report*, 13 Apr. 1991, p. 917.

37. Fred Barnes, "Pregnant Silence," *New Republic*, 19-26 Aug. 1991, p. 12.

cessful electoral challenges to Republican candidates. To stop the challenges, the state Republican Party was forced to agree to share with the alliance the leadership of a PAC that would contribute money to candidates.[38] That in turn brought an angry response from the state chapter of the National Republican Coalition for Choice. In such cases, there is little middle ground for the party; the choice is to be taken over or torn apart. We need to know more about the role of organized interests in party platforms and functions. With respect to presidential nominations, however, the antiparty prospects are very clear.

IMPLICATIONS FOR AMERICAN POLITICS

As we have seen, the impact of citizens' groups on the American parties is complex. These groups are not necessarily party wreckers. For instance, the competition posed by citizens' groups seems to have prompted the national party organizations to respond by becoming more institutionalized and more active in fundraising and service delivery. To a great extent, these party and group changes are part of the same broader social changes: rising educational levels, making comprehension of new issues possible; increased access to mass media, expanding the options for intermediation; a more affluent public, permitting more groups to survive on public contributions; and a government of broader scope, touching more aspects of people's lives, thus provoking more groups to form.

But the discussion of these shared influences should not obscure some very real dangers to the parties. Unquestionably, citizens' groups have benefited from the (at least temporary) weakening of voters' psychological attachments to the major parties and may help to further undermine them. In addition, the expanded participation of these groups in the parties' nominating processes can, in some cases, bring party organizations to the brink of internal warfare. Do these changes strengthen or weaken democracy?

It is frequently alleged that because some aspects of parties have been weakened, there has been undesirable change in the policy process, which has become more fragmented, less stable, and less predictable. In theory, at least, strong parties can provide broad and coherent alternatives for citizens, counter the fragmenting influence of interest groups, and give less advantaged people a chance to be heard. Berry writes,

Because the government's role [in trying to inhibit interest group activities] will always be limited, prospects for further curbing the influence of faction must come from the political parties. They are the natural counterweight to interest groups, offering citizens the basic means of pursuing the nation's collective will. Only political parties can offer citizens broad choices about the major directions of public policy.[39]

38. Beth Donovan, "AuCoin's Challenge of Packwood Divides Rights Activists," *Congressional Quarterly Weekly Report*, 15 June 1991, p. 1609.

39. Jeffrey M. Berry, *The Interest Group Society*, 2d ed. (Glenview, IL: Scott, Foresman, 1989), p. 231.

It is accurate to state that the policy process has become less stable during this time. The stable system of subgovernments that had formerly been described as dominating some policy areas has often given way to a more volatile system of issue networks with an expanded set of players. But is that undesirable? Heclo argues that these issue networks, containing groups, bureaucrats, and other experts with shared policy knowledge and a common framework for policy debate, serve the bridging function between "Congress and the executive branch in ways that political parties no longer can."[40]

With respect to the representativeness of the system, researchers differ as to whether the rise of citizens' groups is beneficial or worrisome. In general, interest politics tend to amplify the voices of narrow, well-organized groups, which are disproportionately well educated and upper income.[41] The interests of broad publics and disadvantaged groups can probably be more effectively represented through the parties and the electoral system.

On the other hand, parties do not always excel at aggregating diverse interests. They do not always work hard to mobilize the public or to facilitate coordination between branches of government. Nor are citizens' groups necessarily the narrow, selfish factions that interest groups are thought to be. Citizens' groups often represent segments of American society that have not made their voices heard in the past, and thus can help to reduce inequalities between interests. With their assertive use of the mass media, citizens' groups may force concerns onto the public agenda that might otherwise be overlooked. Concerns that crosscut both parties, for example, may not be represented effectively through the party system. The damage done by tobacco is not likely to receive issue status from a party system in which there are antismoking advocates as well as tobacco sellers within each party.

These changes in the parties may not, then, pose a danger to representation in one sense. But they may well enhance another sort of threat to representation, by expanding the maneuvering room available to political leaders. The destabilization of the policy process and the increase in citizens' group participation mean that officials probably have more discretion to select policy alternatives; almost any alternative will have some group support. "Where interest groups were seen as the prime motive force pressing politicians to make policy decisions in their favor, now the officials very often exploit the groups."[42] The power of incumbency, attributable in part to the weakness of voters' party attachments, gives officeholders a substantial amount of independence from both party and group demands. The consequence may be that "the parties and the PACs have fought their battle over electoral turf without challenging the primacy of the candidates themselves."[43]

40. Hugh Heclo, "Issue Networks and the Executive Establishment," in *The New American Political System*, ed. A. King (Washington, DC: American Enterprise Institute, 1978), pp. 116-17.

41. Berry, "Public Interest," p. 43.

42. Salisbury, "Paradox of Interest Groups," p. 213.

43. Sorauf, "PACs and Parties," pp. 235-36.

The greatest danger, then, would be a weakening of the processes of deliberation and mediation, which interest groups and parties can provide, in favor of an increasing dominance of elected leaders—especially presidents—with a direct, unmediated, personality-based relationship with their constituents.[44] Whether citizens' groups continue to splinter the parties, complement them, or form new ones, their relationships with the party system will help shape the responsiveness and policy capability of American politics.

44. See Mark A. Peterson, "Interest Mobilization and the Presidency," in *Politics of Interests*, ed. Petracca, p. 240.

ANNALS, *AAPSS*, **528**, July 1993

Impact of Social Movements
on European Party Systems

By ROBERT ROHRSCHNEIDER

ABSTRACT: The evolution of new social movements in Western Europe creates several problems for established political parties. New social movements demand programmatic changes, green parties attract voters who previously supported established parties, and movement activists prefer decentralized party organizations. This article analyzes the success of established parties in coping with these programmatic, electoral, and organizational challenges. The article concludes that while established parties increasingly meet the programmatic and electoral challenge, they are less successful in meeting the organizational demands of new social movements.

Robert Rohrschneider is an assistant professor at Indiana University in Blooming-ton. His previous publications analyze various aspects of public opinion toward new social movements in Western Europe. He is currently engaged in a study of elite political culture in East and West Germany.

157

THE evolution of the environmental, peace, and women's movements has altered the political agenda in Western Europe. While economic issues over the extent of the welfare state dominated policy priorities in Western Europe until the early 1970s, the evolution of new social movements (NSMs) increasingly questions the policy emphasis of European governments on distributional issues.[1] Indeed, NSMs and their persistent success in mobilizing mass publics challenge established parties in their traditional role as mediators between citizens and the political system. If mass movements can emerge despite the opposition of most established parties, does this not indicate the parties' failure to perceive citizens' interests and channel them into the political system?

This question has sparked a debate over the implications of NSMs for European political parties. While the particular emphasis of these studies ranges from analyzing the influence of NSMs on electoral changes to studying the internal structure of green parties,[2] these debates, on the whole, center on three challenges that NSMs create for established parties: a programmatic challenge, an electoral challenge, and an organizational challenge. This article will discuss the nature of these challenges and assess the extent to which parties are able to meet each of them.

For reasons of space, I will confine specific illustrations of the challenges to the environmental movement in Western Europe. I have chosen this movement because environmentalism represents a symptomatic problem for political parties. As I will discuss in more detail shortly, the movement enjoys widespread public support, and supporters of environmental groups are recruited from different social strata.[3] Consequently, all of the established parties may lose electoral support if they do not address environmental issues. We can therefore learn much about the ability of established parties to respond to NSMs in general by studying the particular effect of the environmental movement on political parties.

The first part of this article will discuss the role of political parties in European polities and what characteristics of NSMs put parties under duress. The next three sections will analyze the nature of the three challenges and how parties cope with them. The last section will summarize the broader implications of NSMs for European political parties.

PARTY GOVERNMENTS
AND NEW SOCIAL MOVEMENTS
IN WESTERN EUROPE

Unlike in the United States, political parties have dominated the political process in Western Europe for much of the twentieth century. Parties, for example, train and recruit political elites. Before Chancellor Kohl or French President Mitterrand ascended to the chief executive office, they were trained for decades within

1. Russell J. Dalton and Manfred Kuechler, eds., *Challenging the Political Order* (New York: Oxford University Press, 1990).

2. Herbert Kitschelt, *The Logics of Party Formation* (Ithaca, NY: Cornell University Press, 1989).

3. Robert Paehlke, *Environmentalism and the Future of Progressive Politics* (New Haven, CT: Yale University Press, 1989).

their parties in the institutional values and norms of their respective polities. Furthermore, parties define electoral campaigns because voters choose between parties, not between individual candidates. Consequently, parties control which issues are addressed during electoral campaigns, and they influence which issues are omitted from the political agenda. Parties are also the primary agent of political representation because they formulate political programs that normally reflect and synthesize citizens' interests. These programs serve as a basis for defining public policies, once a party—or a coalition of parties—gains control of the chief executive office. Finally, parties provide a forum for citizens who want to participate in the political process. This extensive control of parties over the political process has led analysts of European party systems to speak of party governments, since parties "are the primary institutions of representative democracy."[4]

The emphasis that party governments give to welfare issues can be traced to the Industrial Revolution, when European parties originally emerged on the basis of those social cleavages—primarily economic—that had developed during the preceding centuries.[5] Although religious and ethnic differences continue to be important in a number of West European countries, virtually every party system features as their major protagonists a socialist—or social democratic—party, largely representing the secular segments and the working class, and a center-conservative party, which primarily represents the religious segments and the old middle class. Supplementing these parties, the industrial cleavage is institutionalized by contending interest groups, such as unions or employers' associations. Consequently, parties and interest groups have integrated citizens into a cohesive network of social institutions that have preserved the industrial cleavage as a basis for European party systems well into the second half of the twentieth century.

From the early 1970s onward, however, the evolution of NSMs suggests that the parties' control over the political process has loosened. This is reflected in three important respects. First, the issue-dimensions represented by NSMs are located outside of the realm of traditional controversies over economic issues. The environmental movement, for example, questions the ideology of unmitigated economic growth and the belief in scientific technology as automatic sources of societal progress. Accordingly, environmentalists often place environmental protection above economic growth, or they value an improvement in quality-of-life indicators more than an increase in quantity-of-growth measures.[6] To be sure, environmentalism has its own historical predecessor in the nature conservation movement, which emerged during the nineteenth century.[7] One impor-

4. Russell J. Dalton, *Citizen Politics in Western Democracies* (Chatham, NJ: Chatham House, 1988), p. 127.

5. Seymour M. Lipset and Stein Rokkan, *Party System and Voter Alignments* (New York: Free Press, 1967).

6. Lester Milbrath, *Environmentalists* (Buffalo: SUNY Press, 1984).

7. John Sheail, *The Environmental Revolution* (London: Hodder & Stoughton, 1976);

TABLE 1

PUBLIC SUPPORT FOR ANTI-NUCLEAR-ENERGY GROUPS IN WESTERN EUROPE

	1982	1984	1986	1989
France	41.0	41.8	42.5	50.1
Germany	35.7	33.5	37.0	54.0
Great Britain	48.6	37.8	55.0	49.0
Netherlands	56.2	57.3	56.5	66.3

SOURCES: Eurobarometers 17 (1982), 21 (1984), 25 (1986), and 31A (1989).

NOTE: Entries are percentages of European publics supporting the anti-nuclear-energy movement.

tant difference between the modern environmental movement and its historical predecessor, however, is that the latter tried to achieve environmental protection within the growth ideology of the then-industrializing nations, for instance, by buying up and protecting unspoiled areas of land. In contrast, the modern environmental movement explicitly questions the premises of industrial economies. Similarly, the peace movement attacks traditional security strategies,[8] and the women's movement attempts to redefine traditional gender roles.[9] Thus, NSMs have confused European party systems because they question premises that are shared by both the traditional Left and the center-conservative parties.

A second, equally important factor is that the modern environmental movement, like other NSMs, has developed a large support base among European publics. As an illustration, Table 1 displays public support for

the anti-nuclear-energy movement in four West European nations. The anti-nuclear-energy movement is the most vocal critic of industrial policy priorities within the modern environmental movement.[10] Yet, despite the fundamental criticism that this movement levels against established policy priorities, it enjoys substantial public support. In 1989, for example, 54 percent of the population in Germany supported the movement.[11] Public support for the anti-nuclear-energy movement in the other nations and viewed over time is of comparable magnitude. Equally important, unlike the nature conservation movement of the nineteenth century, the contemporary movement appeals to a variety of social groups: citizens from the middle class as well as the working class support the anti-nu-

10. Wolfgang Ruedig, Anti-Nuclear Movements (Essex: Longmann, 1990).

11. The data for this analysis stem from representative public opinion surveys that are conducted twice a year in all member states of the European Community (the Eurobarometer series). A detailed description of the construction of these indicators and the data can be found in Robert Rohrschneider, "The Roots of Public Opinion toward New Social Movements: An Empirical Test of Competing Explanations," American Journal of Political Science, 34:1-30 (1990).

Russell Dalton, The Green Rainbow (New Haven, CT: Yale University Press, 1993).

8. Thomas Rochon, Mobilizing for Peace: Antinuclear Movements in Western Europe (Princeton, NJ: Princeton University Press, 1988).

9. Joyce Gelb, Feminism in Politics (Berkeley: University of California Press, 1989).

clear-energy movement. The broad appeal of the anti-nuclear-energy movements to different social classes undermines those explanations that locate public support for NSMs primarily in the new middle class.[12]

A third innovation of NSMs generally and the environmental movement in particular concerns their organizations and their action repertoire. In contrast to such established interest groups as unions or employers' associations, NSMs tend to have decentralized organizations, with a minimal degree of centralized leadership.[13] In addition, NSMs favor direct action tactics whose spectacular character—such as that of climbing up smokestacks—attracts media attention and alerts public opinion to a movement's cause. In sum, NSMs are new because they represent nonmaterial issues, attract widespread support from different social segments of European societies, and favor participatory organizations.

The newness of NSMs partly explains why these movements emerged outside of the relatively rigid and closed structures of party governments. But why did these movements emerge in the first place? One widely cited explanation for the evolution of NSMs is Ronald Inglehart's theory of postmaterial value change.[14] Inglehart argues that the unprecedented affluence and international stability of postwar Western Europe resulted in the satisfaction of the basic material needs—such as food, shelter, and security—of West European publics. Therefore, a growing proportion of, especially, younger citizens—whom Inglehart termed "postmaterialists"—shifted their primary political attention away from economic issues and traditional security strategies. Instead, postmaterialists stress quality-of-life issues as policy priorities, issues such as environmental protection or gender equality. Numerous empirical studies show that supporters of NSMs are disproportionately concentrated among postmaterialist individuals.[15] Thus the change of value priorities combined with existing problems—for example, pollution problems or the perceived threat of nuclear war[16]—contributes to the evolution of NSMs.

In sum, the formation of NSMs throughout the 1970s represents a significant departure from the hitherto existing issue agenda and political style of mass publics. The historical roots of most European parties in the Industrial Revolution explains why parties are well equipped to provide ideological alternatives within

---

12. See, for example, Stephen Cotgrove, *Catastrophe and Cornucopia* (New York: John Wiley, 1982); Claus Offe, "New Social Movements: Challenging the Boundaries of Institutional Politics," *Social Research*, 52:817-68 (1985).

13. Philip Lowe and Jane Goyder, *Environmental Groups in Politics* (New York: Allen & Unwin, 1983).

14. Ronald Inglehart, *Culture Shift* (Princeton, NJ: Princeton University Press, 1990); idem, *The Silent Revolution* (Princeton, NJ: Princeton University Press, 1977).

15. For example, Oddbjorn Knutsen, "Cleavage Dimension in Ten West European Countries: A Comparative Empirical Analysis," *Comparative Political Studies*, 21:495-533 (1989). For a critical appraisal, see Scott Flanagan, "Value Change in Industrial Society," *American Political Science Review*, 81:1303-19 (1987); Harold Clarke and Nitish Dutt, "Measuring Value Change in Western Industrialized Societies: The Impact of Unemployment," ibid., 85:905-20 (1991).

16. Rohrschneider, "Roots of Public Opinion."

the framework of economic issues. Their historical roots in the industrial cleavage also explain why most established parties were initially poorly equipped to offer solutions to the challenges generated by NSMs.

THE PROGRAMMATIC CHALLENGE

The first and most obvious challenge that NSMs represent for European parties is a programmatic challenge. The question at this juncture is, How well do European political parties respond to the issues generated by NSMs? As my discussion so far has implied, most established parties were reluctant to adopt social movement issues into their programs. As the environmental movement expanded from the local to the national level, environmentalism became a viable political force; however, the initial response of most parties in most European countries consisted in minimizing the existence of environmental problems. Since established parties control most political institutions, the regular political process was effectively closed off to the environmental movement.[17] Consequently, green parties were founded from the mid-1970s onward in order to inject postmaterial issues into West European parliaments. By the end of the 1980s, green and other New Left parties had attracted enough voters to be represented in nearly every West European party system. Thus there is considerable evidence that estab-

17. Dorothy Nelkin and Michael Pollack, *The Atom Besieged* (Cambridge: MIT Press, 1981).

lished parties were at first unable— or unwilling—to meet the programmatic challenge.

When green parties had their first electoral successes at the end of the 1970s, established parties, especially Old Left ones, realized that they had to become concerned with voter shifts away from established parties to green parties. Consequently, the 1980s evidenced a growing responsiveness of established parties to issues generated by NSMs. To illustrate the policy reaction of established parties, I will review in more detail the policy response of established parties to the anti-nuclear-energy movement.

Party policies and the nuclear energy debate

One major cross-national consistency of party policies on nuclear energy issues concerns the continuous support of center-conservative parties for the use of nuclear power as an energy source. For instance, the Christian Democratic Union/Christian Social Union in Germany has always promoted the construction of nuclear reactors, and the support remains unwavering in spite of the relatively strong support of mass publics for the anti-nuclear-energy movement (see Table 1). Similarly, French and British conservatives, like other conservative parties, advocate the continued use of nuclear power as an energy source. While some variation in the degree of support for nuclear power exists within the conservative party camp, these parties, on the whole, remain supportive of using nuclear power as an energy source.

In contrast, traditional left-wing parties display the full range of policy positions on nuclear energy, even within a single party viewed over time. Let us discuss in more detail the developments within the German Social Democratic Party (SPD), British Labour Party, French Socialist Party (PS), and the Dutch Labour Party (PvdA) because these parties reflect the full scope of programmatic reactions to the evolution of NSMs. The SPD in West Germany reversed its official policy on nuclear energy after a long and arduous process of intraparty discussions. In the 1970s, the SPD under the leadership of Chancellor Schmidt supported the use and expansion of nuclear energy. Once the SPD became the opposition party in 1982, anti-nuclear-power forces succeeded in changing the official policy position of the SPD, probably as a result of the growing electoral threat from the newly founded green party. Eventually, at a preelection party congress in 1987, the SPD decided to endorse a platform that called for a gradual phasing out of nuclear energy over a 10-year period. By the early 1990s, the SPD had developed a program that attempts to synthesize economic and environmental policies.

The PvdA has the longest association with NSMs, which explains why it was one of the first major socialist parties in Europe to adopt an anti-nuclear-energy position. From the end of the 1960s onward, supporters of NSMs gained access to the leadership institutions within the PvdA. As a result, in 1976, the party proposed a moratorium on the construction of nuclear power plants. During the anti-nuclear-energy debate throughout the mid-1980s, the PvdA confirmed its image as a party representative of the anti-nuclear-energy movement in the Netherlands. In short, of all the established parties, the PvdA was among the first to react favorably to the anti-nuclear-energy movement.

In contrast to the SPD and the PvdA, French Socialists have been generally supportive of nuclear power as an energy source, although the PS has made some overtures to the French anti-nuclear-energy movement. The policy program of the PS toward nuclear energy issues is visibly documented by the rapid construction of nuclear power plants between 1981 and 1985, when France expanded its nuclear energy production faster than any other nation.[18] During 1977, however, Mitterrand, then the opposition leader, demanded a two-year moratorium on the construction of new nuclear power plants; the demand most likely was the result of the strong anti-nuclear-energy sentiments in France during the 1970s. During the 1981 presidential election campaign, Mitterrand made a promise, which he kept, to scrap the construction of a nuclear power plant at Plogoff in order to attract environmentally concerned voters.[19] Still, the policy behavior of the PS reflects a partial responsiveness at best toward the de-

18. Miriam Boyle and David Pepper, "Nuclear Energy in France: A Foretaste of the Future," in *Nuclear Power in Crisis*, ed. A. Blowers and D. Pepper (London: Croom Helm, 1987), pp. 55-84.

19. Howard Machine, "Stages and Dynamics in the Evolution of the French Party System," *West European Politics*, 12:59-81 (1989).

mands of the anti-nuclear-energy movement.

Finally, British Labour has also been reluctant to respond favorably to the anti-nuclear-energy movement, probably because of the strong influence of unions on Labour's intraparty affairs.[20] After Labour lost the 1979 election, internal disputes arose over nuclear energy, but the intensity was considerably less than the disputes within the German SPD because the dominant policy issues for Labour remained industrial conflicts. Between 1983 and 1986, however, pro-environmental forces gained considerable influence within Labour, which resulted in a reversal of its nuclear policy position at the 1986 annual conference: delegates passed a document that called for the closing of older nuclear power plants, a halt on the construction of new plants, and a variety of other measures. While the anti-nuclear-energy stance of Labour appears less firm than that of the PvdA or the SPD, Labour appears to be slowly adopting an anti-nuclear-energy stance.

Explaining variations

There are a number of factors that may account for the variations in parties' responsiveness to the programmatic challenge of the environmental and other movements, but the following three should be considered in any explanation. First, socialist parties respond more favorably than do center-conservative parties because the former share with NSMs a concern for the social and political equality of individuals, although they often disagree over the priorities of economic and noneconomic issues. Second, variations within the Old Left party camp are partially explained by whether party systems operate under plurality or proportional laws. In Germany and the Netherlands, modified proportional laws facilitate the evolution of smaller green parties, which increases the pressure on established Old Left parties to respond favorably to social movement demands. In contrast, the modified plurality system in France and Great Britain shields established Old Left parties from minor-party competition, which delays a favorable response of British Labour and French Socialists to NSMs. Another institutional factor that protects Old Left parties in France and Great Britain from movement pressures is the centralized political institutions, which provide movements with fewer points of access to the political system than do federal systems. Finally, a third factor can be located within parties by focusing on the role of unions within Labour parties.[21] Unions often oppose social movement goals because unions put a priority on improvement in the material conditions of the lower classes. Consequently, the unionized members of Old Left parties, such as British Labour, often oppose adopting an environmental platform.

Despite these variations, however, it seems clear that European socialist parties are increasingly ready to address concerns of the environmental

20. Timothy O'Riordan, "Prospects for the Nuclear Energy Debate in the UK," in *Nuclear Power in Crisis*, ed. Blowers and Pepper, pp. 295-315.

21. Thomas Koelble, *The Left Unraveled* (Durham, NC: Duke University Press, 1991).

movement. Similarly, analyses of the responsiveness of these parties to the peace[22] and women's movements[23] also suggest that established Old Left parties are now more capable of addressing social movement concerns than was true at the end of the 1970s. Thus the policy developments within traditional left-wing parties by the early 1990s suggest that the future policies of established parties should not be assessed merely on the basis of their past unresponsiveness.

THE ELECTORAL CHALLENGE

A second challenge, related to the programmatic one, focuses on the question of whether established parties are able to attract voters who support NSMs. As with the programmatic challenge, the initial answer must generally be negative. Since established parties, by and large, disregarded social movement issues, social movement activists helped to found green parties. Given the programmatic overlap between NSMs and green parties, voters who sympathize with NSMs also represent the primary source of electoral support of green and other New Left parties.[24]

In theoretical terms, the evolution of green parties has sparked a debate over the possibility of a fundamental shift in the partisan attachments of European voters, a so-called "new politics realignment." Most analyses of electoral change agree that historical alignments between social classes and established parties (for example,

between the working class and Old Left parties or between the middle class and center-conservative parties) have weakened since the early 1970s—a dealignment. It is also widely held that this broad trend was initiated by fundamental changes in the socioeconomic structure of advanced industrial societies, such as the growth of the new middle class, the shrinkage of the old middle class, or the increasing affluence of the working class.[25] At the same time, the partisan dealignment coincides with the evolution of NSMs, setting the stage for a reorientation of European voters within the party space: old alliances crumble and new issues and parties emerge, which could serve as a basis for a new coalition between voters and parties—a realignment.[26]

To assess the prospects for a partisan realignment based on New Politics issues, consider that established parties initially did not address environmental and other New Politics issues. Consequently, voters who looked for a partisan home that matched their New Politics preferences often did not feel adequately represented by any established party and increasingly supported green parties. Undoubtedly, the electoral success of green parties represents a serious challenge to established parties since these voter movements, in the long run, may lead to a decline in the aggregate vote share of established parties.

22. Rochon, *Mobilizing for Peace*.

23. Gelb, *Feminism in Politics*.

24. Ferdinand Mueller-Rommel, ed., *New Politics in Western Europe* (Boulder, CO: Westview Press, 1989).

25. Ivor Crewe and David Denver, *Electoral Change in Western Democracies* (New York: St. Martin's Press, 1986).

26. Russell J. Dalton, Scott C. Flanagan, and P. A. Beck, eds., *Electoral Change in Western Democracies* (Princeton, NJ: Princeton University Press, 1984).

The evolution of green parties represents the most visible phenomenon of partisan changes, and, accordingly, most analysts almost exclusively study the link between voters' New Politics preferences and their support for a green party.[27] The growing programmatic responsiveness of established Old Left parties, however, raises the possibility that these parties are able to attract New Politics proponents. In order to investigate this possibility, I analyzed the partisan preferences of supporters of the anti-nuclear-energy movement between 1982 and 1989 (Table 2). For example, in 1989, 18.8 percent of the supporters of the anti-nuclear-energy movement would vote for the Greens in Germany. At the same time, the SPD was chosen by 57.2 percent of movement supporters, which is about 20 percent more than the SPD received in the 1990 federal election. Furthermore, the proportion of group supporters siding with the SPD increased during the 1982-89 period, which suggests that the adoption of an anti-nuclear-energy stance indeed led sympathizers of the anti-nuclear-energy movement to support the SPD. A similar development may be observed even in France and Great Britain, where the PS and Labour have only been partially responsive to the anti-nuclear-energy movement. Finally, center-conservative parties receive less support than their nationwide average from environmental group supporters, which

is consistent with the pro-nuclear-energy stance of these parties. In sum, these developments imply that, as with the programmatic challenge, established Old Left parties are increasingly able to meet the electoral challenge.[28]

THE ORGANIZATIONAL CHALLENGE

The organizational challenge to established parties is concerned with the question, How do participatory demands of social movement activists affect the internal organization of established political parties? Historically, the evolution of hierarchical and rigid party organizations in Western Europe is closely related to the evolution of mass parties at the turn of the century. Since mass communication technologies did not exist, parties, especially leftist ones, developed hierarchical organizations in order to increase their visibility to voters between elections and in order to mobilize voters during elections.[29] The development of parties into large bureaucracies led Robert Michels to coin the famous dictum that parties—or other organizations—inevitably create intraparty oligarchies: the "iron law of oligarchy." Michels argues that any organization experiences a certain degree of oligarchization because organizations need ex-

27. For an exception, see Sidney Tarrow, "The Phantom at the Opera: Political Parties and Social Movements of the 1960s and 1970s in Italy," in Challenging the Political Order, ed. Dalton and Kuechler, pp. 251-73.

28. For a more detailed analysis, see Robert Rohrschneider, "New Party versus Old Left Realignments: Environmental Attitudes, Party Policies, and Partisan Affiliations in Four West European Countries," Journal of Politics 55:682-701 (1993).

29. Leon Epstein, Political Parties in Western Democracies (New Brunswick, NJ: Transaction Books, 1980).

TABLE 2
**PARTISANSHIP OF SUPPORTERS OF THE
ANTI-NUCLEAR-ENERGY MOVEMENT, 1982-89**

		1982	1984	1986	1989
France	Unified Socialist Party/Ecologists	17.6	17.6	11.1	30.5
		(9.4)	(5.8)	(5.3)	(13.9)
	French Communist Party/Socialist Party/	58.9	48.6	58.6	44.4
	Left Radical Movement	(49.5)	(45.3)	(43.5)	(43.9)
	Rally for the Republic/	23.5	33.8	30.2	25.1
	Union for French Democracy	(41.1)	(48.9)	(51.2)	(42.2)
	(N)	(329)	(332)	(303)	(371)
Germany	Greens	16.1	20.6	17.1	18.8
		(1.1)	(1.7)	(1.0)	(1.2)
	Social Democratic Party	45.2	55.4	57.3	57.2
		(28.6)	(36.4)	(36.9)	(36.5)
	Free Democratic Party/	38.7	24.0	25.6	24.0
	Christian Democratic Union/	(70.3)	(61.9)	(62.1)	(62.3)
	Christian Social Union				
	(N)	(334)	(274)	(302)	(512)
Great Britain	Alliance	36.7	18.3	21.9	14.1
		(33.0)	(19.8)	(21.3)	(11.8)
	Labour Party	38.1	52.0	51.5	55.4
		(26.0)	(30.1)	(22.8)	(30.0)
	Conservative Party	25.2	29.7	26.6	30.5
		(41.0)	(50.1)	(55.9)	(58.2)
	(N)	(529)	(318)	(386)	(354)
Netherlands	Pacifist Socialist Party/	29.0	17.2	15.8	18.3
	Democrats 66/Radical Political Party/	(15.4)	(6.4)	(8.9)	(10.4)
	Netherlands Communist Party				
	Labour Party	29.4	49.1	50.4	44.2
		(16.0)	(26.3)	(26.5)	(27.5)
	Christian Democratic Appeal/	41.6	33.7	33.8	37.5
	People's Party for Freedom and Democracy	(68.6)	(67.3)	(64.6)	(62.1)
	(N)	(545)	(453)	(468)	(563)

SOURCE: Eurobarometers 17 (1982), 21 (1984), 25 (1986), and 31a (1989).
NOTE: Entries are the percentage of supporters of the anti-nuclear-energy movement who would vote for the political party specified; except for N, entries in parentheses are the percentage of movement opponents who would vote for the political party specified.

perts who are able to manage them skillfully, creating a division between leaders and the rank and file. Furthermore, rank-and-file members, according to Michels, are psychologi- cally dependent on a party's leadership because "in the organized mass of the labor parties, there is an immense need for direction and guidance. This need is accompanied by a genuine cult for the leaders, who are regarded as heroes."[30] Finally, given that party members are unable to control a party's leadership, party elites often pursue policies and develop preferences against the interest of ordinary party members. In short, oligarchies evolve because large organizations need leaders and because members are presumably passive and unable to control a leadership effectively.

Michels's analysis still influences analysts of political parties who, by and large, accept the iron laws as an accurate depiction of internal party dynamics. Nonetheless, even if one accepts Michels's analyses as accurate for his time, the evolution of NSMs may fundamentally alter the internal processes of political parties. Movement activists introduce not only new issues to the political agenda but also a new style of political activities. Like their counterpart on the level of mass publics, movement activists have a preference for organizations that maximize the opportunity for ordinary members to participate in intraparty affairs.[31] These anti-oligarchical preferences, within the realm of party organizations, find their most visible expression in the organizations of green or other New Left parties.[32] These parties attempt to minimize the dominance of a party's leadership over intraparty affairs, and they attempt to maximize the influence of the ordinary member on party decisions.

Yet there is evidence that movement proponents are increasingly represented within established Old Left parties, which in turn may alter their internal dynamic. For example, arguing that NSMs are changing European party systems, Sartori maintains that New Politics activists radicalize "many of the established parties in most Western nations."[33] Other observers also note the influx of social movement proponents into established parties and their decentralizing influence on established parties' hierarchies.[34] Thus it seems plausible to argue that social movement proponents within established parties may attack existing party oligarchies in order to make party structures more compatible with the activists' organizational preferences.

If this argument is correct, then the organizational challenge aims at the core of European mass parties because it is considerably more difficult to assuage than the programmatic or even the electoral challenge. For instance, the organizational challenge questions the leadership of established party oligarchies, thereby undermining the historical distribution of power among party factions. Meeting the organizational challenge would require a devolvement of party power from the leadership to activ-

30. Robert Michels, *Political Parties* (1915; New York: Macmillan, 1962), p. 88.

31. Dieter Rucht, ed., *New Social Movements in Western Europe* (Boulder, CO: Westview Press, 1991).

32. Kitschelt, *Logics of Party Formation.*

33. Giovanni Sartori, *Parties and Party System* (New York: Cambridge University Press, 1976), p. 150.

34. Joachim Raschke, ed., *Buerger und Parteien* (Opladen: Westdeutscher Verlag, 1983); Alan Ware, *Political Parties: Electoral Change and Structural Response* (Oxford: Basil Blackwell, 1987).

ists or even to the local rank and file. It seems considerably easier for parties to integrate new issues into party platforms than to fundamentally reorganize the internal distribution of power, for example, between unions and social movement proponents. Furthermore, meeting the organizational challenge would create its own electoral repercussions for parties. For example, if the programmatic appeal of a party to the electorate at large is placed second to activists' interests, traditional constituencies may no longer feel integrated by their party, which may affect a party's overall vote share.

Obviously, social scientists have debated for some time which party organization is best suited to function properly in advanced industrialized democracies. In the 1950s, for example, Duverger argued that mass party organizations as exemplified by socialist and social democratic parties were the best suited to compete successfully in elections.[35] He expected that mass parties increasingly would adopt the organizational structures of left-wing parties, a process he termed a "contagion from the left." A quarter century later, Epstein, in contrast, maintained that the growing reliance on mass communication technologies made a mass membership base increasingly superfluous because voters could be reached without an elaborate party apparatus.[36] Accordingly, he expected that parties increasingly would develop into loosely organized, elite-di-

rected organizations. In juxtaposition with Duverger, he termed this process "contagion from the right." The organizational challenge of movement activists to established European parties, however, is new in two senses. First, activists have joined social scientists in the debate over organizational norms. Second, movement activists usually favor neither a contagion from the Left nor a contagion from the Right but a contagion from below: intraparty power should devolve to local party branches and party activists, away from a ruling party oligarchy. For their part, established parties have made the least attempts to master the organizational challenge, precisely because it is the most difficult and serious challenge that NSMs create for established parties.

CONCLUSION

The evolution of NSMs presents established political parties in Western Europe with a number of challenges. While European parties were initially slow to respond favorably to the demands made by NSMs, Old Left parties have especially addressed the programmatic concerns of NSMs. In fact, green and socialist parties even form electoral and government coalitions on the state level against center-conservative parties, as in Germany. Similarly, the peace and women's movements have formed alliances with various established organizations, such as churches or labor parties. These developments suggest that New Politics issues are accepted as legitimate policy dimensions in West European

35. Maurice Duverger, *Political Parties* (London: Methuen, 1954).

36. Epstein, *Political Parties in Western Democracies*.

party systems. The programmatic developments also imply that the electoral challenge may be met by established parties, especially by Old Left ones. Voters who wish to base their electoral choice on New Politics issues find that Old Left parties, in addition to green parties, are an acceptable partisan outlet.

These developments suggest that partisan realignments may occur in two different forms. First, New Politics voters may continue to support green or other New Left parties, a realistic possibility because green parties are the most explicit party representative of NSMs. But a second scenario suggests that Old Left parties may integrate New Politics proponents into their coalition of voters, along with their established clientele. Of course, Old Left parties will encounter difficulties in reconciling the demands of environmentalists and unions. In addition, partisan realignments based upon New Politics preferences are less stable than organizationally based alignments between social classes and political parties.[37] Yet, given the programmatic and electoral developments, it

37. Dalton, Citizen Politics in Western Democracies.

appears that established Old Left parties now meet the electoral challenge of NSMs better than is generally assumed.

Our discussion also indicates that the implications of parties' response to the programmatic and the electoral challenges are closely intertwined: meeting the programmatic one increases the odds for meeting the electoral one; not meeting the former increases the chances of not meeting the latter. By meeting the programmatic and electoral challenges, however, parties are likely to attract social movement activists who have a predisposition to challenging oligarchical party structures. As movement activists are represented within established parties in growing proportions, they are likely to initiate lively debates over the parties' organizational structures. Responding to the programmatic and electoral challenge will therefore exacerbate the organizational challenge for established parties. In conclusion, while the influence of NSMs on the organization of established parties is one of the least-researched domains, the organizational dimension may turn out to be the most serious challenge that NSMs create for established political parties.

Book Department

INTERNATIONAL RELATIONS AND POLITICS

HEADRICK, DANIEL R. *The Invisible Weapon: Telecommunications and International Politics, 1851-1945*. Pp. x, 289. New York: Oxford University Press, 1991. $32.50.

In today's world of instantaneous satellite television transmissions by the Cable News Network (CNN) and constant streams of fax messages, it is hard to imagine a time when diplomatic messages were sent by carrier pigeons and three-masted sailing ships. Daniel Headrick, professor of history and social sciences at Roosevelt University in Chicago, carefully demonstrates how the coming of telegraphy, and then radio, offered the leaders of the world new communication instruments and forever changed all phases of international relations.

For Headrick, telecommunication is narrowly defined as point-to-point communication, not the mass media. Yet, somewhat surprisingly, he chooses to all but ignore the impact of the telephone in the early twentieth century. This is because, until the 1950s, transoceanic telephone calls were rare occurrences.

The main point in *The Invisible Weapon* is that the telegraph and radio principally reshaped the political history of Europe and the United States from 1851 through 1945. Headrick's historical analysis begins with the invention and innovation of the telegraph and closes with changes that radio brought to intelligence gathering and dispersal during World War II.

In particular, Headrick describes in loving detail how the first primitive telegraphy enhanced European imperialism, making it possible for leaders in London, Paris, and Amsterdam to monitor ever so closely their newly acquired colonies. Indeed, for Headrick, the inherent limitations in the telegraph technology in dealing with these far-flung empires hastened the deterioration in international politics that eventually led to World War I.

Radio seems to have had its greatest impact in tipping the balance of power during World Wars I and II. In a fascinating chapter, examining the role of radio communication across the Pacific in 1942 and 1943, Headrick helps us sense how satellite communication has revolutionized our present-day links to Japan, China, and the rest of Asia.

The Invisible Weapon is the third in a trilogy, the first being *The Tentacles of Progress: Technology Transfer in the Age of Imperialism, 1850-1940* and the second *The Tools of the Empire: Technology and European Imperialism in the Nineteenth Century*. We should thank Daniel Headrick for working through, step by step, the impact of a plethora of technological changes that have radically transformed all aspects of international relations and diplomacy.

DOUGLAS GOMERY

University of Maryland
College Park

HOLSTI, KALEVI J. *Peace and War: Armed Conflicts and International Order, 1648-1989.* Pp. xvii, 379. New York: Cambridge University Press, 1991. No price.

This work presents an empirical analysis of the causes of war since 1648. Holsti includes 177 international conflicts, but he leaves out rebellions and civil wars unless they spilled over into war with other states. He identifies 24 issues that led to those wars (Table 12-1). Most can be grouped into larger categories: control of physical space, various aspects of economic competition, sympathy for ethnic or religious fellows, nation-state unification, and ideology. The time span under study is divided into five periods bounded by the great peace conferences of history: 1648-1714, 1715-1814, 1815-1914, 1919-41, 1945-89. For each era, Holsti enumerates the wars and the issues he believed caused them. In some cases, he notes only one cause, usually physical space, for both sides; but in most, he finds that several issues touched off the wars, up to seven for some wars. The issues for an era are summarized in tables, and the tables are then combined for the total period. Holsti uses his totals to find out what issues have been largely constant since 1648, which ones have declined, and which have become more common.

Holsti goes on to study the great peace conferences to determine whether peacemaking also has a discernible pattern. He concludes that all five sought to settle issues that had touched off the wars just concluded. Four of them sought to assimilate the defeated powers back into the international community; the one exception, 1919, saw its settlement quickly collapse because it did not. The author argues that all five conferences were deficient in one important respect: they failed to identify future issues of war-causing potential and thus failed to prevent new wars.

Like any attempt to create an orderly schema for something as nebulous as the causes of war, Holsti's analysis is open to criticism. The most serious problem is his inclusion of truly minor episodes with the great wars. For example, he not only includes the Anschluss of 1938 with the Japan-United States war of 1941-45 but actually gives it greater weight in his statistics by identifying seven issues as its causes compared to five for the far greater conflict in the Pacific.

Considering that the work covers 177 wars over 340 years, the errors of fact are few, but several are jarring. For example, the Thirty Years War is said to have begun as a Bohemian revolt against Spanish rule (p. 26).

This book will be of interest to a wide range of scholars, but I doubt that a present-day statesman using it will be able to predict what will cause the next war.

There is no indication that Holsti, writing two years ago, had any prescience that states emerging in Eastern Europe would be now at war with each other.

FREDERIC J. BAUMGARTNER

Virginia Polytechnic Institute
and State University
Blacksburg

PACKENHAM, ROBERT A. *The Dependency Movement: Scholarship and Politics in Development Studies.* Pp. viii, 362. Cambridge, MA: Harvard University Press, 1992. $42.50.

The purpose of this volume is to examine the impact on and value for the study of the development process in the Third World of so-called dependencia theories. The latter refers to a heavily Marxist-oriented analysis of current problems of the developing countries laced with nationalistic ideology and nurtured predominantly in Latin American academic and intellectual circles, with a sprinkling of a primarily academic following outside the region.

According to Packenham, who teaches political science at Stanford and previously has published *Liberal America and the Third World*, dependency theory has entered deeply into mainstream academic disciplines, as well as quickening scholarly analysis of North-South relations. And yet, according to the author, "dependency ideas are still widely and seriously misunderstood." Also in need of examination is the position advanced by the dependencia movement that social scientific analysis and research must be made subject to politics—a view characterized by Packenham as repugnant to the "classical conception" of learning prevailing in the United States and elsewhere.

To those who thought that the appeals of totalitarian-style social science à la the Nazis and the Soviets had vanished, dependencia's apparent justification of a politicized kind of science may seem rather quaint. Still, whatever one may think about dependency theory, Packenham takes it seriously on its own terms and has given it a thorough and balanced treatment in these pages. There is an initial informative chapter on the genesis and different offshoots of the dependency movement, reflecting Packenham's close reading of the writings of such dependencia protagonists as Jose Mariategui, Fernando Cardoso, Jorge Dominguez, and others. Packenham notes the "eclectic" nature of the dependency writers and their familiarity with and references to a broader, non-Marxist social science literature. How well dependencia writers grasp the importance of this non-Marxist apparatus is not examined, however. Subsequent chapters deal critically, though fairly, with a number of key dependency ideas (for example, various forms of holism—substantive and epistemological) and the varieties of dependency analysis, such as those applicable to socialist or capitalist situations. Concluding chapters deal with the effect of dependency thinking on such scholarly organizations as the Latin American Studies Association and on the scholarship of development generally, particularly in the United States.

Thoroughly annotated and provided with an extensive bibliography, Packenham's study will remain as a useful introduction to a kind of politicized academic writing that seems—from a U.S. vantage point—peculiarly a product of the radicalism of the 1960s. At a time when, from Mexico City to Santiago, Chile—not to mention from Moscow to Delhi—internationalist market economics and its social and cultural correlates are the ascendant public philosophy, dependencia's resentment-ridden blend of Marxism and nationalism and its horrendous jargon—for example, "epistemological holism" and "nonfalsificationism"—seem almost museum pieces, clung to today with fervor primarily in Havana or Pyongyang and, of course, on U.S. college campuses.

Especially noteworthy in the latter context is the extent to which what Packenham calls "dependencist rules of discourse" has now permeated "the subculture" of those scholars in the United States who deal with Latin America and with Third World development problems generally. Violation of "basic academic standards has occurred with remarkably little comment or resistance," the author notes, as the icons of dependencia thought are brandished about and devotees rush to defend their criteria of "political correctness." Packenham's condemnation of this aspect of "holistic dependency" is unvarnished—"anti-scholarly" and "anti-scientific"—and deserves to be read with care by any student of U.S. social scientific fashions. It is the great merit of Packenham's book, however, that before such deservedly harsh judgments are rendered, sufficient factual and objective accounting of the dependency theories has been offered so as to enable the reader to make his or her own way through the literature.

JUSTUS M. VAN DER KROEF

University of Bridgeport
Connecticut

WITTKOPF, EUGENE R. *Faces of Internationalism: Public Opinion and American Foreign Policy.* Pp. xix, 391. Durham, NC: Duke University Press, 1990. $75.00. Paperbound, $24.95.

In a superficial sense, this thoughtful and sophisticated analysis of American attitudes toward foreign affairs between 1974 and 1988 had already been overtaken by events when it was first published at the very end of 1990. Like so much academic writing on foreign affairs in general and the former Soviet Union in particular, this tome is compelled to justify the sacrifice of trees going into its production principally by reference to its conceptual value. Happily, this value is considerable.

One of the volume's great virtues is as revisionist political science. Wittkopf rejects the conclusion of a long line of academic psephologists that the American public is *Homo boobiens* when it comes to foreign policy. More precisely, while conceding that, yes, the public may be bored with and ignorant about foreign policy, Wittkopf argues that its foreign policy beliefs are nevertheless both coherent and politically relevant. Why? Because a citizen does not have to know where in Central America El Salvador or Nicaragua is to have "firm and unwavering convictions" about "whether American boys should be sent to fight in the region. From the point of view of policymakers in Washington, the latter is the important, politically relevant datum."

The volume's conceptual contribution, for which a mass of data is adduced (mainly from quadrennial mass and elite opinion surveys conducted by the Chicago Council on Foreign Relations and the 1987-88 project Americans Talk Security), is a new typology of American public opinion on foreign affairs. With a technical virtuosity that I am incompetent to evaluate, Wittkopf shoehorns respondents into one of four "belief system" cells according to their attitudes along two axes: militant internationalism and cooperative internationalism. To oversimplify, members of the mass public are located along the first axis according to whether they quake or salivate in contemplation of using U.S. troops abroad and how much of a threat they perceive communism to be (have been?). Respondents are distributed along the second axis according to their faith in the United Nations and cooperative as distinct from conflictual strategies. The resulting four types are (1) internationalists, who support both forceful and cooperative solutions to foreign policy problems; (2) isolationists, who cannot abide either; (3) accommodationists, who back only cooperative approaches; and (4) hard-liners, who would shoot first and ask for cooperation later. These are the faces of internationalism, symbolized by the arrows and the olive branch, to which the title refers.

Most remarkable is the finding that, based on this conceptual scheme, between 1974 and 1986 (that is, between the dark days of the Vietnam war's denouement and the return of American self-confidence in the world), the proportions of the public adhering to each of the four underlying belief systems were almost equal—and scarcely changed. A shade less than one-quarter of the public has been isolationist at any of the four data points. In other words, just over three-quarters of Americans have been internationalist throughout this turbulent era.

But while there has been consensus at a very high level of generality concerning whether the United States should be involved abroad, the public has been deeply split over how our involvement should be pursued. Accommodationists and hard-liners have been almost equal in number throughout this era. The public may rally round the flag in the early stages of the commitment of U.S. armed forces abroad, but the stark reality is that deep-seated differences in belief systems will make it difficult over time for the country to sustain a prolonged military intervention—or its avoidance. In light of these data, President Bush's creation of a domestic

and international consensus behind the war to oust Iraq from Kuwait and his immensely successful prosecution of the war stand as an extraordinary achievement, almost a model of how America should, if it must, go to war.

NILS H. WESSELL

U.S. Coast Guard Academy
New London
Connecticut

AFRICA, ASIA, AND LATIN AMERICA

AHMAD, SYED NESAR. *Origins of Muslim Consciousness in India: A World-System Perspective.* Pp. xv, 311. Westport, CT: Greenwood Press, 1991. $47.95.

This book is edited posthumously from a dissertation that was left unfinished by the death of the author at the hands of airline hijackers in Pakistan in 1986. As such, it does not bear scholarly comparison with academic monographs on communalism in British India. Its argument is not new, even as it is framed by the world-system theory of the author's dissertation supervisor, Immanuel Wallerstein. For this theory merely reformulates a materialist explanation for the evolution of an increasingly coherent Muslim demand for a separate state in colonial South Asia that has been shaped by the intellectual legacy of Marx for fifty years. Nonetheless, Ahmad's book merits close attention, for two reasons.

First, it appears at a time when the claim by scholars to objectivity in social analysis has suffered such deep criticism that the epistemological division between objectivity and subjectivity can truly be said to be archaic. The response to this intellectual dilemma by many scholars in Europe and America has been to retreat into a world of subjectivity and representations, where literary images and authorial stylistics replace reality as the preoccupation of scholarship. Ahmad demonstrates the opposite choice. He is forthright in his declaration that scholarship can be a force in the reconstruction of humane societies. His method is designed to show that when real people confront a world of forces beyond their control, they seek political solutions to their problems forged from material at hand, in this case, from the plausibility of Muslim community as a form of political solidarity. The possibility of the Muslim state forms that emerged in South Asia after 1947 arose during the colonial period, as a product of a collective consciousness that was shaped and constituted institutionally within the British Empire. Ahmad's mission here is to demonstrate the historical contingency of that formation and thus to show that collective choices are likewise being shaped in the present, when scholars have the power to exert their own influence over future possibilities.

Second, the very reliance of this work on secondary sources and its preoccupation with a critical reading of existing scholarship make it a good guide to the literature on the subject as of 1986. The tendency of monographs is to cut a narrow shaft into a subject, to establish a secure place for the author in a complex division of scholarly labor. This book has the advantage of presenting an erudite and committed student's broad view of a subject that requires broad vision to remain in perspective.

In November 1986, I had looked forward to seeing Ahmad again, at a conference on the applications of world-system theory to South Asian history, when I learned of his death. This book is a fitting epitaph.

DAVID LUDDEN

University of Pennsylvania
Philadelphia

AHMED, LEILA. *Women and Gender in Islam*. Pp. viii, 296. New Haven, CT: Yale University Press, 1992. No price.

This work is a provocative exploration of "the core Islamic discourses on women and gender . . . and the key premises of the modern discourses on women in the Middle East." Questioning the legitimacy of the customary way in which Arab women are discussed by Middle Eastern Islamists and secularists as well as by Western academicians and media professionals, Leila Ahmed provides a sensitive, phenomenological rethinking of this timely subject. She convincingly argues that the aforementioned debates and discussions often have hidden agendas, such as politics and power, at the root of their treatment of the position of Islamic women.

Part 1 of the text examines the status of pre-Islamic women in Mesopotamia and the Mediterranean Middle East. The non-Muslim reader is soon disabused of any presumption that modern Islamic practices concerning women, such as veiling and seclusion, originated with the Prophet Muhammad. One discovers, rather, that customs and mores regarding women that were already in place in earlier cultures were later incorporated into Islamic practices.

The "founding discourses" on women and gender in Islam constitute part 2 of this study. The role of women at the birth of Islam and the subsequent elaboration of Islamic law, as well as male-dominated scriptural exegesis, from the Abbisid era through the medieval period are clearly analyzed. Relevant religious movements within Islam are also examined.

Part 3 brings the reader to the nineteenth and twentieth centuries, when European colonialism heavily affected the status of Arab women, particularly in Egypt, a "mirror of the Arab world in the modern age." New discourses on the role of women are the result of this intrusion, and it is in her treatment of this topic that Ahmed's feminist perspective is especially helpful to the general reader. Particularly enlightening for the Westerner are the chapters that deal with veiling and with early Islamic feminists.

Because of the focused nature of the material treated in this volume, a non-Muslim reader should already possess a basic knowledge of the history and beliefs of Islam. Should this be lacking, Annemarie Schimmel's *Islam* would fill the void quite well. Professors using *Women and Gender in Islam* as a text or as required reading might want to enflesh the material by showing *Who Will Cast the First Stone?*, a 52-minute video that examines the impact of Islamization on women in Pakistan.

Free of typographical errors and blessed with a helpful index, this perceptive book marks a step toward addressing the deficiency, which Ahmed decries, of objectively valid studies of Arab women. It makes an excellent case for Muslim women's being able to pursue feminist goals within their culture and religion. A case study of the valiant women of Kuwait during the Persian Gulf war and its aftermath would be a welcome sequel from Ahmed's pen.

KEVIN F. DWYER

Merrimack College
North Andover
Massachusetts

ALEXANDER, BEVIN. *The Strange Connection: U.S. Intervention in China, 1944-72.* Pp. xii, 245. Westport, CT: Greenwood Press, 1992. $47.95.

SCHWARCZ, VERA. *Time for Telling Truth Is Running Out: Conversations with Zhang Shenfu.* Pp. xii, 256. New Haven, CT: Yale University Press, 1992. $30.00.

Senator William Knowland of California, the new Chairman of the Senate Foreign Relations Committee in January 1953, instructed the staff of his committee to prepare a revised, and presumably accurate, version of *United States Relations with China, with Special Reference to the Period 1944-49,* the highly controversial China White Paper, published by the Department of State. Having been the principal compiler and author of this document, I was pleased that four years later the committee staff reported that, apart from a few minor details of no substance, the original document faithfully carried out the instructions from President Truman that the State Department prepare a report setting forth the facts about U.S. relations with China, regardless of who might be hurt.

In *The Strange Connection,* Bevin Alexander gives an account of U.S. relations with China that in no respect differs from the White Paper. He does, however, detail what he believes to be mistakes in American policy toward China. I believe it is a fair assumption that the vast majority of officers of the State Department who had any connection with Chinese affairs would agree with the substance, if not necessarily all the details, of his criticism. Even if the passions of that bitter period have now been largely forgotten in the rush of history, it is gratifying to have an independent researcher confirm the accuracy of events that at the time destroyed so many careers and reputations.

It is impossible to do justice to *Time for Telling Truth Is Running Out* in a short review. Zhang was a founding member of the Chinese Communist Party and the one who recruited Zhou Enlai for membership. Being past eighty years of age, he finally agreed to talk extensively with Vera Schwarcz, a professor of history at Wesleyan and the daughter of a survivor of the Holocaust, who, like Zhang, wants to talk and remember. Zhang had been involved in every political movement in China since the May Fourth Movement. It was inevitable that Zhang, who could not control his tongue, would not last in the Communist Party, would largely vanish from sight until rehabilitated some years before his death in 1986, and would then become a sort of official icon and oracle.

Schwarcz is acutely aware of the huge gap between the official, and often changing, versions of history and what and how any given individual chooses to remember. With rare sensitivity as to how slippery her chosen path can be, Schwarcz has raised enough questions that it would be a most opinionated reader who would in the end presume to know the answers. Even the tired old cliché about another man's moccasins is not precise enough.

If there is one cautionary lesson from this fascinating narrative, it is that it is indeed a foolish foreigner who is convinced he or she understands all the subtleties of the Chinese way. I suspect, but cannot prove, that the Chinese would not have it otherwise.

JOHN F. MELBY

University of Guelph
Ontario
Canada

ATTWOOD, DONALD W. *Raising Cane: The Political Economy of Sugar in Western India.* Pp. xviii, 366. Boulder, CO: Westview Press, 1991. $52.50. Paperbound, $19.95.

Raising Cane is an important work as it addresses the issue of variability in social response to the same or a similar set of circumstances—in this case, the commercialization of agriculture. This issue is significant because it questions assumptions and theories of state-society-economy interactions often taken as universal processes. Such studies contribute to theoretical advance, a direction in which this study points but falls short.

Attwood presents an anomaly as he traces the evolution of the sugar industry in western India since the nineteenth century. The anomaly is the general prosperity and relatively open economic mobility following commercialization—in conjunction with the introduction of canal irrigation—without accentuating disparities or the emergence of a kulak or powerful elite class such as often marks the commercialization of agriculture elsewhere and sugar in particular. Politically, the result is a broad-based polity of patron-client structures focused on and acting through sugar mill cooperatives owned and managed by small to large cane producers. Attwood's comparative analysis of cooperatives and their role in this evolution is very good.

Attwood is on target with the argument that commercialization of local economies neither follows a unilinear path nor inevitably produces a single type of polity. The state and outside interests may intervene in different ways. One cannot assume that local societies and people are simply passive, acted upon or victimized. Their interaction produces varying outcomes. Appropriately, his approach is based on interaction theory.

Unfortunately, Attwood directs much polemic against "structuralist" and "Marxist" straw men. This is understandable given the intellectual climate in which he has worked and presented results so at variance with dependency and world systems theory. What is unfortunate is his defensiveness, which at times leads him to overstate findings and away from both recognizing the role of the state and his avowed theoretical perspective.

For instance, his discussion of land relations examines only land ownership patterns—but not operational holdings—that began as highly unequal in the nineteenth century and remain so, with possibly a very slight decrease. True, disparities did not increase, but one wonders if inequality could have increased, particularly given the role of the state in land reform.

Similarly, his defensiveness against "statist" and "bureaucratic" solutions to poverty and development forces him into populist arguments—verging on historical particularism—of enterprising peasants who, if just left to their own devices, create prosperity for all. Only in his very good concluding chapter is the polemic dropped and consideration returned to interaction theory, with comparative asides about Japan, Taiwan, and Korea, where the state plays a positive role in producing equitable distribution and prosperity in agrarian society. One wishes his conclusions had better informed the main body of the study.

BARRY H. MICHIE

Kansas State University
Manhattan

BECK, LOIS. *Nomad: A Year in the Life of a Qashqa'i Tribesman in Iran.* Pp. xiv, 503. Berkeley: University of California Press, 1992. $49.95. Paperbound, $17.00.

Nomad: A Year in the Life of a Qashqa'i Tribesman in Iran, an account of the lives of Qashqa'i tribespeople in the early 1970s, should be of interest to both the general reader and area specialists. Recounting a year in the life of Borzu Qermezi, headman of the Qermezi subtribe of the Darrehshuri tribe of the Qashqa'i, and of the individuals who had significant though not always amicable relations with him, *Nomad* provides a rich description of Qashqa'i life. In particular, *Nomad* recounts the tremendous pressures placed on pastoralists by the

political and economic expansion of the Iranian state under Mohammad Reza Shah, and it gives the reader a detailed view of the relations between political rivals, spouses, parents and children, neighbors, and employers and shepherds as they unfolded in people's daily lives. Readers who are not expert on the Middle East or Iran will, I think, find this intimate view of Qashqa'i lives both accessible and informative. Should they wish to learn more about Iran and Iranian pastoralists, they will find the book's bibliographic essay extremely useful.

Although I am not certain that some of the background information, presented as a series of asides interjected into the narrative flow of the annual round, might not have been more effective if it had appeared in a single introductory section, the text provides more than enough material for the nonspecialist to understand the political, economic, and social context in which the Qashqa'i lived. The nonspecialist reader thus gets an excellent feel both for the larger Iranian society that surrounded the Qashqa'i and for Qashqa'i life itself. Beck's clearly and honestly expressed sympathies for the Qashqa'i and her sensitivity to the issue also helps the book provide insight into how the Qashqa'i—and, by extension, other similar peoples—suffer during the process of modernization. Nonspecialists will find *Nomad* an interesting and moving work and a welcome addition to the literature on the region.

Nomad also has attractions for the specialist. It is the first ethnography, the first relatively detailed view of Qashqa'i daily life to appear in print. As such, it naturally complements, expands, and gives life to previously published material on the Qashqa'i, a good deal of which has been written by Beck herself. It is my impression that in several key areas, the addition of ethnographic detail at least adds nuances to and may to some degree modify these earlier views. Thus for the specialist, too, the text is useful and will reward careful study.

Finally, in a period when ethnography itself seems under attack and concerns with authorial authority and the construction of a narrative often overwhelm readers and the information that a text might impart, Beck's rather straightforward discussion of Qashqa'i life is a pleasant affirmation of the value of describing as well as one can other people's lives.

DANIEL BRADBURD

Clarkson University
Potsdam
New York

CHEN, MARTHA ALTER. *Coping with Seasonality and Drought.* Pp. 254. Newbury Park, CA: Sage, 1991. $29.95.

The dynamics of poverty in village India can best be understood by examining how households cope with seasonality and drought. This is the convincing message of anthropologist Martha Chen's study in Maatisar, Gujarat, the rural headquarters of the Self-Employed Women's Association; the study was carried out during 1987, coincidentally the third year of a devastating drought. Drawing on data from a socioeconomic survey and intensive ethnographic participant-observation, Chen describes the village in terms of its ecological, economic, political, and human resources; the seasonal strategies for employing these resources to cope with poverty and drought; and the 1985-87 drought and responses of specific households. In the final part of the book, she suggests how to use such descriptions of household, village, and state-level responses to hunger vulnerability as a tool for further policy analysis and intervention.

Clearly organized and written, the study offers model descriptive and ana-lytical frameworks for considering livelihoods and coping strategies. These, it is hoped, will be adopted widely by researchers and policymakers. Livelihoods, as detailed here, involve women's multiple activities in multiple sectors—many of them nonmarket—and include not only occupational time allocation but time and skill in networking, negotiating resource distribution and alliances with fellow caste members and kin. To understand coping strategies, Chen tracks the varying rhythms of different occupations and the socioeconomic significance of their worst season or seasons. Importantly, the framework considers the type of strategy (adjustments in work, consumption, assets, social relationships); the level at which the strategy is negotiated (within or between household members, households, village, or government); the degree to which each strategy is reversible; and the sequencing or timing (which households adopt what strategy, when, and why).

The principal findings distinguish between coping mechanisms that affect entitlements to food (such as wage work) or entitlements to produce food (such as land sales), which translate into shorter-term or longer-term effects on hunger vulnerability. Findings also pinpoint where local versus state mechanisms for coping with scarcity prove to be sufficient or superior. Households can count on support from kin in normal times or from government in the worst of times, but they find themselves isolated in slack or bad but not terrible seasons. Not surprisingly, Chen concludes that poverty-alleviation efforts need to address seasonal stress and drought as part of long-term economic planning, not just crisis management. Dryland agricultural technologies, more permanent sources of employment, and seasonal loans and inputs in normal years might help the economy become more drought-proof.

Discouragingly, the analysis suggests that traditional support may be short-lived, as changing demographic, people-to-land, and employment scenarios alter social relations. Unfortunately, we will have to wait to learn what exactly the breaking points are and whether nonlocal organizations, governmental or nongovernmental, will be picking up the slack. In addition, we will have to wait to learn the circumstances under which schooling might be providing a way out of poverty. Even as government and nongovernment schemes together contribute to lessening hunger hardship, the population remains extremely vulnerable, albeit so far resilient, to the vagaries of the weather and the economy. This is the not very happy finding of this careful study.

ELLEN MESSER

Brown University
Providence
Rhode Island

SCHNEIDER, BEN ROSS. *Politics within the State: Elite Bureaucrats and Industrial Policy in Authoritarian Brazil*. Pp. xxii, 337. Pittsburgh, PA: University of Pittsburgh Press, 1991. $49.95.

Politics within the State argues that conventional theories of public administration and organizational behavior are not satisfactory tools for understanding the successes and failures of Brazilian developmental policy.

According to the author, Ben Ross Schneider, high levels of "bureaucratic circulation" within the Brazilian state weaken its formal organizations. Consequently, standard methodologies such as Graham Allison's bureaucratic politics approach, which presume a bedrock of Weberian organizational rationality, are inapplicable to the weak organizational environment of the Brazilian state.

The logic here is that wrangling between multiple interests shapes politics in Brazil just as it does in most states. Political wrangling is shaped, in turn, by the preference structures of state officials. In Brazil, however, high levels of personnel turnover within state institutions prevent actors from keying their preferences to specific agencies. Instead, Brazilian officials are said to be tied to their careers. Thus it is career that shapes decisions through socialization patterns and the "signals superiors send to those who want to advance." The conclusion is drawn that "career paths" better predict the pulling and hauling of Brazilian politics than does bureaucratic location.

The second section of the book attempts to illustrate the heuristic value of this approach through case studies of four major developmental projects. These projects are the administrative reorganization of state steel sector holdings, the construction of the Açominas integrated steel mill, the creation of the Carajás iron ore complex, and the development of export capacity in the bauxite and aluminum industries.

The case studies are quite interesting. They address important milestones in the Brazilian developmental experience and present a surprising amount of information in a very lucid manner. As a result, they should be quite valuable to those seeking insight into the concrete effect of political processes on economic development projects.

The greatest difficulty of the book is that, unfortunately, Schneider's larger analytic framework is fitted only loosely —very loosely—to the cause-and-effect chains used to present the case studies. As a result, the value of the theoretical contribution made by the book is difficult to evaluate. On the one hand, the discussion of the career structures as alternatives to bureaucratic politics is provocative. On the other hand, it is difficult, given the sketchy use made of his model within his own case studies, to see how career structures offer significant improvement in analytic precision or heuristic vigor over the more standard approaches.

DAVID L. NIXON

Oklahoma State University
Stillwater

WICKHAM-CROWLEY, TIMOTHY P. *Guerrillas and Revolution in Latin America: A Comparative Study of Insurgents and Regimes since 1956.* Pp. xx, 424. Princeton, NJ: Princeton University Press, 1992. $59.50.

In an exhaustive analysis of contemporary revolutionary movements, Timothy Wickham-Crowley concludes that, despite their dire conditions, peasants rarely rise up on their own to confront the existing political regime and that their support in a revolt is highly independent of the support given by other social groups to revolutionary movements. Equally important, he concludes, is the fundamental misunderstanding of most analysts in isolating the role of the U.S. government in the revolutionary process.

To reach these conclusions, Wickham-Crowley, a sociologist at Georgetown University, draws upon the memoirs of and interviews with guerrillas, census data, surveys of social conditions in the countryside, and analysis of existing conditions within the selected models. Importantly, he analyzes the strengths and weaknesses of other theories of revolution.

According to Wickham-Crowley, Latin America experienced two distinct phases of revolution, the first from 1956 until 1970 and the second since 1970. The first wave appeared in response to the success of Fidel Castro in Cuba. Having an impact upon intellectuals and existing political parties, these revolutions—in Bol-

ivia, Peru, Guatemala, Venezuela, and Colombia—were short-lived. The second wave, since 1970, was characterized by the emphasis on rural insurrection, but only in Nicaragua were the guerrillas successful. Their contemporaries—in El Salvador, Guatemala, Peru, and Colombia—failed.

Wickham-Crowley proceeds to analyze the age, gender, and philosophy of the guerrillas; the strengths and weaknesses of the political regime and the military in each country; the roles played by other social or political groups; and the impact of outside powers, mainly the United States. Because of the success attributed to Castro and the Sandinistas and due to the long-standing U.S. policy goal for Latin American political tranquility, Wickham-Crowley uses Cuba and Nicaragua as reference points for comparing other revolutionary movements.

While the volume is rich in detail and explanation of theories, the reader is left to make his or her own comparative analysis of the topics examined by Wickham-Crowley during the two revolutionary phases. Still, the volume is an important contribution to an understanding of contemporary Latin American revolutionary movements.

THOMAS M. LEONARD

University of North Florida
Jacksonville

EUROPE

CONNOR, WALTER D. *The Accidental Proletariat: Workers, Politics and Crisis in Gorbachev's Russia.* Pp. xv, 374. Princeton, NJ: Princeton University Press, 1991. $39.50.

Many years ago, in my early postgraduate days, a friend suggested that I take up horse riding. My immediate reaction

—to find not a nag but a book on equestrianism—provoked some mirth. Such, alas, was my response as a would-be academic.

Walter Connor is a fair distance from the object of his study—he is at Boston University—but in terms of academic investigation he has done a thorough job. This is one of the most serious studies of the Russian working class to be published since Solomon Schwarz's *Labor in the Soviet Union* appeared nearly forty years ago.

The work begins with a brief historical overview of Russian workers up to the outbreak of World War I. Next follows a chapter on the formation of the present working class, with its own roots and increasingly distinct from the peasantry. Chapter 3 covers worker training and the role of the education system: the marriage has never been particularly satisfactory. Connor then goes on to consider workers' income and consumption patterns, revealing, inevitably, poverty and their lag behind their American cousins. The statistics are interesting, but I suspect that the writer could have done better than use Professor Gur Ofer's old émigré studies, admirable though they were in their time.

The next major topic is the organization of labor at the workplace and attempts to improve it. A discussion of the problems of political control through the Communist Party of the Soviet Union and the trade unions follows, together with an interesting account of workers' opposition, the "free" trade unions, and a listing of over a hundred strikes after 1956. The last chapter and the epilogue examine the situation of the workers from 1989 to the spring of 1991, though Connor does attempt to update each topic as he goes through. The proletariat, incidentally, is "accidental" because, in Connor's view, it was formed beyond the direct control of the recent leaderships.

Connor is not a Marxist, but he evinces a particular concern with the concept of class and the degree to which Soviet workers form one. This focus may seem superfluous to some readers, especially as there are no broad ideological conclusions. The book seems to me, as suggested earlier, somewhat divorced from reality; there is but little in these pages about the Russian worker's main interests: theft or side earnings—given that wages are almost invariably inadequate—and, of course, alcoholism. But Connor has worked with great care and thoroughness, and his book is a worthy contribution to the subject.

MERVYN MATTHEWS

University of Surrey
Guildford
England

DE GUCHT, KAREL and STEPHAN KEUKELEIRE. *Time and Tide Wait for No Man: The Changing European Geopolitical Landscape.* Pp. x, 256. New York: Praeger, 1991. $47.95.

How to explain the events of 1989 in Europe? A generation or two will have to pass for any durable perspective to emerge. In the meantime, despite its exorbitant price, impatient scholars and general readers could do worse than to pick up this collaborative effort between De Gucht, a Belgian member of the European Parliament, and Keukeleire, a Flemish political scientist. The reader can console himself that the book is really a three-for-one bargain: a journalistic narrative of the events that led to 1989, a discussion of policy alternatives, and, finally, a metahistorical meditation.

For American scholars especially, the narrative provides a useful European perspective. De Gucht and Keukeleire base their work largely on Western European newspapers and scholarly journals in a panoply of languages from French and German to Flemish. At the same time, the reader may wonder about their choice of chronology and focus. Why does the book begin, arbitrarily it seems, in the early 1980s rather than with the post-World War II settlement? Is the focus on Germany overdone?

In their scenarios for the future and their policy recommendations, De Gucht and Keukeleire plead for European political, economic, and military union, with a Franco-German marriage at its core. For them, European confederation will not do. Without genuine union, "a new kind of non-military Yalta, with the USSR and the United States deciding the fate of Europe in discreet but intensive consultations between themselves, would come into being," they conclude. But already events in the former Soviet Union raise doubts about the reliability of their crystal ball. Nevertheless, their ominous warnings about the alternative to European union—the explosive ethnic tensions in Eastern Europe, for example—are all too accurate.

Finally, the reader may enjoy pondering the book's metahistorical musings. The volume opens with Valéry Giscard D'Estaing's preface, a self-congratulatory bit of hyperbole reminiscent of Francis Fukuyama's "triumph of the West" proclamations. The authors follow with oxymoronic statements that the events of 1989 "obeyed a completely individual, revolutionary set of rules." "History is free," they proclaim, yet, in line with their plea for action toward European union, they declare that people can and must take control of their destinies.

Time and tide quickly erode studies of this sort. Nevertheless, future historians, as they assess the meaning of 1989, will turn to such books in reconstructing the mood of the times—the time and tide as they were then.

CLAUDIO G. SEGRÈ

University of Texas
Austin

JOHNSON, PENELOPE D. *Equal in Monastic Profession: Religious Women in Medieval France.* Pp. xv, 294. Chicago: University of Chicago Press, 1991. No price.

Penelope Johnson's book is an engaging, vivid, and useful corrective to the usual monastic history, which contains the records mainly of monks. In Johnson's study, monastic women recover their rightful place as important religious people in the central Middle Ages. Using documents that might, in the hands of a lesser writer, be mute on the subject—charters, visitation registers, cartularies, records of litigation—Johnson brings to light real people and their actions.

Nuns, Johnson shows us, were not undervalued by their contemporaries. Their prayers for the dead were eagerly sought; their goodwill was solicited not only by the highborn and wealthy who might be expected to support religious foundations but by neighboring artisans and peasants as well. Nuns were not cut off by cloistration from the world in the first part of the central Middle Ages; rather, they were active in their families and the wider community around the nunnery.

Johnson examines both the wealthy and the poor female monastic houses of north central France. She confronts the popular mythology of "naughty nuns" and discovers, from the valuable data base of the visitation registers of Bishop Eudes Rigaud, that religious women, and usually just those in small poverty-stricken houses, were only a tiny bit naughtier than their male counterparts. On the whole, nuns kept their vows of chastity, poverty, and obedience, though obedience was perhaps the most difficult since the business of running a monastic house often required the breaking of cloister to venture into the outside world.

The high place that nuns enjoyed in the religious world of the central Middle Ages had deteriorated by the last part of the twelfth century according to Johnson, partly because more and more monks were being ordained as priests. The priests could celebrate masses for the dead, a growing practice avidly supported by Medieval Roman Catholics. This practice brought money into the male monasteries, but nuns, if they were required to have masses said for the dead, had to spend money to hire a priest, since they themselves were not allowed to administer sacraments. Thus there was a greater and greater gap between the income of the nuns and the priests.

All this information is presented in beautiful prose entertainingly laced with vivid language. Nuns "hornswoggle" their opponents and "blow up" at recalcitrant tenants or noblemen. They tear down walls that offend them and march with armed supporters to protect their property rights or block the construction of other religious houses that might become competitors for the resources of their neighborhoods.

The specialist reader and the general reader will both learn from and enjoy this book. I heartily recommend it.

MARY BETH EMMERICHS

University of Wisconsin
Milwaukee

RAMET, SABRINA P. *Social Currents in Eastern Europe: The Sources and Meaning of the Great Transformation.* Pp. xii, 434. Durham, NC: Duke University Press, 1991. $49.95. Paperbound, $19.95.

The speed with which the Communist regimes of Eastern Europe collapsed in 1989 surprised even the experts. Although it was no secret that there was increasing internal opposition, the extent to which the bloc was a house of cards was not recognized until the last few months before it collapsed. Gorbachev's withdrawal of support for the Communist regimes in Central and Eastern Europe and the flight of almost a quarter of a million East Germans in 1989 proved to be more than these regimes could handle. As Sabrina Ramet shows in her remarkable study of social change in Eastern Europe, though, the conditions for this collapse had been developing for many years. While describing the development of new groups and cultures in Poland, Hungary, Czechoslovakia, Yugoslavia, Bulgaria, and East Germany, she chronicles the process of increasing destabilization. The defection of intellectuals to opposition causes, the leaders' loss of credibility, and the increasing factional conflict within leadership circles were all signs of more deep-rooted shifts in the structure and mood of each society. As in the case of the Soviet Union, leaders were unwilling to allow these societies to change in response to the rising levels of urbanization, industrialization, and education. The civil revolt that occurred as a result made the ruling groups even more vulnerable to any reduction in support from the USSR and left them little alternative in the end but to allow the system to collapse.

Those seeking a guide to the social movements that emerged in the two decades preceding the collapse of 1989 will be amply rewarded by Ramet's lively, yet thoughtful and detailed, account. The growth of feminist views, the counterculture created by young people, the resurgence of interest in religion, cultural experimentation, and the emergence of people with the courage to actively engage in political opposition are all chronicled here. As more becomes known, and as the new societies begin to take on a clearer shape, it will be easier to understand the complexities of this great transformation. In the meantime, we are fortunate to have Sabrina Ramet's book to turn to.

ANTHONY JONES

Northeastern University
Boston
Massachusetts

VERHEYEN, DIRK. *The German Question: A Cultural, Historical, and Geopolitical Exploration.* Pp. xii, 228. Boulder, CO: Westview Press, 1991. Paperbound, $35.00.

SMITH, WOODRUFF D. *Politics and the Sciences of Culture in Germany, 1840-1920.* New York: Oxford University Press, 1991. $39.95.

How many books about Germany have titles or chapters referring to "the German problem"? Why is German history—probably more than other nations' histories—so often portrayed in terms of a question? Why are authors obsessed with the problematics of the German identity? These are metaquestions that today strike anyone reviewing the literature on Germany's past and present.

In the end, what is the German question? Over the past century, Germans and non-Germans have posed very different kinds of "the question." For Germans, it has often taken forms like, Where is Germany? Who is German? Why has Germany been so distrusted and mistreated by its neighbors? For non-Germans, the questions are, Is Germany unique? Why did Germany travel a special or separate path in its historical development? How could a civilized nation like Germany support Hitler, bring on World War II, carry out a holocaust against defenseless peoples? Is Germany curable (after World War II)? Is the new united Germany destined to rule Europe, with the slogan *"Deutschmark über alles"*?

Dirk Verheyen's book surveys all these questions. His focus is on a traumatized and fragmented German identity coping with unprecedented problems; his time frame is the period between 1945 and 1990; and his approach is cultural and geopolitical. He points out that each of Germany's problems had a special life of its own in the western part of the country and in the eastern part. They included a

fearfully burdensome past, an unwelcome political division of the country, an accommodation with a foreign occupation, rearmament, the tensions of the cold war between communism and democracy, and, finally, the construction of the Berlin Wall, which physically divided the already ideologically ruptured nation. All of these versions of the German problem were transformed, but not entirely resolved, by the great rush of events in 1989 and 1990.

The value of Verheyen's study lies in its exceptionally lucid review of the major events in Germany's domestic political and foreign policy history. He tells the story with cool admiration for what the Germans have achieved in the postwar era. He makes it clear, however, that the German question is still on the table. What will the reunited Germans do now with their newly acquired power? Are they to be trusted? Will they be responsible Europeans? Or will they try to turn their economic strength into blatant political domination?

Verheyen poses momentous questions about Germany's future. Woodruff Smith, a historian of ideas, examines smaller questions about Germany's past. In the background of Smith's work are two questions: Why did the concept of liberalism fail to take root in German political and intellectual life in the last half of the nineteenth century? How did this failure influence the development of academic disciplines like anthropology, human geography, cultural history, and psychology? For Smith, all of these cultural sciences experienced a severe shock after the collapse of liberalism in the 1848 revolution and in the triumph of Bismarck's nationalism in the late 1860s. His study draws explicit connections between political events and academic thinking.

Many scholars of German history are familiar with the work of Werner Sombart, Georg Simmel, Wilhelm Dilthey, and, most of all, Max Weber. Smith resurrects the life and work of many lesser-known German intellectuals whose influence was widely recognized during their lives. Among these are the student of German folk culture Wilhelm Heinrich Riehl, the cultural geographer Carl Theodor Andree, the educational psychologist Theodor Waitz, the cultural psychologist Adolf Bastian, and, perhaps the most interesting of the group, the anthropogeographer Friedrich Ratzel. What drew all of these scholars together was their dedication to the study of comparative cultural phenomena and to the conviction that the object of all such study should be the uncovering of invariant regularities or laws.

With particular skill, Smith discusses the origin and fate of two theoretical constructs set forth by these cultural scientists. One was diffusionism, a concept that involved the tracing of movements of peoples and cultural traits that helped to explain why peoples in similar environments developed quite different cultures. The other was *Lebensraum*, or living space, a slippery and explosive idea that was to be used and abused many years later by Hitler and his Nazi ideologues.

RICHARD M. HUNT

Harvard University
Cambridge
Massachusetts

UNITED STATES

AXELROD, DONALD. *Shadow Government: The Hidden World of Public Authorities and How They Control Over $1 Trillion of Your Money.* Pp. vi, 344. New York: John Wiley, 1992. $24.95.

The advertising flier for Donald Axelrod's book, *Shadow Government*, suggests that the book is essential, fascinating, and disturbing reading. These statements are correct for the first half of the book. The last half is not essential for anyone and probably would be best avoided except for the final chapter, where the author's policy proposals are so politically unreal that we understand why the shadow governments were created in the first place.

In the first half of the book, Axelrod shows how public authorities from port authorities to light districts have been used to evade state constitutions, to release enormous public debt that goes far beyond the levels that anyone who has not read this book could imagine. The 35,000 public authorities, special districts, and agencies often were created to allow public officials to avoid state debt ceilings and balanced budget provisions in their state's constitution. Axelrod does an excellent job of showing why and how public officials use these vehicles and the abuses that result.

A principal use of special authorities is to issue tax-free bonds to build schools, prisons, and hospitals or to fund any other public improvements. The authority owns the resulting facilities, and user fees pay off the bonds or the state or municipal government pays rent to the authorities. For example, the state of Texas used the Texas Building Authority to construct a state office building. The authority issued the bonds, and the state paid the rent. But the Supreme Court of Texas ruled that this did not constitute the creation of debt by the state. By using such ploys, public officials make actual public debt appear much lower than it is. Axelrod also shows who the major beneficiaries of these arrangements are—bond underwriters, raters, advisers, attorneys, and brokerage firms—and why taxpayers are the losers. All of this is interesting and useful reading. My only objection to its presentation is the complete absence of tables and graphs to help the reader understand the levels and trends of the different uses of these authorities.

The second half of the book deals with the use of public authorities in specific areas where Axelrod supports expenditures: public housing, mass transit, solid waste treatment, and environmental programs. In this section, Axelrod changes from attacking public authorities and their sponsors to attacking the federal government, specifically the Reagan administration. The federal government's cutbacks in these programs forced states to use quasi-public authorities to meet state needs. How does Axelrod suggest that we have our cake—build public housing, provide mass transit, and clean up the environment—and eat it too—have responsible government without the hypocrisy of the shadow governments he opposes? He contends that governments must convince citizens to delete constitutional provisions against public debt and to approve state bonds for unpopular programs such as prisons. From my perspective, the author has identified clearly why we have shadow governments in the first place, to have programs for which the American citizenry does not want to provide and will not provide support. Despite court orders and obvious need, governors and mayors will continue to rely on trickery and hypocrisy because honesty does not work.

R. KENNETH GODWIN

University of North Texas
Denton

BAKER, NANCY V. *Conflicting Loyalties: Law and Politics in the Attorney General's Office, 1789-1990.* Pp. viii, 248. Lawrence: University Press of Kansas, 1992. $25.00.

Most studies of the federal government mainly treat the presidency and Congress and devote insufficient attention to cabinet officers. Nancy Baker's superbly argued *Conflicting Loyalties* corrects this imbalance considerably. Drawing upon a great number of governmental documents and secondary works, Baker examines the historical evolution of the office of attorney general and shows that competition between administrative responsibilities and political obligations have determined the attorney general's actions.

The office experienced minor changes in the late eighteenth and early nineteenth centuries. Attorneys general gave legal advice to presidents and managed various litigation for the national government. The establishment of the Department of Justice in 1870 provided the law officers with a permanent bureaucracy and brought them more complex duties. Their response to this situation developed into what Baker sees as an "advocate" versus a "neutral" attorney general. The advocate type has been receptive to societal demands, sees himself or herself as a member of the presidential team, and has promoted the policy goals of the administration. Neutral officers have adopted a limited view of presidential authority, emphasize the rule of law over partisanship, and have confined policymaking to departmental responsibilities. Baker sees Robert F. Kennedy as the fullest expression of the advocate style. Kennedy used the powers of his office to remedy domestic ills and foreign policy problems, without engaging in illegal activities.

Other attorneys general were not as fortunate. "The advocate traits of partisanship, loyalty to the president, and pursuit of ends over means may take such a law officer into questionable legal and ethical terrain," Baker writes. The role of John Mitchell in the Watergate scandal well illustrates this dilemma. Mitchell secretly directed Richard Nixon's reelection campaign in 1972, authorized the break-in of the Democratic National Committee headquarters, and lied about his behavior to a federal grand jury. These abuses led to the appointment of former University of Chicago president Edward Levi, who was strongly committed to a neutral legal philosophy. Baker relates that Levi enforced standards of nonpartisanship and restored credibility to the attorney general's office.

The pendulum swung back to the advocate attorney general. In the 1980s, Republican activist Edwin Meese sometimes put political views ahead of legal principles and acted unethically and improperly. Baker wisely concludes that the ideal criterion for attorney general should require that the officer accommodate majority sentiments as represented by the president while displaying a firm support for the rule of law.

MARTIN J. SCHIESL

California State University
Los Angeles

CAYTON, ANDREW R. L. and PETER S. ONUF. *The Midwest and the Nation: Rethinking the History of an American Region.* Pp. xxii, 169. Bloomington: Indiana University Press, 1990. $25.00.

American regional history is not only alive and well; it has reached a level of sophistication and self-consciousness that would have astounded previous generations of regional scholars. During the past twenty years a new generation of interdisciplinary scholars skilled in the art and science of cultural analysis has reinvigorated a field once dominated by environmental determinism, myth and symbol, literary cataloguing, and partisan accounts of sectional politics. *The Midwest and the Nation,* an extended speculative essay on the regional culture of the nineteenth-century Midwest, is a prime example of this new regional his-

tory. Prompted by the 1987 celebration of the bicentenary of the Northwest Ordinance, this slim but significant volume provides a thought-provoking synthesis of recent scholarship on the Midwest.

The book begins and ends with a "deconstruction" of Frederick Jackson Turner's epic vision of the midwestern frontier. More participant than observer, Turner was allegedly a willing captive of the regional culture that he was trying to explain. According to Cayton and Onuf, the Turner model represented a logical extension of "the bourgeois culture" that had dominated the Midwest since the late eighteenth century; indeed, Turner and his regionalist apostles "completed the process of regional definition by interpreting its history as a middle class, capitalist success story and by asserting that the history of the Midwest was nothing less than the history of the United States." In the process of developing and refining their own collective identity, Turner and other midwesterners came to see their regional homeland as an ideal model for the nation at large. Beginning with the Northwest Ordinance of 1787, the Midwest served as a laboratory for American national culture, a place where ordinary citizens could experiment with and perfect the proper mix of capitalist enterprise, equality of opportunity, political democracy, individualism, and community welfare. This experimentation did not lead to a middle-class utopia, except in the minds of a few regional boosters, but, ironically, it did ensure the persistence and deepening of regional identity.

In six brief but carefully crafted chapters, Cayton and Onuf present a wealth of information on various aspects of midwestern history, including the legacy of the Northwest Ordinance, the ethnic and religious determinants of regionalism, and the distinctive political culture of the Midwest. All of these matters are handled sensitively and intelligently, although the authors' decision to forgo a comparative approach that integrates the history of the Midwest with that of New England, the Middle Atlantic region, the South, and the West is problematic and somewhat disappointing. Despite this self-imposed limitation, *The Midwest and the Nation* is a path-breaking book that revisits and reopens a fascinating intellectual frontier.

RAYMOND ARSENAULT

University of South Florida
Tampa

EDSALL, THOMAS BYRNES and MARY D. EDSALL. *Chain Reaction: The Impact of Race, Rights and Taxes on American Politics.* Pp. xii, 339. New York: W. W. Norton, 1991. $22.95.

I am grateful that Thomas and Mary Edsall have written this book. Its subject is winning presidential elections. It provides a useful postwar historical overview of those elections. As with many books written by journalists, it provides a provocative thesis that is wonderful lecture fodder. It also provides an irresistible portrait of our two political parties— Republicans as racists who manipulate the working and middle classes to the advantage of affluent partisan stalwarts, and Democrats as brain-dead dupes who are blinded by their liberal ideology in the face of shifting political winds.

Although the book makes a feeble attempt to incorporate taxes and rights as supplementary issues, it is, as the Edsalls state up front, "an attempt to explore race-laden and race-driven conflicts that now structure much of the nation's politics." The text certainly confirms this focus. Chapters 2 through 5 are almost singularly devoted to the history of racial or racially coded issues from 1960 through the Nixon White House. Remarkable in this stretch is that Lyndon Johnson's problem with Vietnam and Nixon's modest problem with Watergate are hardly mentioned. Vietnam is a minor reference on only four pages of the book. In contrast, Willie Horton is referenced on seven pages, with a full description of the incident filling three pages.

Perhaps most remarkable in this one-issue onslaught is chapter 6, entitled "The Tax Revolt." This 21-page chapter does not directly mention taxes until the fifteenth page, and then the issue is linked to "unrestrained partisan conflict over racial policies." The chapter ends with four pages on the Internal Revenue Service's attempt to tax conservative white Christian schools.

This very poorly edited book rests on the repetitious argument that the Republican Party, through exploitation of racial issues, has managed to capture the majority of the white vote in presidential elections since 1960. In the overview chapter, the book also attempts to make more sophisticated class-based, racial hypotheses, but, unfortunately, that effort is hopelessly confused. On a single page, the Edsalls discuss the prospective white Republican coalition as working class, lower middle class, middle class, and affluent. Because this analysis is never developed, the commonality lies in race, namely, being white.

Scholars who make a living trying to understand voting behavior will justifiably be insulted by this simplified, single-bullet explanation for national voting trends. The Edsalls' argument rests on the failure of the Democratic Party to hold white voters following the liberal racial policies of the 1960s and 1970s. The Edsalls tend to specialize in anecdotal city and county returns to support this contention; however, the national vote suggests a very different pattern. Beginning in 1952 and ending in 1988, based on postelection national survey data, the white percentage vote for the

Democratic presidential candidate was, respectively, 41, 40, 49, 65, 40, 32, 48, 37, 37, and 42. A regression line run through these results is essentially flat: loser Adlai Stevenson received a slightly smaller share of the white vote than did loser Michael Dukakis. Deviations occur in favor of Democrats in 1960 (49 percent), 1964 (65 percent), and 1976 (48 percent). The low point occurs in 1972, with McGovern (32 percent). Assuming a halo effect—perhaps 5 percent—for people falsely saying they voted for a winner, these deviations are even less extreme, with 1964 and 1972 the only elections breaking an almost flat trend line. There are obviously many explanations for these deviations other than racial issues.

The Edsalls have had the courage to emphasize a very important ingredient in our understanding of American presidential politics, an ingredient that liberal Democrats have misunderstood. The issue of race is obviously important in American politics. The problem is that a book is not an extended op-ed piece. Understanding the results of presidential elections is much more complicated than this book suggests. Some of the complications are explained in arcane but tough-minded academic journals, using complex statistical models. But the results are also explained by the tired and defeated look on LBJ's late-night face, by the mystified Nixon waving from the helicopter ramp, by the overly serious and consumed Carter, by the simple and smiling Reagan, and now, perhaps, by a frustrated electorate lashing back at the establishment so represented by George Bush. Race is only one issue in a very complicated puzzle that makes American politics absolutely intriguing.

JOHN F. WITTE

University of Wisconsin
Madison

SCHLESINGER, ARTHUR M., JR. *The Disuniting of America: Reflections on a Multicultural Society.* Pp. 160. New York: W. W. Norton, 1992. $14.95.

Arthur M. Schlesinger, Jr., is deeply troubled. American society, he believes, is disintegrating. The danger comes from the "militants of ethnicity" who denounce the ideal of the melting pot, challenge the very concept of one people, and seek "to protect, promote, and perpetuate separate ethnic and racial communities." This "cult of ethnicity," he maintains, regards America as a nation of groups, not individuals, and views ethnic ties as indelible. Further, Schlesinger asserts, "the ethnic ideologues" endorse a separatist outlook that "nourishes prejudices, magnifies differences and stirs antagonisms." The result "can only be the fragmentation, resegregation, and tribalization of American life."

The threat, Schlesinger believes, comes from many directions: from Afro-American educators who would tamper with the public school curriculum, foist "Afrocentric programs" on unsuspecting students, and transform history from an intellectual discipline to a form of "social and psychological therapy whose primary purpose is to raise the self-esteem of children from minority groups"; from Hispanic Americans who, in their zeal to establish bilingual education, fail to recognize that such a system "dooms people to second-class citizenship in American society. . . . Bilingualism shuts doors. It nourishes self-ghettoization, and ghettoization nourishes racial antagonism"; and from all who condemn the nation's "European legacy" and refuse to admit that Europe is "the *unique* source" of the ideas of "individual liberty, political democracy, the rule of law, human rights, and cultural freedom that constitute our most precious legacy." Sometimes,

Schlesinger uses other phrases—such as "the white Anglo-Saxon Protestant tradition" or "British tradition and culture"—interchangeably with the "European legacy" in order to describe the source of what is uniquely American.

A skilled polemicist, Schlesinger successfully demonstrates that many ethnic advocates have been selfish and shortsighted, if not actually unscrupulous. But has he truly located the cause of racial and ethnic discord? Ethnic advocates may indeed exploit rivalries, suspicions, and hatreds, as Schlesinger contends, but they are not primarily responsible for the existence, or even the spread, of this ill feeling. "The awful wedges between races and nationalities," which so trouble Schlesinger, derive from the failure of American society to live up to those very ideals of liberty, democracy, justice, humanity, and freedom that supposedly "constitute our most precious legacy." So long as this is the case, Schlesinger's remedy for the problem of fragmentation—restoring the "old American ideal of assimilation"—is not likely to be effective.

RICHARD POLENBERG

Cornell University
Ithaca
New York

SMITH, BRUCE L. R. *The Advisers: Scientists in the Policy Process.* Pp. xi, 238. Washington, DC: Brookings Institution, 1992. $36.95. Paperbound, $16.95.

LARSEN, OTTO N. *Milestones and Millstones: Social Science at the National Science Foundation, 1945-1991.* Pp. xvi, 285. New Brunswick, NJ: Transaction, 1992. $32.95.

Although rifts between scholars and government officials over the way federal funds are awarded for the arts, the sciences, and humanities projects are not new, recent decisions by Reagan and Bush administration officials—particularly in the National Endowments for the Arts and the Humanities, the National Science Foundation, and the National Institutes of Health—have exacerbated an already contentious situation.

Some scholars aver that government officials should confine their activities to setting broad priorities and budgetary limits for their programs, leaving decisions about the merit of grant applications to outside reviewers, the "self-proclaimed advisory experts" in the several disciplines. Conversely, government bureaucrats and lawmakers contend that, while outside advice is valuable in evaluating and prioritizing grant applications, it is the governmental agencies that must decide how the public interest is best served. In either case, largely because of budget crunches, increased concern for accountability in research grant expenditures has upset the delicate balance between the outside advisers and government officials in making grant award decisions. For this reason, the two volumes reviewed here are most timely.

In *The Advisers*, Bruce L. R. Smith attempts to synthesize and develop a semblance of order from the chaos created by the existence of over 1000 federal governmental scientific advisory committees and their 21,000-plus panel members. Sometimes referred to as the "fifth branch" of government, the manner in which these committees operate has grown increasingly complex. In this well-organized, well-documented, easily readable study, Smith reviews the experiences of advisers in five governmental agencies and the White House. Smith raises the key questions about advisory committees, explores these questions, and provides some of the answers. He shows, for better or for worse, how advisers participate in the American policy process and concludes that the existing maze of counterproductive practices are "clearly in need of reform." For me,

Smith's frankness and intellectual honesty were most refreshing.

Otto Larsen's *Milestones and Millstones* explores the advances, setbacks, successes, and failures of social science in its 45-year effort to achieve legitimacy at the National Science Foundation. Despite his well-deserved national reputation in sociology, Larsen, like Rodney Dangerfield, complains that the social sciences just "don't get no respect" either from those in the more traditional scientific disciplines or from those in government and, therefore, have not been accorded their fair share of federal research dollars.

Larsen details the history of the social sciences' quest for respectability and inclusion during the past five decades. He recounts the quixotic efforts of a handful of scholars who have kept the National Science Foundation's largess open to social science.

Larsen indicates that with each change of administrator, each reorganization, each budget allocation and appropriation battle, the social sciences were called upon to rejustify their existence and scientific importance. Larsen makes a reasoned effort to overcome the problematic image of social science by defining the activities and strategies required by social scientists to achieve greater respectability and support.

Though somewhat repetitious, Larsen's apologia provides a good prologue to understanding the past and current status of social science within the National Science Foundation family.

CHARLES NEWTON POSKANZER

State University of New York
Cortland

WILDAVSKY, AARON. *The Beleaguered Presidency*. Pp. xvi, 358. New Brunswick, NJ: Transaction, 1991. $34.95.

Evaluating a book like this one is difficult, not so much because it lacks some gems of wisdom and insight about the political process in the United States but because so much of its contents has appeared previously in published form. This raises, then, the obvious question— why are the particular topics and themes of this book assembled in the manner in which they are in this publication, and what advantages does such an assemblage have relative to earlier presentations of the author's identical writings? The book has as its title *The Beleaguered Presidency*; its respective chapters reflect Aaron Wildavsky's views about a diverse list of concerns that, in his judgment, variously confound, confuse, overburden, or otherwise have preoccupied the nation's chief executives in trying to satisfactorily discharge their duties. The range of topics dealt with here is considerable; they include, for example, a look at presidential greatness viewed historically, presidential succession, the effect of foreign affairs on domestic achievements, the merits of directly electing a president, Iran-contra, Jimmy Carter's and Ronald Reagan's approaches to administration, Watergate, and an initial assessment of George Bush's first term.

Wildavsky has written widely about the presidency, as well as other components of American government. He is an eminent scholar. One gets the feeling, however, that the present book, viewed primarily from the perspective of its contents and organization, is something of a mishmash. There is an unshakable impression that the articles have been selected for this volume in much the same way that a nursery publication compiles its lists of recommended annuals and perennials for gardeners' consideration year by year. This or that plant has these attributes, performs well or poorly when used under the following circumstances, and adds to or detracts from some larger scheme of things under the following conditions. Users of a nursery catalogue learn a lot about the features or habits of particular plants by consulting the same catalogue year by year. But if not updated each year to include new developments, the catalogue's readers could find themselves at certain disadvantages over time.

It is clear that the articles composing this book, having appeared in print previously, share the disadvantage of all such compendia; they speak to specific issues or observations set in particular moments in time. This observation does not detract from the merits of individual articles; some remain insightful and original and will continue to be definitive for a long time. But simply putting together about a dozen and a half articles that deal with presidential distress of one kind or another concerning task performance, all written by the same author, does not necessarily offer either representative or evenhanded treatment of what beleaguers the nation's chief magistrate. Nor is there a sense of continuity. There is something both arbitrary and less than fully coherent in the selection of articles included in this compendium. Their topical thrusts are selective and conventional, rather than consistently analytical and empirical.

Introductory summaries or commentaries introducing particular articles, or series of articles, would render compendia like this both more useful and more selectively accessible than the present format allows. Articles are lumped together without a sense—for the reader—of their importance, significance, timeliness, or how they are supposed to fit together coherently. These articles' views, while sometimes insightful and usually interesting, shortchange the dynamics that currently beleaguer the presidency—financial questions and domestic policymaking, for example. This omission will probably be remedied in some future compilation of parts of Wildavsky's voluminous writings. It would be helpful if the future selection of articles concerned itself with their coherence and topical relevance to a greater degree than the present compendium does.

HARRY W. REYNOLDS, JR.

University of Nebraska
Omaha

SOCIOLOGY

BERKOWITZ, EDWARD D. *America's Welfare State: From Roosevelt to Reagan.* Pp. xxii, 216. Baltimore, MD: Johns Hopkins University Press, 1991. $38.95. Paperbound, $11.95.

STOESZ, DAVID and HOWARD JACOB KARGER. *Reconstructing the American Welfare State.* Pp. xxix, 197. Lanham, MD: Rowman & Littlefield, 1991. $41.50.

Like most industrialized nations, the United States has implemented a variety of social welfare programs during this century to assure the well-being of its citizens. We have yet, however, to perfect these arrangements for caring for those in need. These two books examine the origins of the American welfare state, as well as the lingering social, economic, and political challenges it presents.

Edward Berkowitz has written a compelling social history of America's attempt to protect its citizens against the vicissitudes of old age, unemployment, and illness. He divides his discussion into three major sections: the birth and evolution of Social Security; our struggle to devise a welfare system that is compassionate yet does not lead to dependency; and our failure to deal effectively with the issue of health care. His primary focus within each of these sections is on the political machinations that led to certain policies or programs or that prevented the adoption of alternatives. He provides great detail on the personalities involved and on the motives that drove Congress, Presidents, or academic advisers. Along the way, he makes several interesting and important points.

Berkowitz draws a clear distinction between social insurance and social welfare, and he argues that it carries implications for America's enthusiasm for specific programmatic options. At the heart of this distinction is our obsession with the individual's responsibility for his or her own plight. For example, Americans tend to have fewer objections to the old-age provisions of Social Security because we tend to think of it as a forced savings plan, rather than charity. On the other hand, we are eager to believe that the single, unemployed welfare mother has made life-style choices that have led to her dependence on public support. Berkowitz makes the point that we, as a nation, have responded to these different perceptions as we have crafted our own version of a welfare state.

A second fascinating undercurrent concerns the changing positions of women and minorities in American society during this century and the implications for welfare policy. Early in the century, when state and local welfare programs were devoted overwhelmingly to the support of widowed white women and their children, moral indignation was muted due to reluctance to hold these women responsible for their husband's mortality, nor could we object to supporting them while they stayed at home with their children. As more women became gainfully employed, resentment grew over those who were on the dole but refused to work. It did not help matters that divorce, desertion, and illegitimacy soon replaced mortality as the leading cause of single parenthood. America's racial prej-

udices also affected development of welfare policies—or at least our attitudes about them—as the dependent population became less and less lily white. These combined changes involving race and gender contributed to our preoccupation with isolating the truly needy from the welfare cheats.

Berkowitz's discussion of these and other issues makes his book insightful and enjoyable.

In *Reconstructing the American Welfare State*, Stoesz and Karger chronicle the trials and tribulations of social welfare policy, especially poverty programs, during the reign of conservatism in the 1980s and early 1990s. In two especially compelling chapters—chapters 2 and 3—they describe how conservatives, fortified by the Reagan juggernaut, orchestrated an all-out attack on the American welfare state. Meanwhile, corporate moguls undertook a massive relocation of production overseas to cheaper, less regulated settings. In concert, these two forces reduced the capacity of American society to care for the economically disadvantaged while, at the same time, increasing their numbers.

This book is not an ideological diatribe, however. Stoesz and Karger also chastise American liberals for their knee-jerk defense of New Deal-style social programs and for their reluctance to design a new welfare paradigm that is more compatible with the new economic environment of the late twentieth century and with the unique character of American culture.

According to Stoesz and Karger, the recent "excesses" of the neoconservatives and the ineffectiveness of the liberals have created a crisis in the American welfare state. Stepping into the void, they propose a plan to restructure the American welfare system. Their proposal is guided by five main principles, represented by emphasis on productivity, the family, social cohesion, the community, and social choice. It also consists of three primary efforts: a Family Conservation Program, a Community Revitalization Initiative, and a National Service Program. Although necessarily brief, their proposal is thorough, comprehensive, and integrated. While not everyone will agree with the entire package, Stoesz and Karger must be given credit for having laid the foundation for a much needed reexamination of the American welfare state. Now, if only our political leaders would forsake 15-second sound bites and pathetic rhetoric—for example, "a thousand points of light"—in favor of thoughtful consideration of excellent scholarship like that offered by Berkowitz, Stoesz, and Karger.

STEWART TOLNAY

State University of New York
Albany

BONNER, THOMAS NEVILLE. *To the Ends of the Earth: Women's Search for Education in Medicine.* Pp. xiv, 232. Cambridge, MA: Harvard University Press, 1992. $34.95.

In *To the Ends of the Earth: Women's Search for Education in Medicine,* Thomas Bonner documents the long, difficult struggle of women in the United States, Canada, and Europe to obtain entrance to first-class medical schools and to win the right, upon graduation, to practice their calling. Bonner's study, using a comparative approach, begins in the 1850s and closes with a brief section extending into the present.

Bonner gives vivid accounts of the opposition that women encountered, particularly in Britain and the United States, due to Victorian prudery; he documents the capriciousness and antagonism of pre-Communist nineteenth and early twentieth century czarist Russia against

women determined to pursue quality medical education (on the grounds that all these women, and not just some, were political activists); above all, he notes the extremely negative view of Austrian and German universities on the subject of medical education for women. The movement for separate but equal education—that was usually not equal—is covered, with due credit to the tremendous effort and achievement involved, especially in the United States and Russia. However, it was the University of Zurich, other Swiss universities, and the University of Paris that led in providing quality coeducation for women. Bonner quotes Edmund Rose, a Zurich faculty member at the examination of the Russian émigré Nadezhda Suslova to defend her thesis: "Soon we will have the practical emancipation of women in every country and with it the right to work." Suslova thus became, in 1867, the first woman to receive a medical degree from a leading coeducational university. Rose's assertion of "soon" was perhaps a bit optimistic in view of the many bitter controversies that were to take place all over the Western world. The acrimony over the admission of women to the medical school of the University of Edinburgh, and the long struggle, from 1867 to 1945, over the right to full admission to the Harvard Medical School, and the fact that, until 1900, no woman fully trained in medicine was to be found in Germany are among the many indications of the difficulties women seeking medical training were obliged to overcome.

Supplementing his well-documented study with a series of brilliant capsule biographies, often accompanied by excellent photographic portraits, Bonner illustrates that women in the Western world have indeed earned the right to enter the medical profession on the basis of merit. Students of higher education, feminists, and those interested in the prominent pioneers in the medical history of the period covered will find this volume worthwhile and highly readable.

DOROTHY RUDY

Caldwell College
New Jersey

DAYAN, DANIEL and ELIHU KATZ. *Media Events: The Live Broadcasting of History.* Pp. xi, 306. Cambridge, MA: Harvard University Press, 1992. $29.95.

A year of momentous, swift, unpredictable, and puzzling changes, all played out on live television, began with the war in the Persian Gulf. Six months later in Moscow, a coup collapsed in a blizzard of defiant imagery. Sandwiched between and around these events were a Senate confirmation hearing in Washington, a rape trial in Miami, a videotaped beating of a black man by Los Angeles police and their acquittal leading to a virtual insurrection. It was the year that tipped the geopolitical scales, shook the gender-based power structure, and exposed the anger and brutalization of urban life.

I wondered what made these media events different from the usual gradual shifting of historical ground. Why did they unloose landslides that swept over familiar territory and changed the historical landscape? The title of this book promised some answers.

The focus of the book is more narrowly defined, but its aim is even broader than the title suggests. Dayan and Katz studied mostly festive ceremonial events, like state funerals, summitry, the Olympics, and papal visits, that enthrall millions. They argue that such media events deserve a genre and theory of their own, and the authors provide both with impressive scholarship and nimble, inventive terminology.

The last chapter of the book pulls all the threads together to describe the short-circuiting of traditional social and historical processes that live mass-mediated communication represents. The term Dayan and Katz invent for this process is "disintermediation," whose virtue seems to be to allow for its reversal, or "reintermediation," which eventually transforms an entire structure of social relations.

This occurs both inside the event (among its organizers and participants) and outside the event (among publics and institutions). Media events test the mettle of their creators and rearrange the status and powers of their distant but extemporaneous observers. They enhance the illusion of being there and displace traditional intermediaries. They can integrate remote experiences into familiar feelings and open up the political process to broader participation, or they can provide opportunities for manipulation and hegemony. Dayan and Katz, ever the optimists, note the threat but elaborate the promise.

The elaboration takes the reader through a discussion of television genres and a typology of media events and their staging, functions, and possible dysfunctions. The rich historical, literary, and sociological context of references, allusions, definitions, examples, and many but equally instructive exceptions, enlivens and at times overcomplicates the model. *Media Events* is the first fullfledged scholarly treatment of a phenomenon that merits continuing attention and study.

GEORGE GERBNER

University of Pennsylvania
Philadelphia

LEWIS, JANE. *Women and Social Action in Victorian and Edwardian England.* Pp. viii, 338. Stanford, CA: Stanford University Press, 1991. $39.50.

SIMON, RITA J. and GLORIA DANZI-GER. *Women's Movements in America: Their Successes, Disappointments, and Aspirations.* Pp. 184. New York: Praeger, 1991. Paperbound, $39.95.

In *Women and Social Action in Victorian and Edwardian England*, Jane Lewis offers an analysis of the work of five prominent social reformers: Octavia Hill, Beatrice Webb, Helen Bosanquet, Mary Ward, and Violet Markham. All but Webb contributed to a shift from the "lady bountiful" concept of charity to the idea that true service to the poor meant eschewing alms giving in favor of helping the individual develop "character." Socialist Beatrice Webb, maverick among this group, sought structural rather than personal solutions to social ills. Lewis demonstrates that the women were not simply following the dictates of the then popular social Darwinism but derived their differing beliefs from various sources.

A parallel theme is the struggle these women faced in their own lives as they strove to integrate their sense of middle-class duty to serve with the dictates of gender role decorum and the need for self-expression. Most experienced discomfort with speaking in public, and all were wary of stretching the limits of allowable behavior for women. All except Helen Bosanquet opposed women's suffrage at first, and Mary Ward did to the end. The subtleties of the suffrage arguments dispel stereotypes of both the suffragist and anti-suffrage movements. Much of the debate centered on whether or not suffrage would distort gender roles and responsibility, many suffragists arguing that women might better fulfill their feminine service role if they had the vote.

In *Women's Movements in America*, Simon and Danziger discuss similar themes as they trace another sort of social action: women's activities in pursuit of women's rights. Notions of appropriate gender roles underpin all women's rights issues, from equal pay to marriage laws

to abortion. Similarly, unexamined assumptions of class, characteristic of the English social reformers, have permeated the thinking of most U.S. feminists to the present time.

Today, in America, gender role expectations continue to influence social reform debates in ways reminiscent of nineteenth-century England. Citing national polls, Simon and Danziger contend that Americans espouse equality for women while simultaneously maintaining the gender role primacy of a husband's job and a wife's responsibility for child care. They argue that feminists have been most successful when these conservative values have been integrated with feminist goals. Challenges to the social structure, in their view, simply serve to alienate the mass of people. Perhaps what should surprise us is the fact that so much has changed in a century. These books together remind us that a great deal remains the same.

DOROTHY C. MILLER

Wichita State University
Kansas

LUBIN, CAROL RIEGELMAN and ANNE WINSLOW. *Social Justice for Women: The International Labor Organization and Women.* Pp. xvii, 328. Durham, NC: Duke University Press, 1991. $45.00.

The history of women workers, their unions, and the work of governmental agencies on their behalf has been well documented by a wide range of monographs and studies over the last two decades. One aspect of this history, however, had been ignored until the publication of *Social Justice for Women: The International Labor Organization and Women,* by Carol Riegelman Lubin and Anne Winslow. The International Labor Organization (ILO) was founded in 1919 in the wave of internationalism that followed World War I. From its inception, the ILO had specifically targeted special groups of workers, children, women, and young people for protection. Its Labor Charter affirms the principle that men and women should receive equal remuneration for work of equal value.

By evaluating this organization over a seventy-year span, this book examines women's issues from an international perspective and what one organization did to contribute to women's resolve. The major resolutions endorsed by the ILO for women have paralleled larger societal trends; they began with the protection of women from exploitation, shifted later to the emphases on equal remuneration and abolition of discrimination in the range of jobs open to women and, more recently, to women as equal partners in the whole society. Lubin and Winslow have offered us much in the way of statistical data, which is important to support their findings and to have this volume stand as an important reference work. Some readers, however, because of this detail may have preferred a direct storytelling approach.

Paradoxically, the book portrays the ILO as an international advisory body supporting the equality of women, on the one hand, and actual discrimination within the dynamics of the organization itself, on the other. While women played a part in each and every conference year of the organization's existence, only rarely were they represented in top positions. This limited access was not only in key delegate positions but also in staff positions. Only a few women have ever achieved a policymaking status.

When it comes to the inherent difficulties in the struggle for women's rights, the book concludes philosophically. It acknowledges that, within the confines of society that limit all organizations, the ILO has behaved rationally, inasmuch as "the avalanche moves, even though slowly, eroding the habits of centuries,

toward the achievement of the 'impossible dream.' "

The significance of this book lies in the importance of the role that the ILO has played and can play within the larger concerns of women workers and the international labor movement. Though it has lacked power, the ILO has pointed out the problems that women workers have faced in the workplace. The lack of a real international labor movement is a frustrating context within which this volume must be read. Nonetheless, the ILO has held out promise to all workers and, as demonstrated by this book, has acknowledged the problems of working women in a very special way.

M. CATHERINE LUNDY

Michigan State University
East Lansing

POSNER, RICHARD A. *Sex and Reason.* Pp. vii, 458. Cambridge, MA: Harvard University Press, 1992. $29.95.

The nexus between Judge Posner's stated aims and ultimate achievements in this thoughtful, carefully footnoted, and provocative volume impresses often as solid, sometimes as rocky, and, at one juncture at least, as ruptured.

Posner is strikingly successful in implementing his goal "to bring to the attention of the legal profession the rich multidisciplinary literature on sexuality —and to shame [his] colleagues in the profession for ignoring it." His prescriptiveness is particularly admirable when he torments and counsels fellow members of the judiciary he deems responsible for the fact that "the dominant judicial, and I would say legal, attitude toward the study of sex is that 'I know what I like' and therefore research is superfluous." Posner invokes a plethora of pertinent examples from economics, medicine, biology, and the social sciences that can inform, if not direct, judicial decision making about many sexual issues.

On the other hand, fulfillment of his aims falters and wilts insofar as he claims "to demonstrate the feasibility and fruitfulness of an economic approach to the subject" and to explain and predict the variance in sexual behavior, attitudes, customs and laws across different eras, cultures, social classes, races, and the sexes themselves through his specific economic theory of sexuality.

That Posner has neither formulated nor accepted pluralistic approaches to relationships between law, economics, and public policy does not legitimate criticism here on that account. He is entitled to be as monistic or didactic as he chooses in expounding and applying his own theory. The problem for me is that he veers at points from demonstrative reliance upon economic or social science theory and seems to succumb to social bias as a rationale for his position.

Most apparent and troubling in this respect is his acceptance as a "good argument" for exclusion of homosexuals from military service of the contention that "the morale of heterosexuals, and hence the effectiveness of the military services, would suffer if homosexuals were allowed to serve." To allow allusions to negative effects on the morale of opponents to triumph over empirical proof of the presence and professionalism of homosexuals in the United States' and other nations' armed forces becomes all the more astonishing and all the less scientific when the author attempts to support his stance by insisting that "the question of morale is separable from the question of the merits of the exclusion." Posner would, in effect, defer to biases of "hecklers' veto" rather than to objective evidence of performance in evaluating such personnel practices.

In *Palmore* v. *Sidoti* in 1984, the justices of the Supreme Court unanimously repudiated yielding to private biases in applying the Fourteenth Amendment. After the Florida courts had ruled that a white child, if raised by an interracial couple, would suffer social stigmatization that warranted transferring custody of the child from the mother to the natural father, the Supreme Court reversed. Chief Justice Burger posed and answered the question of "whether the reality of private biases and the possible injury they might inflict are permissible considerations" in resolving the case. "We have little difficulty concluding that they are not," the Court ruled. "The Constitution cannot control such prejudices but neither can it tolerate them. Private biases may be outside the reach of the law, but the law cannot, directly or indirectly, give them effect."

Pondering and probing this constitutional creed would have been more consonant with a creative researcher's mission than resorting to shaky data and tales to trump the merits on a vital issue of public policy.

VICTOR G. ROSENBLUM

Northwestern University
Chicago
Illinois

WILSFORD, DAVID. *Doctors and the State: The Politics of Health Care in France and the United States*. Pp. xv, 355. Durham, NC: Duke University Press, 1991. $49.95. Paperbound, $19.95.

In this 10-chapter book, David Wilsford sets out to systematically compare why organized medicine has had impacts on health care policy in France different from those in the United States. This book has all the appearances of a revised dissertation, including careful attention to definitions, extensive but sometimes dated evidence and statistical information, and a thoughtful and carefully circumscribed presentation of the qualitative methodology employed. While I enjoyed the book and learned a lot about French medical and political organization from it, I felt that like many revised dissertations its strength and weakness might be one and the same—extensive detail—and depend on the reader's perspective as to whether it is seen as strong evidence to support hypotheses or excessive evidence.

Wilsford's analysis focuses on one dependent variable to be explained and two independent variables that are used as the sources of variation of the dependent variable. The dependent variable is the relative influence of organized medicine in shaping the medical policy in a society. This variable ranges from a strong influence of the medical profession in the United States to a weak influence in France. The indicators of influence on policy center around three areas: the degree of independence physicians have in setting fees, the degree of independence physicians have in making clinical decisions, and the input physicians have in formal policymaking.

The two independent variables that are described, analyzed, and compared at length are (1) the powerfulness of state structures conceptualized as falling along a continuum from a weak political state in the United States to a strong political state in France, and (2) the degree of organization of the medical profession conceptualized as falling along a continuum from a "cohesive" organized medical profession in the United States to a "fragmented" medical community in France. Thus, in the United States, it is concluded that the medical profession has had substantially more impact on health care policymaking because it is better organized and faces a weak and indecisive state structure in comparison to the situation in France. However, in the United States, because so much of

health care financing is in the private sector, that sector is beginning to emerge as a third force to limit organized medicine's power in shaping health care policy.

In addition to the excellent detailed analysis of the hypotheses explored in this book, which are well summarized in the concluding chapter, one finds out a lot about the great differences between French and American political and medical cultures and the recent historical evolution of health care policy in both countries. This comparative cross-cultural analysis provides insight into alternative ways of dealing with health care policy.

DUANE STROMAN

Juniata College
Huntingdon
Pennsylvania

ZWEIGENHAFT, RICHARD L. and G. WILLIAM DOMHOFF. *Blacks in the White Establishment? A Study of Race and Class in America.* Pp. ix, 198. New Haven, CT: Yale University Press, 1991. $27.50.

Blacks in the White Establishment? traces the impressive accomplishments of and persistent obstacles faced by 38 students who participated in the A Better Chance Program (ABC), initiated in 1963 by 16 of the toniest prep schools in the United States, with support from several foundations. During the next twenty years, 5000 students completed the program. After that, funding to participating schools ended, and an important avenue of mobility for lower-class blacks was closed.

In often poignant and thoroughly engrossing interviews, former students provide fascinating accounts of their induction into the rarefied atmosphere of elite prep boarding schools. For example, one student had to rely on local social workers to give him money to buy the requisite sports jackets for Groton.

Richard Zweigenhaft and William Domhoff achieve a nice balance between interviews, larger studies of ABC graduates, and general survey data to make three major points. First, despite homesickness, culture shock, isolation, and occasional familial resistance, a majority of the students compiled noteworthy academic records in a very rigorous environment. Second, the prep school boost made a big difference in college careers. The colleges most often attended by ABC graduates—through 1981—included all eight Ivy League schools. Finally, and most important, despite these educational and ensuing class advantages, graduates of the program continue to face institutionalized racism and, of course, live in a society pervasively organized along racial lines.

Zweigenhaft and Domhoff use their findings to inform their discussion of the significance of race and class in the United States. They argue that the absence of opportunity and persistent racism have created an oppositional identity that shuns engagement with racist institutions, including schools—hence the prohibitions against acting white that are often leveled against young, academically talented African Americans. The authors argue that rather than viewing the oppositional culture as an obstacle to black advancement, a way should be found to define education so that it is less identified with white culture. This is a provocative suggestion that deserved more discussion.

In the debate on the relative significance of race and class, Zweigenhaft and Domhoff make a compelling case for the continuing centrality of race, and they skillfully combine psychological and structural explanations to explain the continuing dynamics of racism. Their book is a very important contribution and should be widely read, especially by those who espouse or are being swayed by culture-of-poverty explanations for declines in life chances for African Americans.

CATHERINE V. SCOTT

Agnes Scott College
Decatur
Georgia

ECONOMICS

ARONSON, ROBERT L. *Self Employment: A Labor Market Perspective*. Pp. xiii, 156. Ithaca, NY: ILR Press, 1991. $26.00. Paperbound, $10.95.

HASHIMOTO, MASANORI. *The Japanese Labor Market in a Comparative Labor Market Perspective with the United States*. Pp. x, 150. Kalamazoo, MI: W. E. Upjohn Institute for Employment Research, 1990. $22.95. Paperbound, $13.95.

Self Employment is, surprisingly, the first book in more than three decades to examine entrepreneurs. Although politicians and business figures wax interminably about the distinct contribution of entrepreneurship to America's economic success, we know remarkably little about self-employment. As the only available compendium, Aronson's useful book merits attention by interested readers despite its poor organization, repetitiveness, and sloppy reasoning on several key issues.

One important question is why self-employment, rather than continue to wither away as it did until about 1970, experienced a mild resurgence. Aronson does not supply an answer, but he convincingly rules out the effect of growing service sector employment, which long predated the rise in self-employment, and franchising. He too readily dismisses, however, the possible impact of the rising share of professional workers in the labor force. Overall growth in the professions far outweighs the small decline in self-employment among some professions.

The growth of self-employment is apparently puzzling because, since the early 1980s, entrepreneurs have reported lower earnings than wage and salaried workers. Aronson again supplies no answer, but he correctly emphasizes the lamentably poor quality of earnings data on the self-employed. But he is asking the wrong question. The issue is how much the self-employed would have earned as employees, not whether the average self-employed person earns more or less than the average employee.

The Japanese Labor Market provides a brief and insightful view of the evolution of labor market developments thought to contribute to Japan's economic success. Radical changes in Japanese work patterns during the twentieth century indicate that fixed cultural traits cannot explain current practices. For example, until at least the end of World War II, high job-turnover rates and frequent strikes characterized the Japanese work force.

As for the other industrialized powers, the explanations behind Japan's success must be sought in the responses to specific historical and economic developments, not in supposedly unchanging cultural patterns. But Hashimoto presents a much weaker case for the preeminent importance of low transaction costs in facilitating harmony in the Japanese labor market. By his own admission, there are no direct data to measure transaction costs. Moreover, he further weakens his argument by defining transaction costs in a manner that is overbroad and circular. Hashimoto also fails to acknowledge some serious deficiencies in his own

evidence. For example, he emphasizes the importance of joint union-management consultation, but two-fifths of unions do not engage in it.

FRANK GALLO

George Washington University
Washington, D.C.

AYRES, IAN and JOHN BRAITHWAITE. *Responsive Regulation: Transcending the Deregulation Debate.* Pp. viii, 205. New York: Oxford University Press, 1992. $39.95.

The first important key to the nature of the materials composing this book is found in the publisher's assignment of category: Oxford Socio-Legal Studies. Economics and political science also play important, and probably equal, roles in the authors' intentions and selection of source materials. Hence the book is quite wide in scope of concern, and since it is well researched and written, it merits the attention of persons curious about regulation from many perspectives. An obvious disclaimer might be offered, however: specialists such as economists may not find theory of the type and abstruseness they customarily seek.

A presentation of the table of contents possibly is the briefest statement of what to expect. The six chapter titles are as follows: "The Politics of an Idea"; "The Benign Big Gun"; "Tripartism"; "Enforced Self-Regulation"; "Partial-Industry Intervention"; and "Delegation and Participation in a Responsive Regulatory Order." There follow notes, references, and an index. "The benign big gun" means something like "walk softly but carry a big stick" for most of us.

Ayres and Braithwaite no doubt are correct in their preconception that regulation of business cannot reasonably be left to laissez-faire market forces, and hence regulation long will continue on the policy agenda for capitalist countries. The book considers regulation in broad areas such as occupational health and safety, the environment, nursing homes, financial institutions, securities and futures markets, and consumer product safety. They argue for the concept of tripartite regulation: regulation by government, self-regulation by industry, plus creation and empowerment of public interest groups. We find it much more believable that modern societies tend to run amok, critically those of capitalist persuasion such as our own, than that regulation—desperately needed—will be satisfactory.

FLOYD B. McFARLAND

Oregon State University
Corvallis

STOPFORD, JOHN M. and SUSAN STRANGE with JOHN S. HENLEY. *Rival States, Rival Firms: Competition for World Market Shares.* Pp. xiii, 321. New York: Cambridge University Press, 1991. No price.

The reader of this book is exposed to a wide-screen panorama of resources, instruments, relationships, and processes that in this half-century have produced remarkable but uneven world economic development.

There is a suggestion that the book relies on the authors' case studies of Kenya, Brazil, and Malaysia, but in fact it calls up a global experience. The principal authors are teachers at the London Business School and contemporaneously at the London School of Economics and Political Science.

The authors' main theme is that development is a product of three sets of relationships: between governments and firms; between governments; and between individual firms. In the most successful development, these are partners respecting the others' interests, and they pursue coordinated strategies to achieve goals.

There are many variations of successful strategies. Indeed, development is eclectic, especially in developing countries; what works in one time or place may fail in another. Effective strategies are the product of imagination informed by empirical studies, and they usually violate the strictures of the most celebrated economic and political theories. To be more specific, the authors think that theoretical constructs, including those based on comparative advantage and choice theory, are not helpful in development. The assumption of public choice theory,

that states are rational actors and interact rationally with each other, has led many scholars in this field to follow the lead of the economists—who in turn were following the mathematicians—to use game theory and make limiting assumptions about the nature and duration of the game. Logical coherence has been gained at the expense of empirical relevance (p. 134).

Conventional frameworks of analysis fail, say the authors, because they do not take into account the broad structural changes in the global economy and also because they ignore the domestic social and political forces with which governments must deal.

Economic development is increasingly a global rather than a country phenomenon. New production technology often encourages large-scale enterprise that is attained through international expansion, and firms find that a multinational presence spreads risk and also allows them more control over their environment. Governments that desire economic development tend to choose a cooperative relationship with the larger, viable multinational firms, usually serving them best not by offering protected markets but by creating an environment of political stability and a developmental infrastructure that includes worker training. Governments, rather than relying on trade mechanisms to achieve a favorable balance of trade, may seek a stage beyond trade when international firms decide to invest in local production in order to serve both domestic and foreign markets. Indeed, the global economy is being achieved not primarily by expanded trade but by multinational investment.

This is not to say that state-controlled development never succeeds. Korea and other rapidly growing countries proved that intervention can work well during the early developmental stages. The authors maintain that, in general, governments lack the competence and political will to execute developmental programs, and, in any case, policies organized by national boundaries tend to cramp development.

In the last analysis, development is a product of partnership achieved by extensive bargaining between governments and firms and even between the firms. "The importance of the new 'triangular' diplomacy has been revealed in almost every project."

This book is not an easy read, but the perspectives to be gained from it are worth the effort.

DON F. HADWIGER

Iowa State University
Ames

OTHER BOOKS

ABRAHAM, HENRY J. *Justices and Presidents: A Political History of Appointments to the Supreme Court.* 3d ed. Pp. xiv, 467. New York: Oxford University Press, 1992. $35.00.

ALBA, RICHARD D. *Ethnic Identity: The Transformation of White America.* Pp. xvi, 374. New Haven, CT: Yale University Press, 1992. $42.50. Paperbound, $17.00.

ALSOP, JOSEPH W. *"I've Seen the Best of It."* Pp. 495. New York: Norton, 1992. $29.95.

ANDELSON, R. V. *Commons without Tragedy: Protecting the Environment from Overpopulation—a New Approach.* Pp. ix, 198. Savage, MD: Rowman & Littlefield, 1991. $34.50.

ARGERSINGER, PETER H. *Structure, Process, and Party: Essays in American Political History.* Pp. xviii, 219. Armonk, NY: M. E. Sharpe, 1992. $39.95.

BAK, JANOS M., ed. *Liberty and Socialism: Writings of Libertarian Socialists in Hungary 1884-1919.* Pp. xxxv, 276. Savage, MD: Rowman & Littlefield, 1991. $46.75.

BARRETT, MICHELE. *The Politics of Truth: From Marx to Foucault.* Pp. vii, 194. Stanford, CA: Stanford University Press, 1992. $35.00. Paperbound, $10.95.

BATT, JUDY. *East Central Europe from Reform to Transformation.* Pp. 129. New York: Council on Foreign Relations Press, 1991. Paperbound, $14.95.

BERBEROGLU, BERCH. *The Legacy of Empire: Economic Decline and Class Polarization in the United States.* Pp. xiii, 130. New York: Praeger, 1992. $39.95.

BJORNBERG, ULLA, ed. *European Parents in the 1990s: Contradictions and Comparisons.* Pp. x, 325. New Brunswick, NJ: Transaction, 1992. $34.95.

BRABANT, MARGARET, ed. *Politics, Gender, and Genre: The Political Thought of Christine De Pizan.* Pp. vi, 240. Boulder, CO: Westview Press, 1992. $39.95.

BROWN, LAWRENCE D., ed. *Health Policy and the Disadvantaged.* Pp. 212. Durham, NC: Duke University Press, 1991. $29.95. Paperbound, $12.95.

BYRNE, JANE. *My Chicago.* Pp. 384. New York: Norton, 1992. $22.95.

CALDWELL, DAN. *The Dynamics of Domestic Politics and Arms Control: The SALT II Treaty Ratification Debate.* Pp. xi, 234. Columbia: University of South Carolina Press, 1991. $32.95.

CHALMERS, DOUGLAS A. et al., eds. *The Right and Democracy in Latin America.* Pp. vii, 321. New York: Praeger, 1992. $45.00.

CHAMBERS, JOHN WHITECLAY, II. ed. *The Eagle and the Dove: The American Peace Movement and United States Foreign Policy 1900-1922.* 2d ed. Pp. lxxxvii, 237. Syracuse, NY: Syracuse University Press, 1991. $29.95. Paperbound, $15.95.

CIMBALA, STEPHEN J. and SIDNEY R. WALDMAN, eds. *Controlling and Ending Conflict: Issues before and after the Cold War.* Pp. viii, 285. Westport, CT: Greenwood Press, 1991. $49.95.

CLAASSEN, EMIL-MARIA, ed. *Exchange Rate Policies in Developing and Post-Socialist Countries.* Pp. xix, 443. San Francisco: ICS Press, 1992. Paperbound, $14.95.

COHEN, ROBIN and HARRY GOULBOURNE, eds. *Democracy and Socialism in Africa.* Pp. xv, 272. Boulder, CO: Westview Press, 1991. $39.50.

COHEN, STEVEN M. *Two Worlds of Judaism: The Israeli and American Experiences.* Pp. xi, 202. New Haven, CT: Yale University Press, 1992. $27.50. Paperbound, $11.00.

COOK, THOMAS D. et al. *Meta-Analysis for Explanation: A Casebook.* Pp. xiv, 378. New York: Russell Sage Foundation, 1992. $42.50.

DEMOTT, BENJAMIN. *The Imperial Middle: Why Americans Can't Think Straight about Class.* Pp. 264. New Haven, CT: Yale University Press, 1992. Paperbound, $14.00.

DIANI, MARIO and RON EYERMAN, eds. *Studying Collective Action.* Pp. 263. Newbury Park, CA: Sage, 1992. No price.

DILLON, MERTON L. *Slavery Attacked: Southern Slaves and Their Allies, 1619-1865.* Pp. 300. Baton Rouge: Louisiana State University Press, 1990. $39.95. Paperbound, $16.95.

DISTEFANO, CHRISTINE. *Configurations of Masculinity: A Feminist Perspective on Modern Political Theory.* Pp. xvii, 206. Ithaca, NY: Cornell University Press, 1991. Paperbound, No price.

DREIFORT, JOHN E. *Myopic Grandeur: The Ambivalence of French Foreign Policy toward the Far East, 1919-1945.* Pp. xiv, 334. Kent, OH: Kent State University Press, 1992. $35.00.

EARLE, CARVILLE. *Geographical Inquiry and American Historical Problems.* Pp. xii, 555. Stanford, CA: Stanford University Press, 1992. $49.50.

ECKARDT, A. ROY. *Sitting in the Earth and Laughing: A Handbook of Humor.* Pp. xviii, 222. New Brunswick, NJ: Transaction, 1992. $29.95.

EMERSON, THOMAS I. *Young Lawyer for the New Deal: An Insider's Memoir of the Roosevelt Years.* Pp. xxi, 337. Savage, MD: Rowman & Littlefield, 1991. $46.50.

FEIN, HELEN, ed. *Genocide Watch.* Pp. x, 204. New Haven, CT: Yale University Press, 1992. $25.00.

FESTE, KAREN A. *Plans for Peace: Negotiation and the Arab-Israeli Conflict.* Pp. xxix, 179. New York: Praeger, 1991. $47.95. Paperbound, $15.95.

FINKELMAN, PAUL, ed. *African Americans and the Legal Profession in Historical Perspective.* Vol. 10. Pp. xi, 529. New York: Garland, 1992. $87.00.

FINKELMAN, PAUL, ed. *African Americans and the Right to Vote.* Vol. 6. Pp. 579. New York: Garland, 1992. $94.00.

GARNHAM, NICHOLAS. *Capitalism and Communication: Global Culture and the Economics of Information.* Pp. 216. Newbury Park, CA: Sage, 1990. $45.00. Paperbound, $18.95.

GITZ, BRADLEY R. *Armed Forces and Political Power in Eastern Europe: The Soviet/Communist Control System.* Pp. x, 193. Westport, CT: Greenwood Press, 1992. $45.00.

GLUCK, CAROL and STEPHEN R. GRAUBARD, eds. *Showa: The Japan of Hirohito.* Pp. lxii, 315. New York: Norton, 1992. $25.00.

GRAHAM, LAWRENCE S. *The State and Policy Outcomes in Latin America.* Pp. xiii, 206. New York: Praeger, 1990. $39.95.

GRANOVETTER, MARK and RICHARD SWEDBERG, eds. *The Sociology of Economic Life.* Pp. vi, 399. Boulder, CO: Westview Press, 1992. $65.00.

GROSS, JO-ANN, ed. *Muslims in Central Asia: Expressions of Identity and Change.* Pp. xiv, 224. Durham, NC: Duke University Press, 1992. Paperbound, $18.95.

GROSSMAN, GENE M. and ELHANAN HELPMAN. *Innovation and Growth in the Global Economy.* Pp. xiv, 359. Cambridge: MIT Press, 1991. $29.95.

GUTIERREZ, RAMON A. *When Jesus Came, the Corn Mothers Went Away: Marriage, Sexuality, and Power in New Mexico, 1500-1846.* Pp. xxxi, 424. Stanford, CA: Stanford University Press, 1991. $49.50. Paperbound, $16.95.

HAMILTON, KENNETH MARVIN. *Black Towns and Profit: Promotion and Development in the Trans-Appalachian West, 1877-1915.* Pp. xii, 185. Chicago: University of Illinois Press, 1991. No price.

HAMPSON, FEN OSLER et al., eds. *The Allies and Arms Control*. Pp. x, 375. Baltimore, MD: Johns Hopkins University Press, 1992. $55.00.

HESKIN, ALLAN DAVID. *The Struggle for Community*. Pp. vi, 195. Boulder, CO: Westview Press, 1991. Paperbound, $24.85.

HOLLAND, JOHN H. *Adaptation in Natural and Artificial Systems*. Pp. xiv, 211. Cambridge: MIT Press, 1992. $30.00. Paperbound, $14.95.

HOWARD, LAWRENCE, ed. *Terrorism: Roots, Impact, Responses*. Pp. x, 193. New York: Praeger, 1992. $42.95.

HOWARD, M. C. and J. E. KING. *A History of Marxian Economics*. Vol. 2, *1929-1990*. Pp. xv, 420. Princeton, NJ: Princeton University Press, 1992. $60.00. Paperbound, $19.95.

HREBENAR, RONALD J. *The Japanese Party System*. Pp. xvi, 319. Boulder, CO: Westview Press, 1992. $59.00.

HSIEH, CHING-YAO and MENG-HUA YE. *Economics, Philosophy, and Physics*. Pp. xxxvii, 169. Armonk, NY: M. E. Sharpe, 1992. $39.95. Paperbound, $16.95.

IBE, HIDEO. *Japan Thrice-Opened: An Analysis of Relations between Japan and the United States*. Pp. 294. New York: Praeger, 1992. $49.95.

IONESCU, GHITA. *Leadership in an Interdependent World: The Statesmanship of Adenauer, De Gaulle, Thatcher, Reagan and Gorbachev*. Pp. xi, 336. Boulder, CO: Westview Press, 1991. $48.00. Paperbound, $22.50.

KAISER, ROBERT G. *Why Gorbachev Happened: His Triumphs, His Failure, and His Fall*. Pp. 522. New York: Simon & Schuster, 1992. Paperbound, $14.00.

KEDDIE, NIKKI R. and BETH BARON, eds. *Women in Middle Eastern History: Shifting Boundaries in Sex and Gender*. Pp. xii, 343. New Haven, CT: Yale University Press, 1992. $35.00.

KELLNER, HANSFRIED and FRANK W. HEUBERGER. *Hidden Technocrats: The New Class and New Capitalism*. Pp. xi, 246. New Brunswick, NJ: Transaction, 1992. $29.95.

KENNEDY, IAN. *Treat Me Right: Essays in Medical Law and Ethics*. Pp. xviii, 428. New York: Oxford University Press, 1991. Paperbound, $28.00.

KENNEDY, ROGER G. *Rediscovering America: Journeys through Our Forgotten Past*. Pp. xvii, 398. Boston: Houghton Mifflin, 1992. Paperbound, $14.95.

KOLBERG, JON EIVIND, ed. *Between Work and Social Citizenship*. Pp. xvi, 199. Armonk, NY: M. E. Sharpe, 1992. $42.50.

KREPON, MICHAEL and DAN CALDWELL, eds. *The Politics of Arms Control Treaty Ramification*. Pp. viii, 486. New York: St. Martin's Press, 1992. $45.00.

KUSMER, KENNETH L., ed. *The Ghetto Crisis of the 1960s: Causes and Consequences*. Vol. 7. Pp. 350. New York: Garland, 1991. No price.

KUSMER, KENNETH L., ed. *Progress versus Poverty: 1970 to the Present*. Vol. 1. Pp. 381. New York: Garland, 1991. No price.

LATYNSKI, MAYA, ed. *Reappraising the Munich Pact: Continental Perspectives*. Pp. 107. Baltimore, MD: Johns Hopkins University Press, 1992. $22.00. Paperbound, $10.95.

LAVER, MICHAEL and NORMAN SCHOFIELD. *Multiparty Government: The Politics of Coalition in Europe*. Pp. xiii, 308. New York: Oxford University Press, 1991. Paperbound, $17.95.

LEDONNE, JOHN P. *Absolutism and Ruling Class: The Formation of the Russian Political Order, 1700-1825*. Pp. xvii, 376. New York: Oxford University Press, 1991. $49.95.

LEE, FREDERIC S. and WARREN J. SAMUELS, eds. *The Heterodox Eco-

nomics of Gardner C. Means. Pp. xxxiii, 363. Armonk, NY: M. E. Sharpe, 1992. $49.95.

LEVINE, HERBERT M. et al. *What If the American Political System Were Different?* Pp. xx, 284. Armonk, NY: M. E. Sharpe, 1992. $45.00. Paperbound, $16.50.

LIJPHART, AREND, ed. *Parliamentary versus Presidential Government.* Pp. xii, 257. New York: Oxford University Press, 1992. $56.00. Paperbound, $19.95.

LIKHACHEV, DMITRII S. *Reflections on Russia.* Pp. xxii, 191. Boulder, CO: Westview Press, 1991. $29.95.

LITTLE, DANIEL. *Understanding Peasant China: Case Studies in the Philosophy of Social Science.* Pp. xi, 322. New Haven, CT: Yale University Press, 1992. $35.00. Paperbound, $18.00.

LYDEN, FREMONT J. and LYMAN H. LEGTERS, eds. *Native Americans and Public Policy.* Pp. vi, 331. Pittsburgh, PA: University of Pittsburgh Press, 1992. $39.95.

MACEDO, STEPHEN. *Liberal Virtues: Citizenship, Virtue, and Community in Liberal Constitutionalism.* Pp. viii, 306. New York: Oxford University Press, 1991. Paperbound, $15.95.

MADISON, JAMES H., ed. *Wendell Wilkie: Hoosier Internationalist.* Pp. xxiii, 184. Bloomington: Indiana University Press, 1992. $19.95.

MADSEN, PETER and JAY M. SHAFRITZ, eds. *Essentials of Government Ethics.* Pp. xii, 468. New York: Meridian, 1992. Paperbound, $15.00.

McWHINNEY, WILL. *Paths of Change: Strategic Choices for Organizations and Society.* Pp. xiv, 273. Newbury Park, CA: Sage, 1992. $45.00. Paperbound, $19.95.

McWILLIAMS, WILSON CAREY and MICHAEL T. GIBBONS, eds. *The Federalists, the Antifederalists, and the American Political Tradition.* Pp.

138. Westport, CT: Greenwood Press, 1992. $39.95.

NOVAK, MICHAEL. *Choosing Presidents: Symbols of Presidential Leadership.* 2d ed. Pp. xxxii, 354. New Brunswick, NJ: Transaction, 1992. Paperbound, $21.95.

OWEN, DIANA. *Media Messages in American Presidential Elections.* Pp. xxi, 198. Westport, CT: Greenwood Press, 1991. No price.

PARET, PETER and DANIEL MORAN, eds. *Carl von Clausewitz: Historical and Political Writings.* Pp. xvii, 397. Princeton, NJ: Princeton University Press, 1992. $29.95.

PIVEN, FRANCES FOX, ed. *Labor Parties in Postindustrial Societies.* Pp. vi, 290. New York: Oxford University Press, 1992. $39.95. Paperbound, $16.95.

PORTZ, JOHN. *The Politics of Plant Closings.* Pp. ix, 207. Lawrence: University Press of Kansas, 1990. $29.95. Paperbound, $12.95.

RHODE, DEBORAH L., ed. *Theoretical Perspectives on Sexual Difference.* Pp. xi, 315. New Haven, CT: Yale University Press, 1992. $30.00. Paperbound, $15.00.

RIDDELL, PETER. *The Thatcher Era and Its Legacy.* Pp. ix, 270. Cambridge, MA: Basil Blackwell, 1992. Paperbound, $19.95.

RIGBY, ANDREW. *Living the Intifada.* Pp. 233. Atlantic Highlands, NJ: Zed, 1992. $55.00. Paperbound, $19.95.

RITTER, ARCHIBALD R. M. et al., eds. *Latin America to the Year 2000: Reactivating Growth, Improving Equity, Sustaining Democracy.* Pp. xiii, 266. New York: Praeger, 1992. $47.95.

ROSENBAUM, ARTHUR LEWIS, ed. *State and Society in China: The Consequences of Reform.* Pp. vii, 240. Boulder, CO: Westview Press, 1992. $43.00. Paperbound, $15.95.

SCHWAAB, EDLEFF H. *Hitler's Mind: A Plunge into Madness.* Pp. xxxvii, 202. New York: Praeger, 1992. $45.00.

SHAMA, AVRAHAM, ed. *Perestroika: A Comparative Perspective.* Pp. xiv, 129. New York: Praeger, 1992. $39.95.

SHAW, RONALD E. *Canals for a Nation: The Canal Era in the United States 1790-1860.* Pp. x, 284. Lexington: University Press of Kentucky, 1991. $28.00.

SHEFFER, MARTIN S. *Presidential Power: Case Studies in the Use of the Opinions of the Attorney General.* Pp. ix, 137. Lanham, MD: University Press of America, 1991. $29.50. Paperbound, $14.50.

SHELDON, CHARLES H. *The Washington High Bench: A Biographical History of the State Supreme Court, 1889-1991.* Pp. xix, 396. Pullman: Washington State University Press, 1992. $35.00. Paperbound, $25.00.

SHOGAN, ROBERT. *The Riddle of Power: Presidential Leadership from Truman to Bush.* Pp. x, 358. New York: Plume, 1992. Paperbound, $12.00.

SIMONIA, NODARI A. *Synthesis of Traditional and Modern in the Evolution of Third World Societies.* Pp. x, 175. Westport, CT: Greenwood Press, 1992. $45.00.

SMOOHA, SAMMY. *Arabs and Jews in Israel.* Vol. 2, *Change and Continuity in Mutual Intolerance.* Pp. xviii, 357. Boulder, CO: Westview Press, 1992. Paperbound, $38.50.

SOH, CHUNG-HEE. *The Chosen Women in Korean Politics: An Anthropological Study.* Pp. xii, 168. New York: Praeger, 1991. $39.95.

SPECTOR, ROBERT D. *Political Controversy: A Study in Eighteenth-Century Propaganda.* Pp. xii, 184. Westport, CT: Greenwood Press, 1992. $45.00.

SZILARD, LEO. *The Voice of the Dolphins and Other Stories.* Expanded ed. Pp. vi, 181. Stanford, CA: Stanford University Press, 1992. $20.00. Paperbound, $8.95.

TONER, JAMES H. *The Sword and the Cross: Reflections on Command and Conscience.* Pp. xiv, 186. New York: Praeger, 1992. $45.00.

TURNER, FREDERICK C., ed. *Social Mobility and Political Attitudes: Comparative Perspectives.* Pp. xxvi, 274. New Brunswick, NJ: Transaction, 1992. No price.

TYLER, TOM R. *Why People Obey the Law.* Pp. vii, 273. New Haven, CT: Yale University Press, 1992. $35.00. Paperbound, $13.00.

WALLERSTEIN, IMMANUEL. *Geopolitics and Geoculture: Essays on the Changing World-System.* Pp. 242. New York: Cambridge University Press, 1991. $39.50. Paperbound, $12.95.

WHITEFORD, SCOTT and ANNE E. FERGUSON, eds. *Harvest of Want: Hunger and Food Security in Central America and Mexico.* Pp. vii, 264. Boulder, CO: Westview Press, 1991. $48.00.

ZIEGENHAGEN, EDUARD A. and KLEOMENIS S. KOUTSOUKIS. *Political Conflict in Southern Europe: Regulation, Regression and Morphogenesis.* Pp. xviii, 148. New York: Praeger, 1992. $45.00.

INDEX

SOCIAL PROBLEMS AND THE POLICY
STUDIES ORGANIZATION

The Policy Studies Organization has published numerous important books that relate to social, economic, planning, technology, and political policy problems. Nearly all of these books are preceded by a journal issue on the topic. Members of PSO receive eight such journals per year by way of the *Policy Studies Journal* and the *Policy Studies Review*. The list below provides a sampling of the PSO concern for social problems in addition to political problems.

I.   SOCIAL POLICY
1. Harrell Rodgers, *Public Policy and Social Institutions* (PSO-JAI Press, 1989).
2. Michael Kraft and Mark Schneider, *Population Policy Analysis: Issues in American Politics* (PSO-Lexington Books, 1978).
3. Marian Palley and Michael Preston, *Race, Sex, and Policy Problems* (PSO-Lexington, 1979).

II. ECONOMIC POLICY
1. Warren Samuels, *Fundamentals of the Economic Role of Government* (PSO-Greenwood Press, 1989).
2. James Anderson, *Economic Regulatory Policies* (PSO-Lexington, 1978).
3. Alan Stone and Edward Harpham, *The Political Economy of Public Policy* (PSO-Sage, 1982).

III. URBAN AND REGIONAL PLANNING
1. Dean Mann, *Environmental Policy Implementation: Planning and Management Options and Their Consequences* (PSO-Lexington, 1982).
2. Roger Montgomery and Dale Marshall, *Housing Policy for the 1980s* (PSO-Lexington, 1980).
3. Alan Altshuler, *Current Issues in Transportation Policy* (PSO-Lexington,1979).

IV. SCIENCE AND TECHNOLOGY POLICY
1. Joseph Haberer, *Science and Technology Policy* (PSO-Lexington, 1977).
2. Robert Blank and Miriam Mills, *Biomedical Technology and Public Policy* (PSO-Greenwood, 1989).
3. Susan Welch and Robert Miewald, *Scarce Natural Resources: The Challenge to Public Policymaking* (PSO-Sage, 1983).

If you are interested, then send a check for $20 to PSO, 361 Lincoln Hall along with the coupon below or a photocopy of it to PSO, University of Illinois, 702 S. Wright Street, Urbana, Illinois, 61801.

- -

Send me the *Policy Studies Journal, Policy Studies Review, Policy Evaluation Newsletter-Journal, Developmental Policy Studies Newsletter-Journal*, Directories, and other benefits. Here is my name, address, and check for only $20. Add $8 for overseas postage.

Name_____

Affiliation_____

Address_____

City/State/Zip_____

THE SOCIAL ORIGINS OF NATIONALIST MOVEMENTS

The Contemporary West
European Experience

edited by JOHN COAKLEY, *Limerick University, Ireland*

Throughout Western Europe, internal nationalist conflicts are threatening the stability of dozens of communities, states, and in some cases, entire nations. In **The Social Origins of Nationalist Movements**, Coakley and a distinguished group of scholars examine the correlation between these nationalist trends and the social factors that fuel them. In particular, contributors explore the conflicting pressures of class and ethnicity as determinants of the process of political mobilization. Next, they present case studies relating to particular regions—or minorities—within the context of the larger state. Sardinia, the Jura, Brittany, Scotland, and Northern Ireland are examined; by way of contrast, the editor highlights the Nordic region, an area where the prerequisites for nationalist agitation are present, but where vigorous nationalist movements have been strikingly absent.

At a time when nationalist fervor is again making headlines, Coakley's collection provides fresh insights into the undercurrents influencing European politics. Professionals and students of political science, history, political sociology, sociology, ethnic studies, and European studies will find this to be fascinating reading.

"This book has proved an interesting read."
—*European Labour Forum*

Sage Modern Politics Series, Volume 31
1992 / 242 pages / $65.00 (h) (8572X)

SAGE PUBLICATIONS, INC.
2455 Teller Road, Newbury Park, CA 91320
(805) 499-0721 / Fax (805) 499-0871
SAGE PUBLICATIONS LTD.
6 Bonhill Street, London EC2A 4PU, England
SAGE PUBLICATIONS INDIA PVT. LTD.
M-32 Greater Kailash Market—I, New Delhi 110 048, India

THE NEW POLITICS OF CLASS

Social Movements and Cultural
Dynamics in Advanced Societies

*by **KLAUS EDER**, European Institute, Florence*

Are contemporary societies organized by class? In recent years the apparent fragmentation of established class structures and the emergence of new social movements—in particular the women's movement and environmentalism—have altered the traditional expressions of class in society. At the same time, these changes have posed fundamental questions for the concept of class in sociology and political science. In this major reassessment, Klaus Eder offers a new perspective on the status of class in modernity. Drawing on a critique of Bourdieu, Touraine, and Habermas, he outlines a cultural conception of class as the basis for understanding contemporary societies. His model re-evaluates the role of the middle classes, traditionally the crux of class analysis, and links class to social theories of power and cultural capital. The result is a cultural theory of class which incorporates the changing forms of collective action and the new social movements of contemporary societies.

An invaluable contribution both to social theory and to the theory of class and stratification, **The New Politics of Class** will be of interest to a broad readership in sociology and political science.

Theory, Culture, and Society Series
1993 (Summer) / 224 pages (tent.) / $62.00 (h) (86874) / $21.95 (p) (88680)

SAGE PUBLICATIONS, INC.
2455 Teller Road, Newbury Park, CA 91320
(805) 499-0721 / Fax (805) 499-0871

SAGE PUBLICATIONS LTD.
6 Bonhill Street, London EC2A 4PU, England

SAGE PUBLICATIONS INDIA PVT. LTD.
M-32 Greater Kailash Market—I, New Delhi 110 048, India